Educating the Baccalaureate Social Worker
A Curriculum Development Resource Guide

Educating the Baccalaureate Social Worker

A Curriculum Development Resource Guide

Edited by
Betty L. Baer and
Ronald C. Federico

Volume II

Ballinger Publishing Company • Cambridge, Massachusetts
A Subsidiary of Harper & Row, Publishers, Inc.

Library of Congress Cataloging in Publication Data

West Virginia. University. Undergraduate Social Work Curriculum Development Project.
Educating the baccalaureate social worker.

Bibliography: p.
Includes index.
1. Social work education—United States. 2. Social work education—Curricula. I. Baer, Betty L. II. Federico, Ronald C. III. Title.
HV11.W48   1979   375'.361   79-11681
ISBN 0-88410-674-8

International Standard Book Number: 0-88410-674-8

Library of Congress Catalog Card Number: 79-11681

Printed in the United States of America.

This book is printed on recycled paper.

Project Staff

Betty L. Baer, Director
West Virginia University
Morgantown, West Virginia

Ronald C. Federico,
Project Associate
University of Cincinnati
Cincinnati, Ohio

Contributors

Winifred Bell
Cleveland State University
Cleveland, Ohio

Laura B. Morris
Digital Equipment Corporation
Boston, Massachusetts

Katherine Hooper Briar
Pacific Lutheran University
Tacoma, Washington

Edna F. Roth
Virginia Commonwealth University
Richmond, Virginia

Jacqueline D. Fassett
Sinai Hospital
Baltimore, Maryland

Bradford W. Sheafor
Colorado State University
Fort Collins, Colorado

Herbert H. Jarrett
University of Georgia
Athens, Georgia

Ramón Valle
San Diego State University
San Diego, California

Fay Coker Walker
Mars Hill College
Mars Hill, North Carolina

Contents

List of Figures

List of Tables

Introduction

This publication is a companion volume to *Educating the Baccalaureate Social Worker: Report of the Undergraduate Social Work Curriculum Development Project* published in 1978. These two volumes complete the work of the Undergraduate Social Work Curriculum Development Project, funded from July 1, 1975 to June 30, 1978 by the Social and Rehabilitation Service of the Department of Health, Education and Welfare to the West Virginia University School of Social Work. The project's overall purpose was to improve and strengthen social work curricula at the undergraduate level. More specifically, the goal became that of further explicating both educational objectives and the curriculum content essential to the achievement of those objectives. The project's findings concerning the basic competencies of the baccalaureate professional social worker and the curriculum content needed for the attainment of these competencies, are presented in the project report noted above.

This book focuses on issues of program structure and curriculum raised by project findings. During the project's third and final year, its staff identified several areas that would need explicit attention by those involved in curriculum development, if the overall project objective of strengthening baccalaureate social work curricula were to be achieved. With a team of curriculum consultants, project staff then developed a series of papers that elaborated on several of these areas. Drafts of the papers were presented to social work educators and practitioner representatives for their reactions and critique, at a series of workshops held at eight different locations throughout the country between April and June 1978. Revisions of the papers were then made, and the revised papers are presented here. They are intended to serve as a resource for faculty, practitioners, students, and others, as they work together toward strengthening undergraduate social work curricula.

ORGANIZATION OF THIS BOOK

The material presented in this volume is divided into four parts. Part I contains one chapter, entitled "Implications and Issues Raised by the Curriculum Development Project." It identifies the major themes and curriculum implications that emerged from the first two years of the project's work. Since these flow from the earlier publication, it is critical that they be understood in that context. This chapter provides a bridge between the project's work of the first two years and the activities of the third year.

Part II includes three chapters addressing the relationships that a social work program and its faculty must develop and maintain with the social work practice community, with the university or college in which the program exists, and with its own students. For each of these constituencies, a somewhat different relationship is relevant. The selection, development, and maintenance of a learning environment and teaching strategies conducive to the development of the future professional social worker are also addressed in this section.

Part III also includes three chapters. These focus on the setting of educational objectives appropriate to the attainment of baccalaureate professional social work practice competencies, as well as on some issues in the assessment of a program's success in achieving its intended outcomes.

The final section, Part IV, contains four chapters on curriculum content. "Social Work Practice," which includes methods and field, is the first. Consistent with the project emphasis on the outcome of the educational endeavor—a competent baccalaureate social work practitioner—other components of the curriculum can be seen as contributing to the attainment of practice competence. Practice, in other words, becomes the application of knowledge within the context of the social work profession's values and ethics, in order to realize the objective of the profession—to be helpful to people. Each of the remaining three chapters elaborates on one of the following major areas of curriculum content: research; human behavior and the social environment; and social welfare services and policy. It is not the purpose of these papers, or indeed any part of the project's work, to mandate particular courses or to present course syllabi, but rather to address curriculum issues, and to consider aspects of these issues that may be helpful to faculties as they decide on the courses and course content appropriate for their particular programs.

USE OF THE MATERIAL

As indicated earlier, the material in this book is intended to serve as a resource to all those involved in curriculum development and other activities that help to strengthen baccalaureate social work education. It is hoped that it will serve as a resource in at least two ways. First, by elaborating on particular areas, it should help colleagues, students, and others to understand more fully the work and the intent of the curriculum development project. Second, the ideas presented in these papers may serve as a stimulus for discussion and the generation of additional ideas in baccalaureate social work programs everywhere.

There are two important points to keep in mind while studying and utilizing the material. First, there are areas of omission as well as areas not fully developed. Not all aspects of curriculum received the attention we might have liked. Time and energy ran out; it was a very full three years. As the material now stands, it represents the point where the curriculum development project ended. We feel comfortable with this, because activities to strengthen and develop curricula are never-ending. We know that others will pick up on, contribute to, and improve the project's work as time goes on. Our work represents only one particular point in time in the long process, begun many years ago and continuing into the future, of continually strengthening undergraduate social work curricula. Users of this material should approach it critically, in order to clarify its limitations and identify the next steps in the process.

The second point concerns the three-year process that the entire work of the project underwent—a process that involved hours of study and discussion between educators, practitioners, and others, and resulted in much reworking of material. In reflecting back, we now understand much more fully the importance of the process and the ways in which it contributed to the final product and each person's understanding of it. A similar process within each program of study, dialog, and debate would seem to be essential, if the material is to be understood and then used critically by individual programs to strengthen curricula.

ACKNOWLEDGMENTS

As with the first book produced by the curriculum development project, the material presented here represents the contributions of many persons. We are grateful to all of them for their generosity in contributing ideas and their ongoing challenge and stimulation to us, as well as for their many expressions of support for the project. We have tried to utilize and present the helpful contributions of others accurately and carefully, but project staff carry final responsibility for the material as it is presented here.

We are especially indebted to the curriculum consultants who worked with us in the development of this material. They were remarkably patient in developing and reworking their contributions to the book. We hope that the experience was fruitful for all of them.

We want also to acknowledge the contributions of all those educators and practitioners who participated in the eight project-sponsored workshops held throughout the country during the spring of 1978 (all of them are identified in the Appendix). We tried to the best of our ability to assure the achievement of mutual objectives, so that participants' understanding of the project's work was enhanced at the same time that we benefited from their critique of the material, then in draft form.

Special thanks go to several of the curriculum consultants who assisted us by providing leadership to workshop groups. Dr. Herbert Jarrett participated in all but one of the workshops. We are grateful to him and to the School of Social Work at the University of Georgia for making so much of his time available to us. Fay Coker Walker, then of Mars Hill Co lege in North Carolina, skillfully led two workshop groups. Jacqueline D. Fassett, director of social services at Sinai Hospital in Baltimore; Laura B. Morris, director of community relations for the Digital Corporation in Boston; and James D. Satterwhite, on the staff of the Mental Health Association of New York City, provided leadership to the practitioner groups who took part in the workshops. We were fortunate to have the participation and contributions of these talented practitioners throughout the life of the project. Ms. Fassett and Charles Wright of the Illinois Department of Mental Health and Developmental Disabilities were designated by the National Association of Social Workers as the liaison persons to the project when we first began our work in 1975. We appreciate their helpful services in this capacity.

The Commission on Educational Planning of the Council on Social Work Education designated representatives to attend the workshops, so as to obtain feedback on the results. We were pleased to have their participation and hope that the work of the project will aid the council in its ongoing activities and responsibilities.

We are particularly grateful to Dr. Pauline Godwin, special assistant to the commissioner and director of the Office of State Management Training, Administration for Public Services of the Department of Health, Education and Welfare, without whose support the third year of the project would not have materialized.

We acknowledge again and with appreciation the support of our colleagues in the School of Social Work of West Virginia University and in the social work program of the University of North Carolina at Greensboro. We were relieved of many other responsibilities in order to carry out the project's work. Finally, the faithful clerical support of Jerry Dobbs, Bonnie Corley, Rita Rendina, Viola Smith, and Vilma Peary greatly facilitated our work.

Betty L. Baer, Project Director
and Ronald C. Federico, Project Associate

I. The Project Context

Chapter One

Implications and Issues Raised by the Curriculum Development Project

**Betty L. Baer and
Ronald C. Federico**

The report published earlier by the project includes a chapter that summarizes the findings and identifies the major implications for curricula.[1] This material was developed at the conclusion of the first two years of the project's work. The reactions to the main substance of the project's work have helped us to clarify further our thinking as well as identify areas that will need ongoing attention. Moreover, they serve to remind us of the need for emphasis and reemphasis of the major thrusts of project findings. The papers that follow can be understood only in the context of those findings.

In this chapter, we will restate the major project findings or themes and their implications for curriculum development. In addition, other issues that emerged from the project-sponsored workshops and are directly related to the implementation of project findings will be discussed. All of these are dealt with fully in the chapters that follow, but are presented here to provide an overview and context for the rest of the book.

MAJOR PROJECT FINDINGS

There are two themes in the project findings from which several others flow. These are the definition of social work and emphasis on the outcomes of the educational program.

Definition of Social Work

Understanding the definition of social work adopted by the project is fundamental to understanding all other parts of the

3

project's work. This definition is as follows: "Social work is concerned and involved with the interactions between people and the institutions of society that affect the ability of people/to accomplish life tasks, realize aspirations and values, and alleviate distress."[2] Therefore, it follows that there are three major purposes of social work: "(a) to enhance the problem-solving, coping, and developmental capacities of people; (b) to promote the effective and humane operation of the systems that provide people with resources and services; and (c) to link people with systems that provide them with resources, services, and opportunities."[3]

This definition of social work, supported and promulgated by others long before the curriculum development project ever came into being, was adopted because, in its view of social work as primarily concerned with the interactions between people and societal institutions, it reflects the uniqueness and the essence of social work. In utilizing it as a final screen to identify activities appropriate for the baccalaureate level of practice and critical curriculum content areas, the project attempted to fully operationalize the definition. In other words, the knowledge, the values, and the skills that provide the underpinnings of social work practice must be supportive of and consistent with the definition of social work and its purposes.

Emphasis on Outcomes of the Educational Program

The major aim of a baccalaureate social work program is to prepare the first-level professional practitioner—that is, to prepare for *practice*. (There are, of course, other purposes, but the project was concerned only with the definition of the objectives and content essential to preparation for practice.) With this aim as the focus, it naturally followed that the project had to specify as clearly as possible the nature of that first level of practice. Without this, the setting of curriculum objectives and the selection of content was impossible. Through the use of a variety of strategies, which are detailed in the original report, the project defined what the baccalaureate worker must be prepared to do in practice. This is summarized in the form of the basic practice competencies that the baccalaureate worker should have when he or she leaves the educational program and enters practice. The focus is more on the outcomes of the educational program than on the inputs and process, unlike the emphasis in the past.

The two themes noted above are central to the entire project and its findings. Additional implications for curricula flow from them.

Need for Greater Emphasis on Analytical and Conceptual Skills

Our view of social work and its purposes demands a worker with the capacity to confront a situation or concern regardless of whether it is manifested by an individual, family, group, community, or organization and to understand that problem in terms of its many dimensions and implications. As a result of that understanding the worker chooses ways to intervene that will best resolve the problem, within the context of worker resources, client system goals, feasible options, and so on.

The importance of critical, analytical, thinking skills cannot be overemphasized. The assessment process must be carried out within a holistic perspective that demands an ability to utilize a conceptual framework in which situations can be analyzed in terms of interacting systems. This is not new to baccalaureate educators; project findings simply indicate the need for greater emphasis on the development of such skills. And, as will be pointed out shortly, the development of problem-solving, analytical skills should not be viewed as the responsibility of social work faculty and course work alone. It is a responsibility shared by faculty in academic disciplines as well as faculty in the professional discipline.

Need for Tighter Linkages with Key Academic Disciplines

The competencies to be achieved by the baccalaureate social work student throughout the normal four years of undergraduate education demand a much tighter relationship with other disciplines than is currently characteristic of many programs. Clearly, those disciplines furnish much of the basic theoretical foundation content. This content needs to be interwoven throughout the educational experience, so that all along the way, students are broadening their understanding in content areas that will help them with the "what" and "why" of practice.

Greater interdependence of social work faculty and faculty from academic disciplines can be enhanced by more clarity in defining social work purposes and the outcomes of baccalaureate social work educational programs. The interactional view of social work, for example, speaks to the need for some rather specific content, in anthropology, economics, sociology, political science, and psychology, just as the development of analytical problem-solving skills speaks to the essence of liberal arts education. Unfortunately, social work faculty as well as faculty from other disciplines have too often been unaware that content from those disciplines provides essential content for the social work student.

The project, in thinking through curricular implications in this area, has found it useful to differentiate between liberal arts-general education content and foundation content. The first area refers to the broad liberal arts-general education courses that are currently mandatory for all students in most institutions of higher education. These requirements, frequently distributed among the arts and humanities, the social and natural sciences, English composition, and physical education, most often provide some degree of choice for students. Unfortunately, however, there is little coherence and much confusion today in American institutions of higher education with regard to liberal arts education, its purposes, and what and how much ought to be required of students. This important point needs to be taken into account by those social work educators who view liberal arts education as a sacred cow.

The second area of curriculum content, foundation content, refers to material drawn from the academic disciplines that clearly and specifically provides the cognitive, theoretical underpinnings of social work and its practice. For example, much understanding of the several systems and social institutions that impact on people's lives will be gained from content in the social science disciplines. Application of that content is obviously the responsibility of social work faculty. Broad liberal arts-general education requirements contribute to this learning, but to assure the depth of knowledge that project findings recommend, curriculum content must be carefully planned.

In fact, this is a very weak area in most social work curricula. A very basic rule-of-thumb curriculum assessment tool might be as follows: one-quarter of total curricular credit devoted to liberal arts-general education; another quarter devoted to the major area of study; a third quarter assigned to theoretical content relevant to the major (foundation content); and the final quarter open for electives. Were we to apply this guide to current baccalaureate social work curricula, we would find, in many instances, that the number of credit hours assigned to liberal arts-general education courses was generally satisfactory; the hours devoted to the major, creeping steadily upward and going beyond the minimal quarter in the rule-of-thumb measure; the electives area, with at least some hours assigned to it; and the time devoted to required foundation content, generally far *below* our rule-of-thumb measure. Project findings indicate that this lack of required foundation or theoretical content is critical. Few social work faculties have the resources to teach theoretical content drawn from the social sciences, not to mention the potential hazards of failing to utilize fully those institutional resources already available. While the project has not attempted to specify in a definitive way all of the essential knowledge content, it has tried to emphasize certain basic theoretical areas, as the papers that follow will demonstrate.

Need to Reexamine Current
Curriculum Content

The definition of social work and its purposes seems to us to mandate a departure from the "sick-well" treatment and therapy model that is currently pervasive in many baccalaureate social work education programs. Clearly, this has implications for the selection of foundation content as well as for all components of the professional curriculum.

The definition suggests the need for content that would help students understand that people cope and adapt to their environment in a variety of ways. Coping and adapting, in this sense, are normal and healthy, although the forms of human behavior that they take are as diverse as the different sociocultural forces that different persons and groups experience. Human difference is something to be understood and valued as a normal biological and sociocultural fact of life, since people have the capacity to learn and develop in many different ways. It must be further understood that, as people interact with a range of institutions like the family, religion, education, social welfare, and political and economic systems, their ways of adapting may be enhanced and enriched, or thwarted and diminished. People and groups, in other words, vary in their capacity to secure and utilize institutional resources, while institutions vary in their capacity to improve people's adaptation skills by supporting and contributing to the capacities people have to secure and utilize resources with greater or lesser effectiveness. In this sense, people's failure to control and enhance their own lives as well as to contribute in meaningful ways to society cannot only be seen as a failure of the individual or group that can be solved by interpsychic means. It must also be viewed as a failure of the institutions that support human well-being.

As indicated earlier, all areas of curriculum should be influenced by this stance if there is to be curriculum coherence. The current heavy focus on the individual must be balanced with content that will help students develop the knowledge and skills needed to intervene at the institutional level. In addition, there is a need for students to understand more about the ways in which people learn as well as about teaching strategies and skills, if they are to help people learn how to cope, solve problems for themselves, and manage their lives more effectively.

The implications for various curriculum areas are clear. In the human behavior and social environment area, the existing heavy reliance on normative life span developmental psychology is not nearly sufficient. Content from biology, cultural anthropology, sociology, and other relevant liberal and social science areas is crucial if students are to comprehend the full spectrum of variables that influence and shape human behavior. In addition, there must be a conceptual framework for looking at and understanding human behavior that views this behavior as intertwined with and shaped by the institutions of our society.

In the policy area, some knowledge of basic economics, political and legislative processes, and the legal system is critical to an understanding of social policy and an ability to analyze it. In addition, services and resources in this country are usually provided by complex organizations. Knowledge of them, their politics, formal and informal networks, decision-making processes, and so on is essential if graduates are to contribute with competence to the development of service structures that are more responsive to people.

In the practice area, a framework is needed for conceptualizing the practice event and interventive modes and techniques, one that is supportive of and consistent with the view of social work as interactional between people and the institutions of society. The capacity to assess a situation and the many systems intertwined with it, as noted earlier, is a critical part of practice. This points directly to the need for strengthening research content in such a way that students understand its applicability and relevance to practice.

Need for a Functional Relationship
with the Practice-Service Community

The basic practice competencies at the baccalaureate social work level were developed in a cooperative effort between educators and practitioners, in a process described in the first volume on the project. They were deliberately stated in broad fashion so as to maximize flexibility and creativity at the local program level. Nonetheless, the competencies do lend direction to the content of the basic curriculum at the baccalaureate level. There are activities to illustrate the level of competence envisioned.[4] The student who achieves the competencies indicated will, we believe, be ready to enter practice at the appropriate level and be able to help the people served.

As the competencies are tested and assessment criteria are developed (a task not accomplished by this project), there must be ongoing feedback from the practice-service community, channeled into further curriculum planning, assessment, and development activity. The project statement of competencies was written in 1977, and already new service patterns as well as changes in ongoing delivery systems in response to changing societal conditions demand that there be opportunities for ongoing modifications, changes, or additions. Competence in practice as reflected by the competencies can, in the final analysis, be assessed only if the student is engaged in practice. In addition, while the project believes that the competencies as stated will prepare graduates for basic social work practice anywhere with any population group, each program will need to assess them against the mission and uniqueness of its own institutions and region. Thus, practitioners, educators, and students working together will need to develop criteria for assessing students' competence. A close working relationship with practice is therefore indicated.

Need for Greater Attention to the Learning Environment

The development of professional social workers who are assertive, inquiring, self-evaluative, and able to practice responsibly and to make professional judgments within the values and ethics of the profession of social work seems to demand that increasing attention be given to the learning environment, in which faculty, students, practitioners, and others work together. All professionally educated social workers, whether they be faculty or practitioners, have experienced being a participant in a learning environment. They are keenly aware of the conditions that engage the student as an active learner and that encourage questioning the "truth" of social work and its practice. To be avoided is an environment where faculty dominate as experts, where questioning is discouraged in both covert and overt ways, and where the social work models to which students are exposed are quite counter to the profession and its ethics. Teaching strategies selected are part of the learning environment. A chapter by Tom Walz that appears in the first volume by the project addresses this entire area;[5] a chapter in this volume specifically discusses teaching and learning strategies.

ADDITIONAL AREAS OF CONCERN

Several additional areas of concern to faculty and practitioners emerged from the workshops and are worthy of mention. Although the material in this book address these issues to some degree, they need and deserve careful and ongoing discussion and study. The termination of the curriculum development project precludes its further involvement in these processes, but it is hoped that identification of the issues here will stimulate others to take up this important work.

Knowledge of Higher Education

Undergraduate social work education must broaden and strengthen its place within the college and university. This means that social work faculty must become more knowledgeable about trends and issues in higher education. Clearly, issues such as the future of liberal arts education and changes in course offerings by academic disciplines deeply affect undergraduate social work education. Yet too often social work faculty are unaware of such issues and are removed from decision-making beyond their own program. Faculty in the project workshops were conscious of this lack and indicated the need for ongoing faculty development activity. Currently, however, there are few resources to help those faculty who have entered teaching from practice to understand higher education as a system.

Role Ambiguity

In relation to the above, many faculty expressed a need for greater clarity about the role one assumes upon entering a career in higher education. Colleges and universities demand that faculty members perceive themselves as academics and educators, yet there is also pressure on them to maintain a close relationship to practice. The result is that many faculty choose one identification or the other, finding it difficult to combine both aspects into their role in an appropriate way. Again, while this issue is discussed in one of the chapters in this book, many faculty identified this as an area for ongoing attention in faculty development activity.

Curriculum Development Skills

During the late sixties and early seventies, rapid growth in undergraduate social work education programs created a variety of opportunities for faculty to participate in workshops and seminars that aimed at helping them develop skills in curriculum building. The Council on Social Work Education, the Southern Regional Education

Board, and other groups sponsored such activities. During the past several years, however, these opportunities have rarely been available. By and large, any assistance to faculty is provided through "self-help" efforts—through baccalaureate educator-sponsored activities at the state or regional level or through faculty development activity independently stimulated by the faculty of a program. While such efforts have considerable merit, and are a tribute to baccalaureate educators and their concern that there be ongoing activities aimed at helping faculty strengthen curricula, there are also limitations to such efforts. There is considerable unevenness from region to region in terms of time for planning, resource availability, participants' level of experience, and other factors, which makes it difficult for local self-help efforts to meet all faculty development needs.

What is needed and was articulated by workshop participants is a nationally sponsored faculty development program with ongoing opportunities for new faculty and practitioners. In addition, experienced faculty and practitioners need to continually broaden their own knowledge and skills as well as share their expertise with others. The lack of such a program has profound implications for the future of the findings of the curriculum development project as well as for future baccalaureate social work education in general. Given the considerable concern expressed by many that there be such a program, one will hopefully be developed by an appropriate body in the not-too-distant future.

In conclusion, the response of our colleagues to the curriculum project material has been encouraging. For many of them the project work merely amplifies and reconfirms their many years of effort toward strengthening baccalaureate social work curricula. They share our belief that bright, able undergraduate students can handle greatly increased academic rigor. They also know, as do we, that undergraduate social work education has come a long way in both quantity and quality since the late 1960s. We hope that the work of the curriculum development project will serve as a helpful resource for the never-ending process of strengthening curriculum.

NOTES

1. Baer, Betty L. and Ronald Federico, *Educating the Baccalaureate Social Worker: Report of the Undergraduate Social Work Curriculum Development Project* (Cambridge, Mass.: Ballinger, 1978), pp. 99-105.
2. Ibid., p. 61.
3. Ibid., p. 68.
4. Ibid., pp. 70-84.
5. Ibid., pp. 13-47.

II. Program Structure and the Learning Environment

Chapter Two

The Common Purpose of the Social Work Practitioner and the Social Work Educator

**Betty L. Baer,
in consultation with
Jacqueline D. Fassett and
Laura B. Morris**[a]

INTRODUCTION

This chapter will identify and discuss specific implications of project findings for the practice-education relationship.

Attention will then be given to the objectives that are shared by educators and practitioners who are part of the educational program. The structure necessary to achieve those objectives as well as some of the obstacles that may impede their achievement is presented. Finally, a process is offered to help programs as they seek to strengthen their curricula. Hopefully the chapter will stimulate educators and practice participants of all programs to join together in dialogue, clarifying their common objectives, identifying problem areas experienced, and working together toward the achievement of shared responsibility for improving the quality of baccalaureate social work education.

Much of the material in this chapter was developed in discussions with the practitioners who participated in the project's regional workshops held during the spring of 1978.

SIGNIFICANCE OF PROJECT METHODOLOGY

From the outset, the West Virginia Undergraduate Social Work Curriculum Development Project assumed that the how and what of

[a]This paper was written by Betty L. Baer, but essential consultation was provided by Jacqueline D. Fassett, director of social services, Sinai Hospital, Baltimore, Md., and Laura B. Morris, director of community relations, Digital Equipment Corporation, Boston, Mass.

a student's preparation for practice in social work were of concern to both educators and practitioners. The project also assumed that the outcome of the curriculum development activity would be more relevant to current and future social needs if planning deliberations included, to the fullest extent possible, those who would be affected by the outcome. Certainly, practice is deeply affected by the result of social work educational programs.

The project did not make these assumptions blindly; it took seriously the recommendations of the Council on Social Work Education (CSWE) Task Force on Practice and Education, as these were adopted by the House of Delegates in March 1976. One recommendation adopted by the house was of particular significance to the project in its choice of curriculum development strategy:

> Educational programs should demonstrate that they provide opportunities for meaningful and continuing participation by practitioners and other representatives from practice settings that would make possible a significant influence on policy decisions that affect the educational program.[1]

This policy seemed to be equally applicable to a national project—the curriculum development project—concerned with strengthening baccalaureate social work education programs. The project was also aware of the CSWE Community Mental Health Project, created to examine the relationship between educators and community mental health practitioners, and funded by the National Institute of Mental Health. Not surprisingly, the mental health project report emphasizes the same theme, that "neither the system of social work education nor [community mental health] practice can, in isolation, meet current manpower needs for knowledgeable, skilled and competent professional practitioners. The two systems must work together for the successful achievement of this goal."[2]

The effort to carry out the commitment to cooperative participation by educators and practitioners in curriculum planning activity influenced the project's processes and outcome profoundly. This is documented in the first volume on the project.

While there was no systematic assessment of the process during the first two years of the project's activity, a few observations are in order. There was some anticipation that educators would align themselves as a group, as would practitioners. This was a naive presumption; no such thing ever occurred. Rather, depending upon the issue, alliances shifted, and the critical variables seemed primarily related to participants' views of the social work mission, life and practice experiences, and conservative or liberal ideologies, among other factors. Finally, it became clear that the end result of those deliberations would be influenced by the dialogue between practitioners and educators. Practitioners and educators began to gather as one group, listening to the contributions of other practitioners and educators, talking with each other, and arriving at substantial agreement together. The result was different and far richer than any product that would have emerged had the two groups worked separately and then invited reactions or contributions to each other's work. The process itself influenced the outcome significantly.

The above experience was instructive for all of us. It seemed, clearly, that we had attempted to operationalize the intent of the CSWE practice and education recommendations as well as the more recent mental health project proposals.

After the project completed the first phase of its work, which resulted in the project report, it then began to consider issues involved in implementation of project findings, with the ultimate objective of strengthening baccalaureate education. During this second phase, it became quite apparent that the curriculum envisioned by the project would demand a rethinking and a reconceptualization of the practice-education relationship at the local level and by each individual program. Because of the project's view that any effort to strengthen baccalaureate curricula should involve practitioners at the outset, it seemed appropriate to cover the issue in the initial chapter of this book.

PROJECT IMPLICATIONS FOR THE
PRACTICE-EDUCATION RELATIONSHIP

Introduction

Some rather specific implications for the future relationship between social work education and social work practice emerge from project findings. However, had there been no curriculum development project, the creation and maintenance of a healthy partnership between the two would still require attention. Such is the demand on any professional educational program that aims to prepare practitioners. As Dolgoff pointed out in the CSWE study cited earlier, some "healthy tension" between educators and practitioners seems almost inevitable, but when the gap becomes too great, serious difficulties arise. This ultimately affects students and the quality of the educational experience as well as social work education and the profession in general. Such is the case when a feeling prevails that education is not responsive to practice needs. Throughout the life of the project, the dialogue with the practitioners suggested that, on the undergraduate social work educational level, the program's relationship with the practice-service community seemed generally quite positive. There were, admittedly, many instances of what appeared to be poor understanding by practitioners of the educational program and its objectives. In still other instances, there was evidence of antagonism, the sense of a lack of mutuality and trust. Enough of the latter was evidenced by practitioners who attended many project-sponsored activities to suggest that, whether a program does or does not choose to deal seriously with the findings of the curriculum development project, attention should be given to assessing and strengthening each program's relationship with its practice-service community.

Specific Implications

The following section discusses certain project findings that have specific implications for the way in which practice and education will interact.

Need for Ongoing Assessment of Basic Competencies. The ten basic competencies were developed by the project in partnership with some major segments of the practice community and the profession. They emerged from a process that included examination of task analysis studies, discussions with practitioners and educators, review of other curriculum studies, and so on. As nearly as possible, an effort was made to identify those competencies that would be fundamental to practice at the baccalaureate level and that should be held by all graduates from accredited baccalaureate social work programs.

In studying these competencies, it is important to note, first of all, how the project intends them to be used. They should be tested in the range of educational programs in the months ahead, modified over time, and continually reassessed in terms of how well they satisfy current practice demands. Second, while an educational program will develop criteria (however simplified at the outset) to assess students' mastery of the basic competencies, the fact that the student has fulfilled the expectations of the educational program simply asserts that he or she is ready to enter practice. How well the student will perform in practice is obviously another matter altogether and can be assessed only as the baccalaureate social worker actually engages in practice. Ongoing feedback from the practice community as well as the graduates themselves will be essential in assessing the "fit" between the readiness for practice, or mastery of the competencies, and actual performance in practice.

The above issues suggest the need for extensive practice involvement in the educational endeavor. Otherwise, the competencies as they are now presented could become "final" or "set," instead of representing flow and change in response to testing in the field and to changing practice demands and realities. It is possible, of course, for educators alone to make modifications and shifts in the competencies based upon their perceptions of what is needed in actual practice. This would, however, undermine both the process by which the competencies were developed and the content of each of them.

Need to Assure Local Practice Relevance. A routinized, uncreative curriculum could well result if educators simply borrow the competencies as defined in the first volume by the project and "lay" them into their own programs. While the project felt that the basic competencies should be reflected in every educational program, the way in which they are put together should represent each program's uniqueness of mission, students, faculty, and local practice-service community. Each program will need to evolve a study structure to review and assess the basic competencies defined by the project as well as the program's own statement of anticipated educational outcomes. Such a study-review process, which obviously should include opportunities for understanding the totality of project findings, will serve to identify competency areas and service needs relevant to the local practice-service community that are not included in program's current statement of basic competencies. For example, many programs already go beyond the basic required core by preparing students with specific competencies in special fields, such as child welfare, aging, and work in rural areas.

Emphasis on Outcomes is New. The project emphasis on educating for competent practice represents a less exclusive preoccupation with the process and form of education and a greater emphasis on the outcomes of education. Whether the student at the point of leaving the program has the competence that he or she is asserted to have is critical. Obviously, the competencies do not exist in a vacuum; they are critical to the achievement of the major purpose of the profession which, broadly stated, is to provide quality services to people.

The emphasis on competencies may have strong implications for social work practice and social work education. For example, final mastery of the competencies must be demonstrated in practice or in the practicum situation. The student must be able to draw upon, put together, and utilize the basic competencies in order to achieve the objectives of the intervention effort and to be helpful to the people served. This must be clearly understood by practicum supervisors and educators alike as the development of criteria for the assessment of student performance will need to be a joint practice-education responsibility.

There is a second consequence of the emphasis on educating for practice competence. A series of unique practice principles flow from the competencies. Chapter 4 offers a basic explication of them, noting in full detail how *analytical tasks* and *interactional tasks* are indicated by each of the principles. The principles, then, guide practice by indicating tasks that are operationalized in carrying out each specific practice event. Therefore, while learning may take place at many times and in many places, the ultimate test is to assess whether the student's performance in practice situations is guided by practice principles or whether the tasks of "thinking" and "doing" are carried out appropriately and meaningfully to help the client-service consumer. Clearly, such an assessment cannot be carried out by the educator alone.

The Clarity of Outcome Allows for a Variety of Learning Experiences.   One of the most significant features of the emphasis on educational outcomes is that it permits and even encourages utilization of a rich array of learning experiences, depending upon each student's learning needs. Thus, opportunities are provided for faculty, students, and field instructors to maximize creatively the opportunities inherent in the learning environment. Identification of student learning needs can be much more actively shared between student, field instructor, and faculty because all are equally aware of the competencies to be mastered. Practitioner's knowledge of the outcomes sought enables them to identify and develop additional field experiences to enrich student learning. Indeed, knowledge of the competencies required makes it possible to utilize settings where appropriate learning experiences are available, but that have frequently not been utilized because they were not viewed as "social work" settings in the traditional sense. Women's centers, alternative schools, and group homes are examples of such settings.

Importance of a Broad Learning Environment.   While the curriculum development project emphasizes the outcomes of the educational endeavor, it also stresses the need for the creation and maintenance of a learning environment that stimulates and supports the development of a professional social worker. The competencies themselves indicate the need for a social worker who is committed to ethical practice, to furthering the knowledge of the profession, and to working in cooperation with others, including other professionals, in order to develop and maintain more humane service structures and opportunities for people.

These qualities are not developed in the classroom alone. They are fostered in a learning environment where students see practitioners, educators, and clients working together in an atmosphere of regard and respect for each other as well as for students, service consumers, and persons in other disciplines. In such an atmosphere, students see faculty learning from practitioners and practitioners learning from faculty. There is a common concern for helping students understand the dilemmas that arise as one attempts to translate the values of the profession into the ethical practice behaviors the profession demands. Students, educators, and practitioners can be openly critical in questioning each other's professional behaviors. Obviously, the development and maintenance of such a learning environment demands a practice education relationship characterized by mutual regard and trust. While this may seem difficult to achieve, it is critical to the development of a competent baccalaureate level humanistically oriented professional practitioner who has pride in her or his identity with the profession and its commitment to serving people.

A Strong Practice-Education Relationship Maximizes Resources. While the immediate priorities and goals of both educators and practitioners differ, both are ultimately concerned with making better services and opportunities available to people. Neither group can exist without the other if this common objective is to be realized. Social work education cannot prepare competent practitioners without the support and participation of practice, and practice needs the constant infusion of newly educated practitioners, to increase and improve its ranks. Resources to achieve the common purpose are limited in both the educational institution and the practice community. Cooperative activities, however, maximize the resources that are available.

OBJECTIVES OF THE PRACTICE-EDUCATION RELATIONSHIPS

A rationale for a close practice-education relationship has been established. Let us now examine some of the more specific objectives of that relationship.

As members of the same profession, social work educators and practitioners share some common commitments and concerns. The overriding common objective is that of developing, delivering, and maintaining adequate and effective services, resources, and opportunities for people. This cannot be accomplished without an ongoing supply and replenishment of personnel, well prepared by their education to carry out in practice the profession's mandates and purposes. In this sense, the education of the future professional social worker is merely the means to an end—that of achieving the profession's purposes. All members of the profession have a very large stake in the educational endeavor, because all are affected if the graduates of educational programs are not as effective in practice as they should be. Thus, all must have responsibility for developing and maintaining quality in social work education.

In working toward the achievement of common purposes, another factor must be considered. Students in social work education programs are learning to become competent practitioners. The practicum experience is powerful; it is here that students test out and develop their competence as practitioners. The quality of the practice students observe, learn from, and model after is fundamental to the development of a competent practitioner. Therefore, social work educators have a very large stake in the quality of practice and in its relevancy. Assurance of quality in practice is the responsibility of social work educators as well as practitioners. The resources of the educational program and their accessibility to practitioners can be critical to the development and maintenance of a practice community that grows in skill and sophistication.

Specific Practice-Education Objectives

Project findings identify some specific objectives that guide the way in which practice and education work together. Through a formalized structure (which is covered in Part III), practitioners and educators can work cooperatively in order to come to agreement on the following features of the educational program.

Outcomes of the Program and Criteria to Assess Performance. The curriculum development project identifies the basic practice competencies that should be included in every baccalaureate social work program. Their applicability to the specific mission, location, and resources of each program as well as how they are operationalized become a matter for local discussion and agreement. In addition, the development of criteria for the assessment of students' performance as they progress through the classroom and field components of the program is the responsibility and concern of practitioners as well as educators.

Ongoing Assessment of the Total Curriculum. The most significant data for the assessment of total curriculum will come from the assessment of student performance. The latter occurs at regular intervals throughout the student's experience in the program and provides considerable insight into program strengths as well as weaknesses. Use of this assessment data to indicate ways in which curriculum should be modified and/or changed is a responsibility that must be shared by practitioners, educators, and students, since "total curriculum" includes field learning experiences and how these are sequenced throughout the curriculum. (See Chapter 8, "Social Work Practice," for discussion of the field program and its place in the curriculum.)

Creation of a Total Learning Environment. The project places considerable emphasis on the need for devoting greater attention to the total milieu in which students learn to be social workers. Appropriate socialization into the profession, including development of a professional identity and ethical behaviors, is most significantly learned by observing the behaviors of other professional social workers. Practitioners and educators need to work together to create and maintain such an environment in the classroom as well as in the field. Ways must be found in which the entire professional community can support students who are placed, for legitimate reasons, in agencies and organizations without professional social workers on the staff. For these students, the development of professional identity may be difficult unless some special attention is given to the situation.

Maximizing Resources. As was pointed out earlier in this chapter, resources are not limitless for either practice or education. It is essential, therefore, that those available be used to the maximum and that ways be found to develop additional resources where necessary and appropriate. Together, practitioners and educators should take stock of the kinds of resources that are necessary and conduct an inventory of those already available. How these can be developed and utilized to enhance both the educational program and practice in the community can be a topic for mutual discussion. The inventory of resources should include: total teaching resources, including those within the practice community; teaching materials available within the college or university and within many agencies and organizations in the community; other resources within the college or university community, including research data and the special expertise of other disciplines; and the students themselves, who represent a very special kind of resource to the service structure of the community.

Developing a Continuing Education Plan. A well-developed plan is needed to meet the educational needs of practitioners, especially field instructors, who are directly involved with the implementation of curriculum in the field. Workshops, seminars, and other activities will be meaningful to the extent that planning becomes a mutual endeavor. Greater attention must also be given to ways in which the practice community helps social work educators keep current with practice. Faculty must openly recognize that when one leaves direct, day-to-day involvement with practice and assumes new responsibilities and priorities as a social work educator and academic, there can be lessening awareness of changes in current issues and practice. It is highly unlikely, despite good intentions and effort, that faculty can find the time to engage directly in practice, especially given the range of responsibilities in the educational sphere. Moreover, the college or university system itself places additional constraints and demands on faculty. Faculty may consciously learn from practitioners, however, if there is sufficient recognition of the need to do so.

Understanding Differences in Priorities and Values. While the ultimate objective of practitioners and educators is the same, immediate priorities and values are not. The first priority of the practitioner is service, with value placed on the quality of the service provided. The immediate priority of the educator is the education of the student, with value placed on the quality of the student's learning experience in the field. For the practitioner, however, the student in the agency can affect the quality of service provided. These differences between education and practice are natural and will always exist, but they can lead to great tension and even conflict unless each understands and respects the role of the other. Understanding and respect may be enhanced when opportunities exist for practitioners and educators to discuss their differences openly and to explore ways of working together.

Mutual Collaboration on Issues and Programs. There are times when, given sufficient information, each of the partners could be helpful to the other. Educators confront issues that could be resolved more adequately with the understanding, assistance, and collaboration of an organized practice community. Colleges and universities, on the whole, are anxious to have the goodwill of their community, and there are times when they can use the practice community's help in interpreting the needs of the educational program. For example, securing resources essential to competent faculty supervision of the field program is an area where practitioners are as concerned and articulate as educators. Having a faculty with sufficient practice experience even though all may not hold the doctorate, is another area that impacts on the practice community and in which the practice community might be helpful to university and college administration. On the other hand, there are many times when the assistance of the educator is invaluable in dealing with a particular practice issue or concern, through help with needed information and data or through direct involvement and assistance with interpretation.

Recognition of Contributions. Recognition for one's contribution is, as every social worker knows, a common human need. Even so, it appears, at times, that too little consideration is given to the need for recognizing the valuable contributions made by all in the effort to prepare competent practitioners. Practitioners who participate in the program do so with a sense of commitment to the profession. Time and energy as well as patience are demanded, particularly for those engaged in helping students develop practice skills in the midst of agency demands and pressures. Recognition for such efforts can do much to promote feelings of satisfaction and reward. Recognition may be offered in a variety of ways, ranging from adjunct faculty status to use of college or university facilities for formalized end-of-year recognition activities. This requires planning, so that recognition goes beyond the serendipitous "thank you" and is relevant to those being recognized.

By the same token, probably little attention is given to faculty's similar need for recognition and reward. While many faculty are recognized by the system in which they work, several others at the baccalaureate level are without the doctorate, and, despite competent performance, stand little chance of promotion and tenure—the major way a college or university rewards its faculty. Therefore, recognition from the professional practice community would provide encouragement and satisfaction.

DEVELOPING A STRUCTURE TO
ACHIEVE OBJECTIVES

The CSWE-sponsored mental health project report mentioned earlier in this chapter points out that for educators and practitioners, to simply talk with each other is not sufficient. Structure, formal and informal, must be established for productive and continuing interaction on agreed-upon goals. We support this position and in this section will touch briefly on some of the areas that should be considered as educational programs undergo reassessment and move to strengthen their working relationship with the service community. We recognize that some programs have already evolved a structure that is well-suited to their particular situation, and this is, of course, as it should be. Each community is different, so that in developing a structure, each program must consider such things as resources available, local traditions and customs, distances involved, weather conditions that may make travel uncertain during several months of the year, and other factors pertinent to the local situation.

Three issues appear to need careful consideration by all programs. These are (1) the definition of service community; (2) development of appropriate structures; and (3) potential problems.

Definition of Service Community

The most immediate and perhaps most difficult task will be to define who and what comprises the service community with which the educational program should be involved. Dolgoff's comments of several years ago are especially relevant here:

> The most frequent assumption on the part of both educators and practitioners is to equate agencies which serve as field instructional placements with the profession and the social work practice community. Logically, schools and programs of social work education have an implied relationship to the profession of social work and the practice community in addition to the agencies which provide field placements. The fact that both educators and practitioners usually equate the "field placement agency" and social work practice does have causes and inevitable consequences.[3]

Dolgoff goes on to point out that the educational system's lack of relationship and communication with other parts of the practice community cuts back on some of the essential information that it ought to receive and limits the contributions of the broader practice community.[4]

Even more significant is Harm's observation that "a total emphasis upon traditional models and agencies of service delivery is not adequate to meet emergent needs of large populations of consumers."[5] The implications of this position are supported by the curriculum development project. That is, the educational program must find ways to identify and relate to the entire range of service structures found in a given community. Traditional as well as nontraditional and/or emerging service groups, organizations, and agencies are all part of the service community to which the program must relate. The agencies involved with the program have opportunities to impact on the curriculum, and that in turn has enormous implications for current and future practice. For example, if the educational program relates itself primarily to field instruction settings in the traditional agency structure, there is, as Dolgoff points out, the very real possibility that graduates are channeled in certain career directions.[6]

Thus, we need to think about "service community" in a way that goes beyond what is normally considered the social work practice community. The service community would then include, in addition to the social work practice community and the structures through which social workers are currently providing services, settings where social workers may not now be employed but where services, resources, and opportunities are or could potentially be provided to people. Business and industry are examples of these settings. Other examples are many of the community-based groups and organizations concerned with people and their problems.

In addition to the above and including the traditional public and private agency structure and current field instructors, there is the range of associations and organizations that vary in significance from one community to another. Each program would need to review and assess such groups in terms of their appropriateness for participation. These groups include professional social work organizations, health care associations, child care groups, employment security, and developmental disabilities groups.

Hopefully, in carrying out the review to identify those groups in the community with whom the educational program will attempt to develop a relationship, the program will have the full support and assistance of the local chapter of the National Association of Social Workers (NASW). The program ought to expect, it would seem, that the NASW would be helpful and eager to provide some leadership to the educational program in its endeavor to strengthen this aspect of its functioning. The NASW must be recognized as unique; it is the largest of the social work professional associations and it carries the responsibility for setting and monitoring standards for the entire profession. NASW asserts that it is *the* professional association, the umbrella organization for all other professional social work groups. Whether one accepts this assertion or not, it is clear that the NASW is a significant group and that efforts to secure its active support and involvement ought to be carefully considered. At the very least, providing an opportunity for the NASW chapter to participate with educators in identifying and assessing the service community and in developing and maintaining the structure for ongoing interaction could go a long way toward breaking down the barriers of nonacceptance for the baccalaureate social worker (BSW) that presently seem to exist in some areas of the social work practice community. This is critical because, as project findings indicate, there is need for an ongoing professional support system for BSW's in practice.

In any event, the service community must be defined. This activity, at the outset, will need to be stimulated by educators.

Development of Appropriate Structure(s)

Once the major elements of the service community have been identified, faculty will need to provide strong and effective leadership to pull this community (or the appropriate representatives, if size is a factor) together to develop a plan and a structure to realize common objectives. If there are several educational programs in the same community, some collaboration between them may be indicated. Faculty should share this leadership role with an appropriate social work practitioner, such as a designated NASW representative, if appropriate. Many programs already have organizations of field instructors, so the appropriate practitioner at the beginning might come from that group. However, at the very outset of any effort to strengthen the program's relationship with the service and social work practice community it is critical that faculty demonstrate a genuine desire to share responsibility and work in partnership.

As the structure evolves, whether it takes the form of an advisory committee, a community relations task force, or other structure, the program's field instructors require particular attention. They are a special group with special needs. They are in an excellent position to assess the curriculum in a very special way, as they see the results in practice. The structure that develops should assure the opportunity for the voice of field instructors to be heard. The structure should also assure that the voice of other segments of the service community is heard. Finally, the structure should be developed and organized in a way that promotes respect for the contributions of all of the people participating in it.

Potential Problems

The material in the chapter does not intend to suggest that there are no problems or obstacles to the development of a stronger relationship between educators and the service community. Rather, it is believed that, if their intent is sincere, educators and practitioners, working together, can overcome or minimize many of the problems as they emerge. It might be helpful, however, to identify the kind of problems that tend to arise.

Role and Authority Ambiguity. Most frequently, faculty enter social work education directly from practice and receive very little assistance in learning to carry out their new roles as social work educators and academics. They may even show a reluctance to be viewed as educators and academics and a desire that others continue to view them as social work practitioners. This is due, perhaps, to some discomfiture at being removed from practice. If this situation prevails, with a failure to accept that there are a different set of roles and expectations within the system of higher education, difficulties may arise. These educators will be unable to interpret their appropriate role in relation to practitioners and, if their definition of role has remained that of practitioner, competition with practitioners leading to tension and conflict may ensue. (In chapter 3 the project attempts to help faculty by clarifying some of the expectations of the higher education system.)

On the other hand, practitioners who serve as field instructors clearly carry a teaching role and wish others to perceive them in this way. For example, when faculty reserve for themselves the final judgment on the student's performance in the field, practitioners feel that their teaching role and professional competence are undermined. Clearly, assessment of student competence in the field must be characterized by appreciation of role difference as well as the competence of one's colleagues.

The issue of authority and accountability, if not understood, may also create difficulties. There are different kinds of authority. Faculty, for example, are responsible for the total curriculum and its direction and carry institutional authority for carrying out this responsibility. However, when the individual student is placed in the agency for field instruction, faculty do not have authority over the specific interventions to be implemented.

Time. Time is a precious commodity. How it is used and toward what ends are critical issues for educators and practitioners alike, and must be dealt with by both groups working together. Practitioners, on the whole, raise serious objections to participating in activities that take a lot of time with little payoff. In addition, there are differing timetables and priorities in education and practice. Much of the educational program's timetable is related to the quarter or the semester, which is certainly not true of the practitioner's timetable.

Leadership. Both faculty and service community participants have important leadership roles. Service community representatives may and probably would carry the direct leadership roles in a formalized structure. Faculty, however, would need to assume major responsibility for planning activities, selection of necessary materials, presentation of information, and so on.

How comfortable people are with sharing leadership is critical. The ability of faculty to support the development of strong leadership within the service community group, even though that leadership may at times challenge faculty ideas or develop its own agendas, is of major significance and a primary factor in the success or failure of the educational endeavor.

Status and Power. Harm points out that, in the CSWE community mental health project, in which educators and practitioners worked together on committees, "practitioners often perceive educators as having higher status and power and they reacted to them with deference. . . . Also, some educators acted as though they were of higher status and with more power." She says further that, as both groups worked together, practitioners "sometimes discovered that their perceptions [of educators having more status and power] were not accurate."[7]

These perceptions do exist. Throughout the life of the curriculum development project and the many meetings sponsored by the project that involved both educators and practitioners there were occasions when educators could have dominated the situation. Fortunately, practitioners and educators associated with the project understood the significance of their roles and were able to handle such situations. This is, however, a potential problem area, and a great deal of self-awareness and sensitivity is called for, as well as candor in discussion.

Support Services. Support services involve costs. If an effort is viewed as an essential component of developing and maintaining a dynamic, viable, and changing curriculum, there must be a willingness to lend it financial support. The cost may not be great, but providing the resources certainly communicates the seriousness of intent to the practice community.

SUMMARY

This chapter has attempted to discuss why, consistent with the stance of the curriculum development project aimed at strengthening baccalaureate social work education, a reassessment of the relationship that programs have with their service community is essential. Curriculum objectives cannot be achieved without the active participation of the service community, and both segments share the goal of providing quality services to people. More specific objectives to guide the working relationship between the service community and the educational program were presented and discussed. Interaction between the two to achieve the objectives cannot be left to chance; the relationship must be formalized in a way that reflects the unique situation of each program and its community. Also reviewed were obstacles and problems that may hinder the practice-education relationship.

Hopefully, the material in this chapter will stimulate discussion of local programs between educators and practitioners, leading toward a strengthening of the relationship.

NOTES

1. *Policy Statements on Social Work Practice and Education and Structure and Quality in Social Work Education* (New York: Council on Social Work Education, 1976).

2. Harm, Mary Gay, ed., *A Report of the Community Mental Health Practice-Education Project* (mimeo) (New York: Council on Social Work Education, 1978), p. 15.

3. Dolgoff, Ralph, *Report to the Task Force on Social Work Practice and Education* (New York: Council on Social Work Education, 1976), p. 8.

4. Ibid., p. 9.

5. Harm, p. 23.

6. Dolgoff, p. 9.

7. Harm, p. 28.

Chapter Three

The Social Work Program: Its Place in Higher Education

Bradford W. Sheafor

INTRODUCTION

The development and maintenance of a high-quality baccalaureate program in social work requires considerable effort by those persons primarily concerned with the outcome of this educational endeavor (i.e., faculty, students, and the practice community). At one level the task involves finding an appropriate fit between the expectations of two major social institutions—the social work profession and higher education. At another level it involves developing a sound curriculum design that can be effectively implemented within the particular college or university in which a social work program is located.

For many programs, serious consideration of the Undergraduate Social Work Curriculum Development Project findings requires a rethinking of their relationship to both social work and to the college or university in which they are located. It points to the need for social work education to be responsive to emerging trends in various fields of social work practice. Baccalaureate social work programs are preparing students with a broad base of knowledge, values, and skills that allow for versatility in approaching the needs of practice. They should also provide leadership in the development and testing of new practice approaches that are responsive to changing needs in the field. Here the challenge of inquiry and experimentation, which is part of the fabric of higher education, serves the profession well.

It is evident that social workers bring many strengths to higher education that may contribute to positive changes in that social institution. Having worked in large bureaucratic organizations (e.g., most social agencies), social workers who are moving into faculty roles can more easily understand how a college or university operates. As classroom teachers social workers have a special value commitment to developing the potential of each student. In addition, their practice competence includes skill in promoting individual development and in working with group processes that can facilitate student learning. They also offer a perspective of the community, through ties with the social service delivery system that can help the school avoid an "ivory tower" orientation. Finally, social workers bring to the college or university a rich background in interdisciplinary teamwork that can facilitate the increasingly important collaborative efforts among disciplines on the college campus.

It is clear that social work has much to gain from its association with higher education, and that higher education also stands to gain from social work. This chapter is concerned with an examination of issues confronting social work educators as they operate at the interface of social work and higher education. It first discusses the more general question of the fit of social work into the fabric of higher education. It then turns to the place of the social work program within a college or university and examines how the faculty and the structure of the program can support the achievement of program objectives.

SOCIAL WORK AND HIGHER EDUCATION

Should professional education be conducted in academic institutions? The history of social work education reflects a long-standing struggle between persons who favored technical training for social workers in agency-sponsored institutes and those favoring a more general educational approach provided under the auspices of an academic institution.[1] The prevailing side in this issue, those favoring alliance with higher education, effectively demonstrated that as a profession social work must have a scientific base that extends beyond the apprentice training goals of any individual agency. Although social work education is now clearly established in academic settings, tension still exists in satisfying the academic expectations of institutions of higher education and, at the same time, meeting agency demands for trained workers.

The appropriateness of including social work education in institutions of higher learning lies in both the scope of the material to be learned and the value of exchange with other academic disciplines. Social work, particularly at the baccalaureate level, has increasingly broadened its scope to include the basic knowledge, values, and skills for intervention in a broad range of practice situations. The range of competencies identified by the project clearly suggests a scope well beyond technical or apprentice training. Further, as in many other professions, social work has recognized that the competent practitioner is a person who can view human behavior from a number of perspectives. These perspectives on the human condition are enhanced by knowledge gained from the study of history, biology, philosophy, literature, and the arts, as well as the more specific knowledge that might be acquired from the social sciences and the practice knowledge of related disciplines. In short, a sound general education is essential for the social worker.

Educational Philosophy of Social Work

Derrick, in his insightful article entitled "Liberal Education and Social Work Education," identifies four schools of thought in twentieth-century American higher education. These can be described as:[2]

1. Humanist-traditionalist school—This school of thought stresses knowledge of the ideas that have influenced human behavior, understanding of the tradition in which humans live, and ability to communicate clearly. It has opposed the view that ulitarianism is to be valued in higher education and opposed both the elective system and vocationally oriented courses.
2. General education movement—Characterizing this school of thought is the perception that knowledge of modern innovation and change is just as important as understanding traditional thinking. This school has focused on the social and emotional growth of the student, in addition to his or her intellectual development.
3. Pragmatist-progressive school—John Dewey, a clearly identified leader of this school, believed that education should liberate students' ability to think rather than focus on content. This liberation, according to Dewey, could occur in both liberal education and vocationally oriented courses.
4. Professional school model—This model has tended to devalue the importance of liberal education. It has substituted advanced technical knowledge in one profession for the more liberalizing knowledge in courses offered by a variety of academic disciplines.

In his assessment of the current status of baccalaureate education, Derrick concludes that while the desire for some degree of vocational education is clearly entrenched, it is generally accepted that this must be balanced with a liberal-general education.[3] The general education movement, then, perhaps best reflects higher education's contemporary educational philosophy.

The current educational philosophy of social work is reflected in the baccalaureate accreditation standards that require a program to demonstrate that it "builds on, and is integrated with, a liberal arts base that includes knowledge in the humanities, social, behavioral, and biological sciences."[4] Whereas the graduate model in social work education has been that of the professional school, the undergraduate model has broken precedent and is more closely identified with the general education movement. There is little question that much of the content in social work courses at the baccalaureate level is liberating for the undergraduate student. Thus baccalaureate programs are more than "junior" professional schools; they are programs with an educational philosophy that spans both vocational training and the accepted view of liberal education. They are best typified as a blend of the general education and pragmatist-progressive conceptions of higher education.

Is social work's conception of baccalaureate education viable in higher education? Although members of academia who are strongly identified with either of the more extreme schools of thought—humanist-traditionalist or professional—may seriously question the educational philosophy underpinning baccalaureate social work programs, there is little question that they fit into the mainstream of higher education. It is important to recognize that most institutions of higher education are characterized by multifaceted programs that include elements of all four schools of thought. Hutchins has described institutions of higher education as "a series of disparate schools and departments, united by nothing except the fact that they have the same president and board of trustees."[5] This disparity makes it possible for social work programs to establish objectives that aim to produce liberally educated graduates who are also prepared to discharge the duties of the profession.[6] Thus, from the standpoint of educational philosophy, baccalaureate programs have the opportunity to play a significant role in enhancing the liberal education provided by the college or university. From this vantage point social workers have an opportunity to help shape the future of liberal education so that it might be more concerned with the impact of society on the lives of individuals and social groups.

In summary, baccalaureate social work education has found a legitimate place in higher education. It has valuable contributions to make to academic institutions as well as having much to gain from the association with these institutions. Although students and the practice community should play a key role in determining program goals and objectives, the final responsibility rests with the program director and faculty. They must take the initiative to maximize the benefits that can accrue from this relationship.

Differences with the Traditional Academic Orientation

Despite its relative goodness of fit with the traditional orientation of academic institutions, there are areas of difference that the social work program might expect to encounter as it seeks to develop a solid place in the structure of the college or university. Although these differences are presented as polarized positions, the reader should be cautioned to recognize that there is considerable middle ground between these positions.

First, the traditional mission of higher education has been to impart knowledge to students. That goal has resulted in an emphasis on the student's intellectual development to the neglect of other aspects of that student's life. In helping to prepare the student for practice, the social work program must assume a more holistic concern and seek to facilitate the student's intellectual, social, and emotional growth and development. However, emotional activities that promote the broader goals of growth and development are often viewed with suspicion and perhaps considered not worthy of academic credit.

Second, the social work field and the traditional academic approach differ greatly in their treatment of values. Values are the heart and soul of social work. The social worker simply must develop strong value commitments and concern for individual development and social justice.[7] Thus the educational experience must help the student examine and arrive at a personal position in relation to those value issues. On the other hand, much of academia is committed to rigorous application of scientific method as a tool for understanding truth. The social work concern for value development stands at the opposite pole from this "value-free" approach.

Third, the academic tradition provides for the various programs to have considerable autonomy in building a curriculum. The only restraints are usually confined to the general requirements of the college or university and the established turf of other programs. Social work, however, faces many other guidelines and constraints. Through the Council on Social Work Education accreditation standards are established that reflect the prevailing view of social work and, therefore, influence the direction of program curriculum. In addition, most social work programs actively engage the practice community, as well as students, in their activities, and this involvement is meaningless if it cannot impact on program operation. This "external" influence on the program has many benefits, but it is not a factor to which academia is usually accustomed or sympathetic.

Finally, a sacred area of life for faculty members in higher education is academic freedom. The protection it affords faculty allows them to speak openly on controversial questions and gives them the freedom to pursue research questions to wherever they may lead. When carried to an extreme, that freedom permits the individual faculty member to teach whatever he or she may choose. For a sound social work program, however, the curriculum must be carefully integrated and the courses planned to allow appropriate sequencing of the required content. Once again, support for this approach as well as the machinery to implement it are not typically found in academic settings, where individual autonomy for the faculty member often takes priority over the need for a planned curriculum.

OPERATIONALIZING THE SOCIAL WORK PROGRAM

Faculty Roles and Responsibilities

Once the viability of social work education in institutions of higher learning is recognized, it is possible to turn attention to factors influencing the ability of a social work program to successfully accomplish its objectives. To work effectively within a college or university, the social work faculty members must become integral parts of that organization and play an active role in enhancing its ability to fulfill its mission.

Interface with the University. The faculty member should seek to develop an historical perspective of higher education as well as an understanding of current trends. Some of these trends are the merits of liberal and professional education, the similarities and differences in public and private universities, the effect of unionization on college campuses, developments in community colleges, implications of second majors, minors, and concentrations, the growth of human services education, the relationship between job preparation and college education, and the public view of the place of higher education in American society.[8]

The social work educator must also seek to become thoroughly familiar with issues and trends in social work education. In addition to reading the professional literature related to his or her own special interests and teaching assignments, the social work educator should become familiar with current and historical documents related to social work education.[9]

Another important factor is the school's investment in faculty development. The college or university should encourage and support faculty participation in meetings that relate to social work education and allow for exchange of ideas and approaches with other social work educators.

Finally, social work educators must seek to become effective change agents in their own colleges or universities. Jarrett observes that in higher education "change can occur at any level in the system and no power prerequisites should be imposed which will limit who can be an effective change agent."[10] It is appropriate in the context of higher education that all faculty members consider themselves agents of change who can enhance the viability of any college or university.

In his identification of the desirable characteristics of change agents in higher education, Jarrett helpfully draws attention to the following qualities these persons should possess:[11]

Attitudes:

- institutional loyalty (in addition to loyalty to profession or discipline)
- commitment to collaboration
- openness and flexibility
- willingness to risk failure

Knowledge:

- organizational structure
- education and higher education
- human behavior
- the particular college or university
- self-knowledge

Skills:

- diplomacy
- formation and maintenance of meaningful relationships
- development of coalitions
- bring order out of chaos
- assess, evaluate, plan, and implement a change strategy
- a sense of objectivity

When engaged in efforts to change the college or university, the faculty member must make use of all his or her social work skills. Faculty must make clear when they are representing their own views and when they are presenting a position of the social work program. Further, they must at least consider the implications of how they express their personal positions on controversial issues, as those positions may have repercussions for the entire program. Just as in working in a social agency, the program director and faculty members must learn the formal and informal structure of their school and seek to build positive relationships with key people in that structure. They should maintain their own creditability by stressing value positions consistent with those of the social work profession, for example, the importance of equality and opportunity for all persons associated with the college or university. Yet, on most issues social work educators can ill afford to assume an unyielding position and refuse to accept the inevitable tradeoffs that are part of every political process. Whenever possible, the faculty and program director should present a reasonably united front on key issues that face the school and/or the social work program. In short, the social and political skills of the faculty members can have much impact on the success of the social work program and the establishment of its appropriate place within the college or university.

Interface with Social Work Practice. In addition to the need to function effectively within the college or university, the social work program must also be prepared to work effectively with the immediate practice community. As part of the instructional faculty of the program and also as social workers with a major investment of time and energy in social work practice, field instructors have a great deal to contribute to the growth and development of the program. They need to have open channels for input into the program. Many programs have successfully formalized this opportunity for input by building a governance structure that includes field instructors (and students) in the significant policymaking groups for the program (e.g., faculty council, curriculum committee, and personnel committee). Full voting privileges for field instructor representatives on these bodies can produce most helpful results not only by obtaining practitioner input in the program but also by having persons in the practice community able to interpret the program.

Social work can set an excellent example for other departments by the meaningful involvement of the community in the affairs of the department and the program. The practice community may not only participate in departmental decisionmaking but also help to support social work interests in college or university decisionmaking. Social work faculty sometimes have difficulty interpreting the profession and the need for social work education to university administration. Community practitioners can do this very persuasively, and can utilize their ties to community decisionmakers (politicians, agency directors, the business community, etc.) to further the interests of social work education. These pressures are significant in all schools that depend on community goodwill, and are especially important in the case of public colleges and universities that rely on public funds. No school can afford to be totally isolated from its surrounding community, and practitioners from the community can be used to demonstrate how social work enhances these ties.

Another important means of maintaining a sound relationship with the practice community is for all faculty to serve in a field instruction or field liaison capacity. The dichotomy between classroom and field teaching often found in faculty assignments works against effective integration of the class and field dimensions of the program. In addition, the regular contact of faculty with social workers in agency practice and with students engaged in field learning helps them stay attuned to the changing needs of social work practice.

Finally, both the program and the community are benefited by faculty involvement in local professional organizations and social agencies. Assuming that faculty are usually experienced practitioners (although a trend toward new Ph.D.'s with little practice background is evident), their background can be most valuable to agencies through consultation, board membership, or volunteer service. There is, of course, a payoff for the program, as this activity provides another vehicle through which faculty can gain additional insights on current practice needs—to say nothing of the fresh "war stories" that can be used for illustration in the classroom.

Faculty Evaluation. The significant role of field instruction and service is one point where social work often differs from many academic disciplines. Schools with an orientation that leans in the direction of the humanist-traditionalist school may tend to undervalue nonclassroom instruction and service while overvaluing scholarly productivity. When this philosophy is expressed in the faculty reward system, through promotion, tenure, salary, and sabbatical leave, for example, the social work faculty members are disadvantaged and ultimately the program is damaged. Certainly a vital role for the faculty is to impact on such an evaluation system so that it will appropriately reward activities that are supportive of good practice-education relationships. The practice community can be especially helpful in interpreting significant faculty activities as they relate to the profession.

It is likely that even an evaluation system that fairly weights the expected activities of a social work faculty member will include the anticipation that there be scholarly productivity and research. That is one of the normal expectations for a faculty member in academia. This matter consistently poses a dilemma for social work educators. The MSW is accepted as the terminal practice degree in the profession and, as such, is intended to equip the graduate for competent social work practice. With very few exceptions, the "graduate teaching assistant" approach of preparing the student with the teaching, writing, and research skills to compete in the academic world is not followed in master's-level social work education. Thus the new teacher with the terminal practice degree and considerable practice experience brings many valued assets to the program, but is required to invest a great deal of effort in developing these other skills. Without considerable motivation and support, the faculty member may be disadvantaged when promotion and tenure decisions are made. On the other hand, the recent development of preparing many young doctoral candidates with the skill to survive in academia has yielded a body of social work educators with very limited practice experience to bring to the teaching situation. This difficulty in matching practice and academic expectations is a problem that social work has yet to resolve.

One approach to this difficulty is for the social work faculty to develop evaluative criteria that fairly measure the quality of their teaching in both class and field. This might appropriately involve student, peer, and self-evaluation of the faculty member's ability to carry out the teaching role.

Second, evaluation must also reflect the scholarly productivity and research activity expected of members of the academic community. This should include publications, monographs, papers, and workshops prepared and presented to an audience of peers. These activities are not only supportive of the interests of higher education, but are also consistent with the social work "Code of Ethics," which states that one should be aware of the "professional responsibility to add [one's] ideas and findings to the body of social work knowledge and practice."[1] [2]

Finally, evaluative criteria must recognize the professional, university, and community service activities of the faculty member. It should not only recognize leadership roles, but also be cognizant of the faculty member's ongoing effort to do the homework that makes committees function effectively and his or her willingness to spend the many hours of time in student contact that makes the latter's education as smooth and productive as possible. The value of faculty participation in community affairs can be interpreted by professional colleagues from the practice community. Once the difficult task of identifying these criteria is completed, they can then be weighted according to the proportion of time the faculty member is expected to devote to each activity. In their capacity as change agents, the faculty can then seek to interpret to the college or university the importance of using a flexible approach to faculty evaluation that is responsive to the workload expectations of each discipline. With a clear plan for their own evaluation in hand, the social work faculty has an improved chance of being evaluated by criteria appropriate to their activities.

Administrative Structure of the Program

An important factor contributing to the ability of a social work program to find a meaningful place in a college or university is the administrative structure of that program. Where a new or small faculty and student body exists, the social work program might appropriately be housed in the department of a related discipline or might even be part of a department made up of several disciplines. Larger and more established programs might expect to be independent departments within the college or university, while those programs, regardless of size or maturity, that operate as part of a school of social work offering multiple levels of social work education face an even different set of administrative issues. Each of these structural arrangements offers certain advantages to the program, and every effort must be made to build on the strengths of a structure while minimizing the losses that may be experienced.

Types of Administrative Auspices. In the past few years many baccalaureate social work programs have experienced changes in administrative auspices as they have grown, matured, and increasingly become an important part of higher education. While there has been little change in the percentage of programs housed in schools of social work, there has been a significant decline in the percentage located in the department of another discipline and related increase in structural arrangements providing the social work programs with more independence and visibility. Although the following categorization of administrative structure does not cover all of the unique arrangements that exist in social work programs, it provides a general picture of the changes that occurred between 1971 and 1977.

Administrative Auspice
of Social Work Program

	1971[1 3]	*1977*[1 4]
Program in academic department	56%	37%
Multidisciplinary department	11%	18%
Independent department	16%	27%
School of social work	16%	18%

It is clear that there are several structural arrangements that are viable for achieving social work objectives. The accreditation standards for baccalaureate programs recognize this phenomenon and state that the "ultimate determination of suitability depends on the degree to which the administrative structure supports the implementation of the objective of preparation for beginning social work practice."[1 5] The choice of an appropriate administrative structure for a given program will depend on program size, maturity, and resources as well as the political climate of the college or university and the potential for building mutually satisfying relationships with other disciplines.

Strengths and Limitations of Structural Patterns. Recognizing that each of the structural patterns enables social work programs to achieve their goals, the advantages and disadvantages of each structure can be examined. In this analysis special emphasis will be given to the internal and external issues that each program will need to address if it is to be a stable part of the college or university.

The most common administrative structure for a social work program is location in the *department of another academic discipline.* With the emergence of social work education on many college campuses in the past ten to fifteen years, it has been a common pattern to house these developing programs within an already established department. This pattern has continued to exist in higher education for many years as it has several advantages. It does not inflate the administrative costs for a small program that might not otherwise survive financially in that school, while at the same time it provides the emerging program with the protection afforded by a certain degree of anonymity and the academic creditability acquired through association with the established parent discipline. In most colleges or universities one can currently observe or historically identify this pattern of relationship between other disciplines, for example, between sociology and anthropology, or speech and English.

For many social work programs the most desirable approach may be to continue this structural arrangement for an indefinite period of time. Where positive collegial relationships develop and adequate resources are available to the social work program, this is a most productive arrangement. The social work program director and faculty can devote more energy to teaching and curriculum development and less to departmental administration. Further, the increased opportunity for interaction with members of the parent discipline can provide intellectual stimulation for the growth and development of both the social workers and the faculty from the host discipline. However, if the host discipline sees this as a means to syphon off resources from the social work program, or to control the social work curriculum by forcing students into their courses in an effort to maintain or increase credit hour production at a time of declining enrollment, this can be a dysfunctional relationship for social work.

Outside the department, this structure requires considerable effort from the social work faculty to keep its needs, interests, and contributions evident to other units of the college or university, to the students, and to the community-at-large. A faculty with substantial political and public relations abilities can surely minimize the difficulties experienced in external relationships.

A second administrative structure, the *multidisciplinary department*, exists where two or more disciplines develop equal partnerships under one umbrella department. This might typically be a department of social work and sociology or a department of social sciences made up of several disciplines. In these instances the department chair might be a social worker, someone from another discipline, or the position might be rotated every few years.

Internally, this pattern is also dependent on positive relationships among the disciplines and formalized agreements that protect each of the disciplines from exploitation by the others. This arrangement offers social work the opportunity for very close collaboration with one or more other disciplines, resulting in faculty stimulation and curriculum integration among the disciplines involved. This integration may benefit students by allowing greater flexibility in selecting an appropriate major field. There is, of course, the possibility that an unequal power balance will exist and the more dominant members of the department will inequitably allocate the resources of the department or promulgate a curriculum that is not in the best interests of each discipline. Compatibility of the disciplines involved, therefore, is an important variable in the success of these arrangements. Richan describes one issue of compatibility with academic disciplines that the social work faculty may experience:

> Unlike the academician, who needs a degree of insulation in order to work,
> the social worker must live and breathe the vitality of the world around
> him. No less the social work educator, who cannot afford to become
> isolated from the community if he is to prepare his students for relevant
> practice.[16]

Externally, this arrangement allows each discipline to have a moderate degree of general exposure and an influence over its fate. Where social work is part of the department title its presence is clearly recognizable in the school's literature, and where several programs share a common department title more consistent efforts are usually made to be sure that each is clearly identified. On the other hand, schools often generate composite planning and evaluation data at the departmental level, which nullifies their value for each discipline involved and hinders each one's ability to secure a fair share of the available resources. Further, unique features of social work, such as its efforts to involve students and the practice community in its decisionmaking process, may often be given little credence by the other disciplines. Clearly, there are strains with this type of structural arrangement.

The *independent department* is the third form of administrative structure commonly found among social work programs. This structure allows for a high degree of program independence. It is clearly identified on the campus and in the promotional materials distributed by the college or university. There is also relative flexibility in establishing policies and procedures, which makes it relatively easy to build a governance structure that includes contributions from both students and the social work practice community. As a self-contained administrative unit (i.e., one discipline, one curriculum, one budget), the program director and faculty of the independent department do not face the problems of interdisciplinary competition within the department and can concentrate their energy on program development and other issues that confront the program.

While internal problems are reduced for the independent department, some external problems are increased. This type of program is highly visible in the college or university as well as in the general community, and thus it is placed in direct competition with other departments. Data on program cost, credit hour production, faculty activity, and so on is openly reported, and the program must be prepared to defend itself against challenges concerning its productivity, service to other programs in the university, quality of students, and the performance of the faculty in teaching, scholarship, and service. Unfortunately, this comparison may not be made in

work in higher education. First, it is essential that the *identity* of social work as a unique discipline with its own knowledge, values, skills, purposes, and professional culture be recognized. It is not simply the applied arm of sociology or any other discipline. Rather, it derives its fundamental knowledge from a range of social science disciplines and its general knowledge from the arts, humanities, and sciences, and selects from that fund of information those items that enhance social work practice. The college or university must be prepared to recognize the distinctiveness of social work if it is to offer sound social work education.

Once the identity of social work is established in the college or university, the social work program is in a position to build bridges to other parts of the school without risk to its own standing. The findings of the curriculum development project point in the direction of establishing close ties with several academic disciplines to facilitate access to their specialized knowledge that may underpin social work practice. At the same time, a program adopting the project's competency-based approach might consider the importance of developing closer relationships with disciplines concerned with the skill development of students (e.g., education, clinical psychology, and child development), as opposed to limiting its relationships to the more traditional social science disciplines.

For the social work programs located within another academic department, or even those in a multidisciplinary department, considerable continuous effort must be made to interpret the unique identity of social work. This interpretation must consistently be made to colleagues from the other disciplines within the department as well as those from the larger college or university. This does not differ from the task of public interpretation of social work faced by most social workers, but specifically involves clarification of social work's similarities with and differences from other academic disciplines in regard to the knowledge, values, and skills required for entry-level social work practice. Programs located within a school of social work often face the problem of interpreting baccalaureate social work education and practice within the school, while all four structural forms require ongoing attention to this activity within the broader college or university and community.

Second, the social work program must be *visible* on the campus and in the public information released by the university. With the growing demand for baccalaureate social work education and only about 240 accredited programs scattered throughout the United States, prospective students are not well served by a school that does not clearly identify the existence of a social work program in its catalog and other promotional materials such as posters, bulletins, and news releases. While student interest in higher education has declined, the sector on most campuses that has experienced growth has been professional and career-related education.[17] A survey conducted by the Carnegie Council on Policy Studies on Higher Education compared the proportions of undergraduates majoring in several areas between the academic periods of 1969-70 and 1975-76. This survey found that while social science majors were decreasing from 18 to 8 percent, majors in the professional fields were increasing from 38 to 58 percent.[18]

That social work has shared in this professional growth is evidenced by the fact that the number of full time degree students in accredited baccalaureate social work programs increased nearly 27 percent between the 1975-76 and 1977-78 academic years alone.[19] This is likely to continue because of social work's appeal to the older, nontraditional students who are attending colleges and universities in increasing numbers. For with declining enrollments, potentially declining enrollments, or smaller proportions of traditional students, the presence of a social work program becomes a valuable resource. Making it visible is in the interest of the total college or university. Further, it is essential that prospective employers, licensing boards, and graduate programs know if a student has completed the accredited curriculum of the social work program. This information can be clearly communicated if the program is visible in the community and there is provision for including such information on the transcript of each graduate.

The problems of visibility are greatest for the social work program located within the structure of another academic department. Prospective students often find it difficult to discover the existence of the program by reading the university's bulletin or examining the promotional materials. In those schools where social work is not an independent major or must be taken in conjunction with another major, the public—and especially potential employers—do not receive clear evidence of the comprehensiveness of an accredited social work program. These problems often exist in the multidisciplinary department (especially if it serves as an umbrella for several disciplines), while those programs located in a school of social work frequently face a different problem, that of making the baccalaureate program visible within the context of the other social work education programs offered by the school. The social work program functioning as an independent department is the one structure that can be relatively free of the need for concentrated efforts to enhance visibility.

Third, there must be recognition of the *autonomy* required to maintain an effective social work program. Autonomy is needed to support professional goals when these are not the same as university goals. For example, some perceive social work professional goals as a challenge to the traditional sanctity of academic freedom because they require a sequenced and integrated curriculum. Further, professional goals encourage a new approach to governance by encouraging community involvement in decisionmaking, expecting release time for program administrators (e.g., the program director and the field coordinator), and requiring adequate support staff, space, and library resources.

For the social work program that is located in the department of another academic discipline or is part of a multidisciplinary department, the achievement of necessary autonomy requires considerable effort. To insure program quality, the department may be required to reallocate money and power to social work. When funds are reallocated within the constraints of scarce department resources other programs must suffer, and the social work program must deal with the inevitable loss of support that ensues. Further, the serious involvement of students and the practice community in program governance is more readily accomplished in those programs located in schools of social work or operating as independent departments. Those programs that are within a school of social work, however, face a difficulty in assuring that the baccalaureate program has adequate autonomy to secure and assign resources to achieve its specific program objectives. Finally, in the area of criteria for faculty evaluation, it is important that the program have some degree of autonomy to establish criteria appropriate to the background and activity of the social work educator. The social work programs in another academic department and in the multidisciplinary department often must live with criteria developed for other disciplines.

Fourth, the faculty of a social work program must have opportunities for *participation* in the governance of the college or university. Social work faculty members who are sensitive to the needs of the community can help the university avoid some of the pitfalls of adopting policies that may isolate the school from its constituency. Further, the value orientation of social work that stresses the development of individual potential is often a valuable perspective that is not expressed by others in the consideration of policy issues. This voice from the social work perspective helps to keep the university's focus on the needs of students and society.

Because of the distinctiveness of the social work program, it is also important, through formal or informal arrangements, that the director of the program be a part of any "council of department heads" that makes or recommends policy affecting the program. The program director should have direct access to the next higher level of administration—usually a dean—and be included in such critical decisions as budget determination, the allocation of faculty and staff positions, and the assignment of space. In addition, the program director should have access to other administrative officials of the university whenever their understanding of the program is essential to its continued growth and development. Finally, the social work faculty should be represented on faculty advisory or decisionmaking groups that are concerned, for example, with curriculum, promotion, and tenure.

The guarantee of participation in college and university governance, is usually provided, at least at a minimum level, for some faculty in independent departments and schools of social work. Beyond that opportunity, the skill, knowledge, and active commitment of time and energy are what allows faculty members to extend that contribution more fully within the college and university. The faculty members from programs within academic departments and multidisciplinary departments are not usually assured representation in university governance and must compete with colleagues within the department for the available positions. If there are not good collegial relationships in the departments and the social work faculty members are outnumbered, they often have limited opportunities for participation in the decisionmaking structure of the college or university. If good collegial relationships exist, however, the support from other disciplines in the department can be a decided advantage in gaining opportunity for this involvement.

Fifth, a social work program should have available, and, where possible, be in control of, the necessary *resources* (e.g., money, staff time, and space) for the maintenance of that program, and the program director should have authority to allocate these resources to achieve program goals. Although university budgets usually have only a few discretionary items, the social work program should have access to those few flexible dollars, to be able to support creative and innovative plans.

Compared to most academic disciplines, social work programs have been successful in securing outside funding to support their development. As these sources of outside funding have eroded, the more popular social work programs are thrown into direct competition with the declining social science disciplines for the scarce resources available to support staff and operating expenses. To maintain enrollment levels, many of these disciplines have begun to move toward "applied" aspects of their disciplines, which again places them in direct conflict with social work. When a social work program shares a department with the competing disciplines, it takes considerable effort to secure and maintain the necessary resources to support the program.

The independent social work department can negotiate directly for these resources with a dean. The program in a school of social work shares this advantage, yet must compete for the social work dollars with other programs in the school. The ability to acquire the necessary resources in a school of social work, then, requires that the baccalaureate program have direct access to the school's decision-making structure.

The ability to secure resources is in no way assured for the independent social work department, but direct access to a dean or other person who allocates large enough sums of money and other resources to have a significant impact on a program is an important asset. For the programs with other structures, the ability to secure resources is often dependent on the goodwill of department heads from other disciplines.

Project findings underline the importance of social work programs building collaborative relationships with other disciplines in the college or university in order to maximize the achievement of objectives. Albright notes that:

> to a considerable extent a university is similar to a holding company which owns the securities of the affiliated companies but leaves the operations to its individual affiliates. In effect, many universities have become conglomerates without actually providing the networks or directions by which the parts can be related.[20]

In this environment, which is formed of relationships similar to those that exist among the disciplines sharing responsibility in social agencies, the social work program can bring considerable skill and experience to the promotion of teamwork. These contributions can significantly influence the viability of the college or university and, at the same time, enhance the position of social work among the disciplines represented on the campus.

The ability to collaborate with other divisions of the college or university can specifically enhance the quality of the social work program. A thrust of the project recommendations is for greater integration of social work programs into the fabric of higher education, so that the full range of educational resources are used in the provision of curriculum content. The maintenance of positive working relationships with related departments becomes even more critical when the social work curriculum is built on the assumption that students will acquire specific knowledge from courses offered by those departments. This collaborative activity requires the negotiation for specific content to be included in these courses and monitoring to be sure that it is maintained in all sections. The ability to trade off required student enrollment for the inclusion of specific content places the social work program in a strong bargaining position.

This situation also may promote consideration of new arrangements that could benefit the entire university. Social workers might suggest the consideration of minors, concentrations, or second majors as options that will benefit students as they explore career decisions. It is, of course, essential that such options be designed in a way that does not compromise the integrity of the social work program. Finally, exploring the possibility of interdisciplinary programs and courses in areas such as criminal justice, women's studies, gerontology, human sexuality, helping processes, ethnic studies, and human diversity is a potentially important leadership role that can be played by social work.

When endeavoring to build collaborative relationships with other disciplines, the program located in a multidisciplinary department or the department of another discipline appears to have the advantage. The daily activity with those disciplines provides an opportunity to build positive relationships with them. However, the program must be careful not to allow the close contact with a few disciplines to cut off the opportunity for developing linkages with a number of other disciplines within the college or university. The independent programs are usually in regular contact with other liberal arts departments and require only a moderate expenditure of energy to build these collaborative relations. Programs in schools of social work tend to be more isolation and must actively build linkage arrangements with the appropriate disciplines.

The last major issue facing baccalaureate social work programs is that of building *linkages* to other social work programs. If clients and the general public are to be well served, it is important that programs of social work and social service education in a given geographic area be carefully planned and articulated with each other. Certainly, programs offered at the community college, bachelor's, master's, and doctoral levels must be carefully linked to each other. Social work programs also have a responsibility to provide continuing education and staff development opportunities for the local social work practice community.

The program modifications required for the necessary linkage arrangements are difficult under any program structure. The independent department, the program in a multidisciplinary department, and the program in the department of another discipline all must expend considerable effort to develop and sustain such linkage arrangements, as none of these structures encourages interaction with other social work programs. The program in a school of social work does have the advantage of being a structure that facilitates contact with the other programs in that school, making it possible to develop clear bachelor's-master's linkages and to tie into schoolwide continuing education programs.

In summary, there is no evidence to support an argument that resolution of any of the above issues can be achieved entirely through a specific administrative structure. Nor does any structure preclude resolving all the problems. Rather, this discussion suggests that structure helps to determine the issues on which the faculty members and program director must expend their time and energy.

CONCLUSION

As relative newcomers to higher education, baccalaureate social work educators have developed an educational philosophy that is quite compatible with the dominant philosophy in undergraduate education, although somewhat different from the professional education model of MSW programs. They have found that they possess valuable tools for effective functioning in academic settings and have learned that they can make significant contributions to the direction that higher education will be taking.

Although higher education has proven to be a satisfactory arena for social work education, programs must make a substantial effort to develop and maintain a good fit with several aspects of that environment. They must make ongoing efforts to enhance their interface with both the college or university and the community. Because the effort required in these activities differs from that of the academic disciplines, social work must give special attention to developing and gaining acceptance of faculty evaluative mechanisms that recognize the uniqueness of social work education and the demands on its educators.

Four dominant patterns of administrative structure have evolved in social work education. Each has certain strengths that allow the program to evolve in particular directions. None of the structures prohibits the program from achieving objectives, but many require the expenditure of additional effort to resolve issues of program identity, visibility, and autonomy, while influencing the opportunity for participation in the college or university and access to faculty and supportive resources. In addition, structure also impacts on a program's ability to build collaborative relationships with other disciplines and linkage with other social work programs. Each program must seek a structure appropriate for its unique situation and utilize the interpersonal competence of the faculty members to overcome the limitations inherent in that structure.

NOTES

1. Lubove, Roy, *The Professional Altruist* (Cambridge, Mass.: Harvard University Press, 1965), pp. 140-56.
2. Derrick, Paul, "Liberal Education and Social Work Education," *Journal of Education for Social Work* 4 (Winter 1978):33-35.
3. Ibid., p. 35.
4. *Standards for the Accreditation of Baccalaureate Degree Programs in Social Work* (New York: Council on Social Work Education, 1974), p. 1.
5. Hutchins, Robert Maynard, *The Higher Learning in America* (New Haven: Yale University Press, 1936), p. 59.
6. Mayhew, Lewis B., and Patrick J. Ford, *Reform in Graduate and Professional Education* (San Francisco: Jossey-Bass, 1974), p. 3.
7. Morales, Armando, and Bradford W. Sheafor, *Social Work: A Profession of Many Faces* (Boston: Allyn and Bacon, 1977), pp. 69-87.
8. It might be useful to the faculty member to read Tyler, Bloom, Mayhew, Hutchins, Whitehead, Dewey, and Bruner. In addition, major evaluations of higher education, such as the reports of the Carnegie Commission on Higher Education, are valuable. In relation to teaching, one might find the following books useful:

Austin, Alexander, *Four Critical Years* (San Francisco: Jossey-Bass, 1977)
Cross, K. Patricia, *Accent on Learning* (San Francisco: Jossey-Bass, 1976)
Eble, Kenneth E., *The Craft of Teaching* (San Francisco: Jossey-Bass, 1976)
Levine, Arthur, and John Weingart, *Reform of Undergraduate Education* (San Francisco: Jossey-Bass, 1974)
Milton, Othmar, and associates, *On College Teaching* (San Francisco: Jossey-Bass, 1978)

To stay abreast of developing issues in higher education, *The Chronicle of Higher Education* and *Capsules: A Review of Higher Education Research* (published by Concordia College, Moorhead, Minnesota 56560) are helpful.
9. Useful resources related to social work education are sparse. One might review its history by reading about the educational efforts of such social work pioneers as Mary Richmond, Edith Abbott, Edward T. Devine, Julia Lathrop, Sophonisba Breckenridge, and Porter R. Lee. Another useful approach is to examine the histories of the American Association of Schools of Social Work,

the National Association of Schools of Social Administration, and their eventual merger into the Council on Social Work Education (CSWE). Significant evaluation of social work education may be found in the following curriculum studies:

Hollis, Ernest, and Alice Taylor, *Social Work Education in the United States* (New York: Columbia University Press, 1951)
Boehm, Werner, ed., *Council on Social Work Education Curriculum Study*, 12 volumes (New York: Council on Social Work Education, 1959). (See especially Herbert Bisno, *The Place of Undergraduate Curriculum in Social Work Education*, vol. 2.)
Madison, Bernice, *Undergraduate Education for Social Welfare* (San Francisco: Rosenberg Foundation, 1960)
Barker, Robert, and Thomas Briggs, eds., *Manpower Research on the Utilization of Baccalaureate Social Workers: Implications for Education*, 2 vols. (Washington, D.C.: U.S. Government Printing Office, 1972)
Teare, Robert, and Harold MacPheeters, *Manpower Utilization in Social Welfare* (Atlanta: Southern Regional Education Board, 1970)
Ryan, Robert, and Harold MacPheeters, *A Core of Competence for Baccalaureate Social Welfare* (Atlanta: Southern Regional Education Board, 1971)
Baer, Betty L., and Ronald Federico, *Educating the Baccalaureate Social Worker: Report of the Undergraduate Social Work Curriculum Development Project* (Cambridge, Mass.: Ballinger, 1978). (For a summary of the studies listed above, see pp. 33-38.)

One can stay current on issues and developments in social work education by keeping up with books and pamphlets published by CSWE and regular readings of the *Journal of Education for Social Work*.

10. Jarrett, Herbert A., Jr., "Change Agent Qualities and Situation Feasibility in Higher Education," *Liberal Education* 59 (December 1973): p. 445.

11. Ibid., pp. 445-48.

12. "Code of Ethics" (Washington, D.C.: National Association of Social Workers, 1960; amended 1967).

13. *Colleges and Universities with Accredited Undergraduate Social Work Programs* (New York: Council on Social Work Education, July 1977), pp. 1-17.

14. Stamm, Alfred, *Analysis of Undergraduate Social Work Programs Approved by CSWE, 1971* (New York: Council on Social Work Education, 1972), p. 12.

15. *Standards*, p. 4.

16. Richan, Willard C., "The Social Work Educator's Dilemma: The Academic vs. the Social Revolution," *Journal of Education for Social Work* 9 (Fall 1973):54.

17. Cheit, Earl F., *The Useful Arts and the Liberal Tradition* (New York: McGraw-Hill, 1975), p. 13.

18. "Surveys Show Drop in Social-Science, Humanities Majors," *The Chronicle of Higher Education* 15 (Dec. 19, 1977):7.

19. Rubin, Allen, and G. Robert Whitcomb, *Statistics on Social Work*

Education in the United States: 1977 (New York: Council on Social Work Education, 1978), p. 23.

20. Albright, A.D., "The University and the Social Professions," in Harry M. Barlow, ed., *Higher Education and the Social Professions* (Lexington, Ky.: University of Kentucky College of Social Professions, 1973), pp. 83-84.

REFERENCES AND BIBLIOGRAPHY

Barlow, Harry M., ed. *Higher Education and the Social Professions.* Lexington, Ky.: University of Kentucky College of Social Professions, 1973.

Carnegie Commission on Higher Education. *Less Time, More Options.* New York: McGraw-Hill, 1971.

Cheit, Earl F. *The Useful Arts and the Liberal Tradition.* New York: McGraw-Hill, 1975.

Derrick, Paul, "Liberal Education and Social Work Education." *Journal of Education for Social Work* 4 (Winter 1978):31-38.

Dolgoff, Ralph. "Administrative Auspices for Undergraduate Social Welfare Programs: Advantages and Disadvantages." *Social Work Education Reporter* 17 (Sept. 1969):22-24.

Facing the Challenge. New York: Council on Social Work Education, 1973.

Feldstein, Donald. *Undergraduate Social Work Education: Today and Tomorrow.* New York: Council on Social Work Education, 1972.

Gartner, Alan. *The Preparation of Human Service Professionals.* New York: Human Sciences Press, 1975.

Glick, Lester J., ed. *Undergraduate Social Work Education for Practice: A Report on Curriculum Content and Issues.* Vols. 1 and 2. Washington, D.C.: U.S. Government Printing Office, 1971.

Henry, David D. *Challenges Past, Challenges Present: An Analysis of American Higher Education Since 1930.* San Francisco: Jossey-Bass, 1975.

Hockenstadt, Merl C., Jr. "Higher Education and the Human Service Professions: What Role for Social Work?" *Journal of Education for Social Work* 13 (Spring 1977): 52-59.

Hughes, Everett C., *et al. Education for the Professions of Medicine, Law, Theology, and Social Welfare.* New York: McGraw-Hill, 1973.

Hutchins, Robert Maynard. *The Higher Learning in America.* New Haven: Yale University Press, 1936.

Issues in Planning for Undergraduate Social Welfare Education. Atlanta: Southern Regional Education Board, 1970.

Jarrett, Herbert A., Jr. "Change Agent Qualities and Situation Feasibility in Higher Education." *Liberal Education* 59 (December 1973):442-48.

Kraft, Ivor. "Governance and the Professional School." *Journal of Education for Social Work* 11 (Spring 1975):68-75.

Kristenson, Avis. "Autonomy in the Administrative Relationships of Schools of Social Work in the United States to Their Parent Institutions." *Journal of Education for Social Work* 4 (Spring 1968):21-30.

Leslie, Larry L. *Innovative Programs in Education for the Professions.* University Park, Pa.: Center for the Study of Higher Education, 1974.

Levine, Arthur, and John Weingart. *Reform of Undergraduate Education.* San Francisco: Jossey-Bass, 1974.

Mayhew, Lewis B., ed. *General Education: An Account and Appraisal.* New York: Harper, 1960.

_____. *Colleges Today and Tomorrow.* San Francisco: Jossey-Bass, 1969.

Mayhew, Lewis B., and Patrick J. Ford, *Reform in Graduate and Professional Education.* San Francisco: Jossey-Bass, 1974.

Richan, Willard C. "The Social Work Educator's Dilemma: The Academic vs. the Social Revolution," *Journal of Education for Social Work* 9 (Fall 1973):51-57.

Schein, Edgar H. *Professional Education: Some New Directions.* New York: McGraw-Hill, 1972.

Shimer, Eliot R. "Social Work Education in a Hostile Environment: Programs Under Academic Attack," *Journal of Education for Social Work* 13 (Spring 1977):107-13.

Smith, G. Kerry, ed. *The Troubled Campus: Current Issues in Higher Education.* San Francisco: Jossey-Bass, 1970.

Chapter Four

Teaching/Learning Strategies to Support the Attainment of Social Work Practice Competencies

**Edna T. Roth and
Ronald C. Federico**

INTRODUCTION

The educational outcomes for the entry level baccalaureate professional social worker identified by the Undergraduate Social Work Curriculum Development Project are most likely attained in a teaching/learning environment that models and supports their development. This environment should promote systematic, analytic thinking that emerges from a clearly defined knowledge base. It should also provide models of effective, purposeful, and ethical interpersonal behavior while facilitating self-directed, collaborative, responsible interaction between students, and between students and others related to the program.

This chapter will discuss teaching/learning principles that help to create the educational environment described above. It begins with a summary of project findings that have implications for the teaching/learning environment. Then, after a brief review of relevant teaching/learning theories and principles, some specific strategies for using these principles to attain the educational outcomes specified in the project are considered.

PROJECT FINDINGS

There are five major project findings that seem to have the greatest relevance for the teaching/learning environment.

1. The development of *analytical skills* is basic to holistic assessment. The view of social work practice espoused by the project emphasizes the social worker's ability to understand the multiple aspects of a person and his or her situation. Adequate planning for problem-solving purposes cannot occur without this ability. The development of such analytical skills as a basis for interactional skills requires a teaching/learning environment that exposes students to the diversity inherent in all people and situations and that enables them to master and integrate knowledge in ways that encourage its application to concrete life situations.

2. Entry level baccalaureate professional practice requires an understanding of appropriate autonomy and self-direction. The teaching/learning environment should help students interact collaboratively and make maximum use of the expertise and resources they and others possess. Autonomy and self-direction are not synonymous with isolation, autocracy, and willfulness. Rather, they are to be understood as indicative of the ability to make professionally sound decisions after having utilized all the resources available. This reflects a need for autonomy and self-direction to be placed within the context of the values of the profession. Since baccalaureate social workers often practice in settings offering limited professional support networks, they must learn how to utilize whatever support networks exist, while still preserving their social work perspective. Clearly, the teaching/learning environment is crucial, in terms of providing students with opportunities to learn to work collaboratively yet still be responsible for their actions. Self-evaluation as part of professional autonomy is also either facilitated or negated by the teaching/learning environment.

3. Baccalaureate social work practice includes the use of existing knowledge that is relevant for practice. Students must learn to be active learners, rather than passive consumers of knowledge that they view as unchallengeable or otherwise beyond their influence. Learning how to find and use knowledge becomes as important as mastering the knowledge itself. Being able to assess one's own knowledge, and knowing how and when to make it available to others are also important skills. The teaching/learning environment plays an important role here, either by encouraging students to participate in their own growth as learners and as teachers, or by discouraging their active inquiry by using a model that clearly separates teachers from learners and that defines learning as a passive activity controlled by teachers.

4. Baccalaureate social work education utilizes the total curriculum, not just social work courses. Learners need to see knowledge as a

group of components that are combined into a relatively unified package with which to better understand the world, rather than as discrete bodies of information that rarely relate to each other. Bridges between social work and other disciplines are constantly built and used, so that social work becomes embedded in a rich and interlocking fabric of theoretical and applied knowledge and action. Faculty are important modelers of this approach to the degree that they actively discourse and collaborate with colleagues in other departments. Those who remain exclusively within social work model a view that sees the discipline as static, thus isolating social work from other disciplines whose theoretical and practical concerns are basic to seeing human behavior as a complex, everchanging system.

5. Competent social work practice involves using interventive skills within the value and ethical boundaries of the profession. Throughout the student's learning in the program, he or she must be made aware of personal values in a thoughtful, supportive way. As discussed earlier, an active orientation is crucial, so that the learner takes responsibility for his or her own values, and begins to make professionally sound decisions about the wisdom of social work as a career choice. Autonomy and self-direction should prevail over passive acceptance of decisions by others about one's own suitability for the profession. The utility of professional values and ethics must be part of learning how to use knowledge, so that arbitrary distinctions between knowing and doing are avoided. Here, as throughout the curriculum, analytical and interactional skills go together, and learners must constantly be exposed to values and ethics as underlying both types of skills.

OVERVIEW OF TEACHING/LEARNING
THEORIES AND PRINCIPLES

Strange as it may seem, there is no well-defined activity called teaching; it seems to be a different phenomenon for children than it is for adults. The concept of teaching that seems most consistent with project findings is that used by Carl Rogers. He sees a teacher as a facilitator of learning who has three important attitudinal qualities: realness and genuineness; nonpossessive caring, prizing, trust, and respect; and empathic understanding and sensitive and accurate listening.[1]

A teacher has to choose between a basically pedagogical (literally, leading children) and an andragogical (leading men, that is, adults) approach to learning. The differences are significant, and reflect different views of why people learn, how they learn, and their readiness to learn. These differences are summarized by Knowles as follows:[2]

1. Whereas children are dependent, growth toward adulthood involves increasing self-direction. Enforced dependency in learning situations tends to generate resentment and resistance in adults who value their self-direction.
2. As individuals mature, they accumulate life experiences that then become learning resources as well as a context in which new learning is understood. Knowledge transmittal techniques that ignore this experience is perceived by the learner as personally devaluing and irrelevant. Furthermore, individual cognitive styles (ways of processing information) are generally more important determinants of learning for adults than for children.
3. As people grow, learning readiness is related more to the desire to perform evolving social roles more adequately than it is to biological development and academic pressure. Therefore, learning occurs most readily when the adult learner sees its relevance to the performance of life tasks.
4. Adults tend to have a problem-centered orientation to learning rather than the subject-centered orientation that children have. Learning for adults is generally facilitated when it relates to their ability to solve a problem, and may be most readily organized by beginning with an experienced problem and then moving to knowledge that relates to its solution.

Whichever approach a teacher takes, three major theories are used to explain the learning process itself. *Behavioral theories* emphasize stimulus-response learning based on classical and operant conditioning principles. *Whole learning* or *gestalt theories* emphasize patterns of action, with learning resulting from the relatively sudden perception of the relationship between different factors. These patterns are then carried over to new situations. This theoretical approach emphasizes the relationships between objects and events in the learning environment rather than viewing response as occurring primarily between isolated stimuli. Gestalt theories also emphasize motivation as an important element in learning. Finally, *field theories* emphasize the importance of the learner's life space in the learning process. The individual's frame of reference invests learning situations with meaning and is an important determinant of the learning that occurs.[3]

The above is obviously just the barest sketch of a massive body of theory and, as is so often the case, the practitioner (i.e., the teacher) has to decide what parts of the theories to use. Each of the areas of theory has something to contribute to those seeking to become more effective teachers, and Knowles has tried to synthesize them into an andragogical approach that he feels is especially useful with the adult learner. His synthesis results in sixteen principles of teaching:

1. The teacher exposes students to new possibilities of self-fulfillment.
2. The teacher helps each student clarify his own aspirations for improved behavior.
3. The teacher helps each student diagnose the gap between his aspiration and his present level of performance.
4. The teacher helps the student identify life problems they experience because of the gaps in their personal equipment.
5. The teacher provides physical conditions that are comfortable and conducive to interaction.
6. The teacher accepts each student as a person of worth and respects his feelings and ideas.
7. The teacher seeks to build relationships of mutual trust and helpfulness among students by encouraging cooperative activities and refraining from inducing competitiveness and judgementalness.
8. The teacher exposes his own feelings and contributes his resources as a colearner in the spirit of mutual inquiry.
9. The teacher involves the students in a mutual process of formulating learning objectives in which the needs of students, of the institution, of the teacher, of the subject matter, and of the society are taken into account.
10. The teacher shares his thinking about options available in the designing of learning experiences and the selection of materials and methods and involves the students in deciding among these options jointly.
11. The teacher helps the students to organize themselves (project groups, learning-teaching teams, independent study, etc.) to share responsibility in the process of mutual inquiry.
12. The teacher helps the students exploit their own experiences as resources for learning through the use of such techniques as discussion, role playing, case method, etc.
13. The teacher gears the presentation of his own resources to the level of experience of his particular students.
14. The teacher helps the students to apply new learning to their experience, and thus to make the learnings more meaningful and integrated.
15. The teacher involves the students in developing mutually acceptable criteria and methods for measuring progress toward the learning objectives.
16. The teacher helps the student develop and apply procedures for self-evaluation according to these criteria.[4]

From these sixteen teaching/learning principles, it is possible to derive six that summarize the major points and that are especially useful to the social work educator.

1. Learning should be an opportunity for individual growth and personal goal attainment.
2. Teaching/learning experiences should build on the learner's existing knowledge and life experiences, and should emphasize the integration and application of knowledge as part of this process.
3. The teaching/learning process should build on and further develop respect and support between teachers and learners, and among learners.
4. Teaching/learning should involve the sharing of resources between teachers and learners, and among learners.
5. Teachers and learners should engage in mutual decisionmaking from identified options, especially in regard to goal identification, selecting effective individual learning strategies, and developing assessment procedures.
6. The learning environment is a crucial component of the teaching/learning process and includes the physical environment, the context for interpersonal behavior, and support for diverse cultural values and behavior.

APPLYING TEACHING/LEARNING PRINCIPLES

A social work educator is concerned with curriculum content that is essential to the attainment of professional competence and with ways to structure learning experiences so that the content is mastered. In order to accomplish this, the educator needs—

1. to know the content area, including what learning opportunities are needed and what educational resources are available;
2. to break the content area into its component parts, which address the application of knowledge, decisionmaking, and the specific relationship of the content to professional social work practice;
3. to assess obstacles to the effective teaching of the content;
4. to examine connections to other relevant content areas;
5. to construct a format that is appropriate for his or her students at the time, the specific school or organization with its particular mission, and his or her specific teaching style.

Content Precepts

Two informal precepts about teaching are teach only what you know and overprepare. Overpreparation refers here to efforts to master the anxieties of being unfamiliar with a situation or a content area. For the educator who is an open learner, overpreparation, when it confronts student experiential knowledge head-on, may reveal some of the gaps and shortcomings in theory. It may also point to the intricacies of individual, group, and organizational behaviors. It invariably means that the educator knows more than is necessary to teach. At this point of knowledge surplus it becomes possible for the educator to step back, observe, think, and test the content area. Whether the content falls within a class, a course, a field assignment, or a field practice experience, the educator needs to ascertain the boiled-down, positive minimum that any student must learn about the content area.

Essentiality of Content. As soon as the educator, from the point of knowledge surplus, finds him or herself making a list and consulting resources in order to decide what is essential or nonessential in a content area, it is useful to stop. Professional education requires that knowledge be put to use. In other words, it should be in the head and bones, as accessible as energy, for the educator as well as for the student. Tying critical knowledge about a policy, for instance, to job performance provides educational clarity and increases the motivation to learn.

Students can be depended on to want to know more than the essentials. Usually there are only two, three, or four essential points to be mastered in a given learning period. For instance, intake might be divided into two major points: (1) determining the need of the client, and (2) determining whether the organization can provide service to meet that need. Given the two major points, the educator can flesh out the subpoints. The students will usually ask: What if the organization cannot meet the need? This question fits, of course, under point two, and is a natural inquiry. Experienced educators count on natural inquiry, knowing that it signals engaged learning. Teaching the essentials is one method of capitalizing on natural inquiry, because it tends to provoke the "What if . . . ?" questions.

Learning Decisionmaking

Students must be informed about essentials in order to make appropriate decisions. This is part of learning to be self-directed. In the course of a professional day, the social worker makes many decisions. Some decisions are minor, some are incremental, and a number are of major importance. Decisionmaking carries responsibilities, as well as personal and professional risks. Students have to face those risks and learn responsible decisionmaking.

Decisionmaking is a process that can be observed, built into learning situations, and taught. Learning the process cognitively and experientially may reduce the number of professional decisions based on inadequate knowledge, impulse, or panic.

Janis has identified five stages of decisionmaking:[5]

1. Appraising the challenge—This is a "startle" stage, for some disturbing information or event has posed a challenge to the usual course of action or inaction.
2. Surveying alternatives—This is a searching stage, a time for looking around for advice, additional information, and resources; it is an uncomfortable time because the person has decided against the status quo and is just beginning movement in other directions.
3. Weighing alternatives—This is a stage of vacillation and is painful; the person has found alternatives and is trying to decide among them; he or she is positive about not returning to the former course of action, but is trying to assess the gains and losses of each alternative.
4. Deliberating about commitment—This is an introspective stage, before the person decides to "go public"; it is a stage when the person evaluates the effects of sharing the decision; making the decision public knowledge strengthens the resolve, since failure to carry through would also be public knowledge and evoke reactions.
5. Adhering despite negative feedback—This is a resolute stage, at least outwardly; it is a time of living with the decision in all its real life dimensions, of consolidation and of tolerating negative feedback (unless, of course, the negative feedback is sufficiently disturbing to pose a challenge of step 1 force).

Decisionmaking's Connection with Performance. The ten basic competencies discussed in the first volume on the curriculum development project serve as referents to the determination of the basic knowledge and the kind of decisionmaking required—minor, incremental, or major—of the baccalaureate social worker.[6] Examination of the competencies will also reveal that some learning processes have centrality. For instance, data collection and analysis is identified in several competencies. Ericksen has pointed out that "students should overlearn those concepts that help to order the complexities of human behavior and social ambiguities and finally, the specific facts that support the concepts and procedures of the profession." He further states that " . . . concepts and principles and problem-solving techniques are . . . likely to remain as lasting educational benefits to the student."[7] Thus, the processes of data collection and analysis should be overlearned by the student so that the knowledge becomes a permanent and essential part of the student's professional armamentarium.

A learning process, such as data collection and analysis, is itself dependent on learning how to use relevant tools.[a] Using specific, tested tools wherever possible and early in social work training develops confidence in students. They learn the purposes and limitations of these tools, their application, the relevance of critical data to measurements, and self-identification as a successful tool user. Much the same process has occurred for professionals in medicine, nursing, physical therapy, and so on. One of social work's concerns, however, has been that tool use can become mechanical. Part of education is teaching the differential use of tools as well as the interactional aspects of tool use, and not making the tool more important than the individual(s) for whom it is being used or the student who is applying it. Throughout the educational experience, tools must be taught as having relevance only to the degree that they will help attain the purposes of social work.

The emphasis on overlearning basic processes and the use of tools is part of a shift in understanding that social work education needs to be more precise. In teaching a "generalist" student, educators somehow did not recognize the need to be precise. School-based faculty struggled to combine a little interviewing, a little work with groups, and a little work about community concerns into one base course, only to find that students knew too little about methodology. Field- or community-based faculty also struggled to expand practice opportunities, so that the student could experience many aspects of social work. Generally, the experiences have led to the consensus that social work needs to be definitive about its tasks and responsibilities, explicit about its knowledge, and precise about its skills. The project helps accomplish this task at the baccalaureate level.

Learning Obstacles

After the educator has mastered the content and examined it for parts that are indispensable to professional performance, it is impor-

---

[a]The steps in data collection, problem solving, and decisionmaking are tools, just like application forms, monthly reports, and computers.

tant to search for obstacles and problems inherent in the learning task. Two major sources of learning problems are interactive inhibition and groupthink.

Interactive inhibition refers to the negative effect of one set of learnings upon another set of learnings.[8] For instance, the impact of a situation can be so powerful that it clouds and overwhelms previous knowledge of how to deal with the situation. Such learning situations as trying to secure important information from an involuntary client, or watching a film that shows evidence of physical abuse, or encountering a "closed" system can and should evoke strong reactions. As much as possible, the educator should anticipate and deal with these reactions during the learning period, so that the student will learn not to withdraw to avoid potentially painful material. Reactions are facts. When reactions are an acknowledged, factual part of learning, it is possible to tie them to relevant concepts and make the material meaningful. Meaningful learning has been described as the recognition of relationships between knowledge expressed as concepts and principles and the situations about which students are concerned. Numerous studies have attested to the positive results of meaningful learning.[9]

Another example of interactive inhibition is life experience that the student may find to be in conflict with learning. In the course of living, everyone has to deal with stress and with pathology. At a given moment, a sample of any student body and of any group of educators will disclose persons who are or have experienced loss, severe deprivation, mental illness, substance abuse, discrimination, physical illness, and so on. These personal experiences may inhibit their helping another person who is facing a similar problem, particularly if there is an implicit or explicit stigma. Social work educators need to de-stigmatize and to normalize stress in everyday life. This opens the door to disclosure and new perceptions, facilitates the development of self-awareness, and makes available the strengths of people from diverse backgrounds.

Groupthink is a term developed by Janis to describe concurrence-seeking behavior of groups.[10] Janis was particularly interested in the effects of groupthink on national welfare through small numbers of persons in high governmental positions. The same principles may obtain among educators and the staffs of organizations. Groupthink thrives in situations where one group has power over others.

Janis has described eight major characteristics of groupthink or concurrence-seeking behavior:

1. an illusion of invulnerability, shared by most or all of the members, which creates excessive optimism and encourages taking extreme risks
2. collective efforts to rationalize in order to discount warnings which might lead the members to reconsider their assumptions before they recommit themselves to their past policy decisions
3. an unquestioned belief in the group's inherent morality, inclining the members to ignore the ethical or moral consequences of their decisions
4. stereotyped views of rivals and enemies as too evil to warrant genuine attempts to negotiate, or as too weak or too stupid to counter whatever risky attempts are made to defeat their purposes
5. direct pressure on any member who expresses strong arguments against any of the group's stereotypes, illusions, or commitments, making clear that such dissent is contrary to what is expected of all loyal members
6. self-censorship of deviations from the apparent group consensus, reflecting each member's inclination to minimize to himself the importance of his doubts and counterarguments
7. a shared illusion of unanimity, partly resulting from this self-censorship and augmented by the false assumption that silence implies consent
8. the emergence of self-appointed "mindguards"—members who protect the group from adverse information that might shatter their shared complacency about the effectiveness and morality of their decisions.[11]

Reactions to groupthink may take the form of protest and fighting, but more often there is a cessation of inquiry, with a resultant spread of concurrence or accord. Students, for example, infer that the field coordinator's decisions are unchangeable because they are unquestioned by colleagues, or that the unit team will never develop recordkeeping so long as it believes that team members know everyone who is in the institution. Groupthink inhibits learning, change, and decisionmaking itself.

Groupthink can be altered by purposive inquiry, from within the group or from the outside. A change in groupthink is an organizational change, and one safeguard against the tyranny of groupthink is a continuous update on new information.[12]

Use of Relevant Content Areas

Learning is reinforced when it is connected to other relevant content areas. For example, an essential to understanding groupthink is that the inhibition of relevant inquiry fosters concurrence behaviors. The same concept is essential for understanding biased sampling in research, recognizing the purpose of silencing strategies in families, grasping the perpetuation of stereotypes and prejudices, and developing communication skills.

Appropriate Format

A format that utilizes reciprocal connections between concept and application will facilitate meaningful learning. As Knowles has pointed out, professional education is adult education and adults seek problem-centered learning, which has immediate application to the problems about which they are concerned.[13] Andragogy, or the education of adults, places experiential learning in a central position:

> The assumption is that as an individual matures he accumulates an expanding reservoir of experience that causes him to become an increasingly rich resource for learning, and at the same time provides him with a broadening base to which to relate new learning. Accordingly, in the technology of andragogy, there is decreasing emphasis on the transmittal techniques of traditional teaching and increasing emphasis on experiential techniques which tap the experience of the learners and involve them in analyzing their experience.[14]

Constructing a format that will highlight the essentials for learning and permit clear opportunities to connect knowledge and application requires time and imagination. Practice and feedback are great aids in stimulating new ideas and variations in format. For instance, in a class dealing with the interface between institutions and people in need, there was an assignment to read four articles on de-institutionalization. Subsequently, the instructor realized that the students would pick up points in common among the articles, but probably could not discern one reading from another. A check with the students supported this assumption, so the instructor devised a format in which there were four small groups, each charged with examining one of the articles and culling from it two or three critical points, and then devising a means of presenting those points to their peers. The test question for each group was: What should the other three groups remember three weeks later about a given facet of de-institutionalization? The biggest problem for the students was narrowing or condensing the literature to its essentials, and they quickly made useful comparisons of this task to the job of condensing the information in the numerous memos that always crossed their desks, of keeping up with professional literature, and so on. Three weeks later, the recall on de-institutionalization was excellent.

Another example concerns a field faculty member who wanted students to understand the many realistic factors influencing the involuntary client's reluctance to use services. Instead of having the three students read about Appalachia, the field faculty member arranged for them to drive to the neighboring areas where each had one or two clients, seeking information on the realistic inhibitors to motivation. The students returned with impressive lists, tales of experiences, and dozens of questions.

Both of the foregoing examples were carefully structured around the essential knowledge to be learned. Both examples also drew on peer teaching and learning.

Professionals must be able to count on one another for feedback, information, support, and development of new ideas. Whether the format for presentation of essentials is a lecture, a role-play, or a use of multimedia material, it is important to facilitate interaction, sharing, and discussion. Students increase communication skills, interactional skills, self-awareness, and development of peer resources through the use of teaching/learning formats that enable them to be active learners.

Organizational Mission

The mission of a school or a community organization helps determine the essentials to be taught. What is essential in one setting, with its particular functions, may be nonessential in another. The school's mission is a template for designing specific content areas in which the basic competencies are to be taught. It is important to emphasize often to the students that many undergraduate programs are handicapped by too narrow a range of human diversity. One educator, for example, helped a small group of female students, only one of whom was black, to understand that they needed to consider the perspectives of men, the elderly, people with physical impairments, those with different life styles, and so on. The students began checking for perspectives, presenting a learning problem—somewhat cautiously—to boyfriends, children, people of other faiths, etc. Some students brought guests to class, and all students brought in illustrations of other persons' perspectives.

Teaching Style

The teaching of essentials is a focus, a unifying concept for professional education, and it can be presented in varying formats, using various techniques. Style, however, is the characteristic expression of a person, and the professional use of self, whether as an educator or as a student social worker, requires awareness of one's style in order to build on and develop it. The use of humor, gestures, other nonverbal communication, a lot of talking, being methodical in procedure, being reserved, and so on are all parts of style. Recognizing one's style and accepting it improve the ability to use it naturally and purposefully.

Each educator must "remake" assigned content areas, so that the delivery of material is in keeping with his or her style. Otherwise, the material will appear unconvincing, and the educator will be put in the awkward position of defending, amplifying, and encouraging discussion pro and con of the material.

In the process of learning the essentials for professional performance the students acquire complex professional behaviors with little or no direct tutoring. The social work educator models the teaching/learning process and the practice of social work; they are not separate processes. Each educator presents a distinctive approach to professional behavior, but all of the modeling to which students are exposed should reinforce the learning objectives of the program and be consistent with high standards of skillful, ethical practice.

CONCLUSION

The teaching/learning process is as important to the attainment of educational outcomes as the actual learning content. The competencies identified in the Undergraduate Social Work Curriculum Development Project can best be attained in a teaching/learning environment that facilitates active learning and that operationalizes an adragogical approach to education. The chapter addresses two continual questions of field-based and school-based faculty—what does the learning situation provide that is absolutely indispensable at attaining a given competency and how can the experience be structured to promote appropriate decisionmaking. The specific teaching/learning techniques discussed in this chapter maximize student learning of professional competencies. The project's focus on a total educational environment and the need for sequential, cumulative, integrated learning emphasizes the need for a teaching/learning environment that is carefully planned and executed. While each individual's particular teaching style is a part of this environment, the basic integrity of a program's teaching/learning approach must not be destroyed by one or more faculty members' idiosyncratic behavior.

NOTES

1. Knowles, Malcolm, *The Adult Learner: A Neglected Species* (Houston: Gulf, 1973), pp. 62-63.
2. Ibid., pp. 45-47.
3. Kidd, J.D., *How Adults Learn* (New York: Association Press, 1959), pp. 133-56.
4. Knowles, pp. 70-72.

5. Janis, Irving, and Leon Mann, *Decision Making: A Psychological Analysis of Conflict, Choice and Commitment* (New York: Free Press, 1977).

6. Baer, Betty L., and Ronald Federico, *Educating the Baccalaureate Social Work: Report of the Undergraduate Social Work Curriculum Development Project* (Cambridge, Mass.: Ballinger 1978), pp. 91-98.

7. Eriksen, Stanford, "Transfer of Learning and the Maturation of Private Knowledge," *Journal of Education for Social Work* (Spring 1978):18.

8. Bigge, Morris, *Learning Theories for Teachers*, 2nd ed. (New York, Harper & Row, 1971), p. 294.

9. Ibid., pp. 289-90.

10. Janis and Mann, p. 130.

11. Ibid., pp. 130-131.

12. Pruger, Robert, "Bureaucratic Functioning as a Social Work Skill," in Baer and Federico, *Educating the Baccalaureate Social Worker* (Cambridge, Mass.: Ballinger, 1978), pp. 161-163.

13. Knowles, p. 104.

14. Ibid., p. 46.

REFERENCES AND BIBLIOGRAPHY

Baer, Betty L., and Ronald Federico. *Educating the Baccalaureate Social Worker: Report of the Undergraduate Social Work Curriculum Development Project.* Cambridge, Mass.: Ballinger, 1978.

Bigge, Morris. *Learning Theories for Teachers*, 2nd ed. New York: Harper & Row, 1971.

Day, Peter R. *Methods of Learning Communication Skills.* New York: Pergamon, 1977.

Eriksen, Stanford. "Transfer of Learning and the Maturation of Private Knowledge." *Journal of Education for Social Work* (Spring 1978).

Ingalls, John D. *A Trainer's Guide to Andragogy*, rev. ed. Waltham, Mass.: Data Education, 1972.

Janis, Irving, and Leon Mann. *Decision Making: A Psychological Analysis of Conflict, Choice and Commitment.* New York: Free Press, 1977.

Kidd, J.D. *How Adults Learn* New York: Association Press, 1959.

Knowles, Malcolm. *The Adult Learner: A Neglected Species.* Houston: Gulf Publishing, 1973.

Pruger, Robert. "Bureaucratic Functioning as a Social Work Skill." In Baer and Federico, *Educating the Baccalaureate Social Worker* (Cambridge, Mass.: Ballinger, 1978), pp. 149-68.

III. Setting and Assessing Program Objectives

Chapter Five

A New Importance for Program Objectives

Fay Coker Walker

INTRODUCTION

The report of the Undergraduate Social Work Curriculum Development Project yields a new and strong consensus regarding the basic knowledge, skills, and practice competencies deemed essential as outcomes of the entry level educational program. The competencies are broadly stated and offer faculty in individual programs freedom to define anticipated outcomes more specifically and/or to add competencies over and beyond the ten identified by project findings. Regardless of further refinement, there is now a widely accepted definition of minimal practice competence expected of the entry level professional practitioner. This definition will profoundly impact on the educational outcomes of undergraduate social work programs.

While most social work educators welcome the project report as a new and positive development toward defining and strengthening the role of baccalaureate social work (BSW) practitioners within the profession, a lingering misunderstanding may hinder the utilization of project findings in undergraduate social work programs. Programs may resist the findings for fear that standardization of minimal educational outcomes may lead to standardization of the methods and means for achieving those minimal outcomes.

Such uniformity in means is not indicated by project findings. While the basic educational outcomes are clear, the project assumes that each program will have a unique set of program objectives that will impact on these basic outcomes, making them specific to its own needs. In other words, how the outcomes are operationalized in individual programs is highly variable.

The desired program uniqueness is achieved as the diversity and resources in the educational context are brought to bear on attainment of competence. Prior to the curriculum development project, programs posited fairly consistent program objectives (preparation for practice, graduate school, citizenship, etc.) and fairly diverse educational outcomes. The impact of project findings may be to reverse this. Programs, while sharing a common definition of the entry level professional and his or her competencies, are now expected to vary widely in the program objectives and curriculum structures that will produce a common outcome, a competent practitioner. This implies a new importance for program objectives.

The purposes of this chapter are: 1) to clarify the place and function of program objectives; 2) to identify analytical and interactional processes that are helpful in analyzing the environment for diversity and resources;[a] 3) to offer some basic principles to employ when formulating program objectives; and 4) to point to the implications that operationalizing program objectives have for curriculum.

THE PLACE AND FUNCTION OF
PROGRAM OBJECTIVES

Distinguishing Mission Statements,
Educational Outcomes, and
Program Objectives

Initially, it is necessary to position program objectives within the broader purview of institutional setting and curriculum structure. Colleges and universities posit *mission statements* that point toward what the institution intends to accomplish. These institutional mission statements tend to be broadly stated and vary widely depending on uniqueness of location, constituency, history, funding sources, and so on. For example, a land-grant college historically relates to the concept of service to its state. A private college, on the other hand, may define its mission in terms of regional thrust, curriculum specialization, or an identified constituency.

At the other end of the general-specific language hierarchy are *educational outcomes*, i.e., competencies, which are specific statements of what a student must know and be able to do prior to certification that he or she is eligible to be graduated. Undergraduate social work programs bring to all institutional settings a set of basic

---

[a]Analytical and interactional processes as part of social work practice are described in Chapter 8.

educational outcomes that most recently and cogently have been defined by the curriculum development project. The ten competencies identified by the project form the minimum without which no student would be graduated to enter professional practice. It should be restated, however, that this consensus definition of practice competencies for baccalaureate social workers in no way limits the BSW student or program to attainment of basic competence alone. Project findings encourage continuing professional growth and development. Additional competencies, i.e., those over and beyond the ten basic competencies, are encouraged and may be posited by any given social work program as additional educational outcomes. Educational outcomes, then, state specific competencies each student will master prior to graduation. They are accompanied by procedures for assessment of minimally acceptable performance.

Program objectives stand between statements of institutional mission posited by the college or university and statements posited by the program of educational outcomes or competencies expected of social work graduates. These statements are more specific than those of institutional mission but less specific than educational outcomes. The concern is neither the institution nor the individual student, but the social work program itself.

For instance, a common statement of institutional mission for the undergraduate college may be to prepare students to continue their education in graduate schools. The social work program posits as an educational outcome for each student the ability to "continually evaluate one's own professional growth and development through assessment of practive behaviors and skills," and the ability to "contribute to the improvement of service delivery by adding to the knowledge base of the profession as appropriate . . ."[1] The interface between this somewhat general institutional mission and these specific educational outcomes is a program objective. Such an objective might read: "The social work program will encourage and provide a range of ongoing learning situations designed to expand and broaden professional practice competence for students, graduates, and practitioners in the surrounding area." This statement demonstrates consistency with the mission of the parent institution while focusing on the intent and uniqueness of the social work program.

The Focus of Program Objectives

Program objectives, as the above illustration suggests, focus the intended interactions between the social work program and relevant institutions, publics, and constituent groups in the environment. The parent institution is only one among many publics with which the social work program interacts. The social welfare institution, the broader professional community, and professional associations such as the National Association of Social Workers (NASW), the Council on Social Work Education (CSWE), and the American Public Welfare Association (APWA); the immediate practice community and local professional organizations; the student community; and consumers of social welfare services in the area all constitute entities in the societal fabric with which the social work program will want to interact. Program objectives are statements that focus this interaction and incorporate it into the program design in such a way as to enhance the attainment of practice competence.

The Function of Program Objectives

Program objectives, as conceived here, are statements of direction that the program intends to take to enable students to attain practice competence. These are strengthening statements asserting how the social work program intends to structure for success. To the extent that they are skillfully negotiated and carefully stated, program objectives empower the program to carry out its intentions.

Program objectives provide guidance and direction for decision-making. As a central statement of what a program intends to accomplish, program objectives anchor the program and keep it consistent with intent. For example, without the integrity provided by program objectives, a program shifts in purpose with every wind that blows funds in a new or different direction. If program objectives are strong, however, funding is sought to implement them. At the same time, program objectives must be flexible enough to respond to the changes in context that constantly occur in undergraduate social work education.

Program objectives point to the curriculum content that needs to be implemented. Structural linkages between the program and the parent institution, the professional community, the local practice community, the student community, and the social welfare institution and its consumers can be identified in program objectives. These linkages enable many constituencies to participate in preparing competent entry level practitioners, acknowledging the impact of these constituencies on the social work program while strengthening the program's ability to influence related institutions. Resources in the program's unique context are exchanged and the attainment of practice competence is enhanced.

Finally, program objectives provide the criteria for assessment. Effective assessment is dependent upon the scope and specificity of program objectives. These must be formulated in such a way that they allow for and encourage ongoing program development rather than ongoing reformulation. As practice competence requires that one be able to "evaluate the extent to which the objectives of the intervention plan were achieved"[2] so educational competence requires that a program continually assess the extent to which program objectives are achieved.

There is no easy way to identify program objectives. The purpose of this chapter is not to identify general objectives in a prescriptive fashion, but rather to suggest a process and an orientation that will utilize the diversity and resources of a program's specific context in pursuit of quality education and program uniqueness.

ANALYZING THE ENVIRONMENT FOR DIVERSITY AND RESOURCES

Program objectives emerge as the practice competencies identified in the project report are grafted onto the contextual diversity of a given environment. These situational variables and resources, when operationalized, will enable the program to produce practice competence as well as program uniqueness.

Contextual diversity is the critical raw material. No program objectives can be selected until the context in which practice competence will be developed has been thoroughly analyzed. Such an analysis calls for assessment of the parent institution, the faculty community, the student community, the local practice community, and human needs in the service area in light of the needs and resources of the social work program. The goal of such an assessment is resource identification, exchange, and establishment of an open and ongoing process of reciprocity between the program and its environment that will foster the attainment of practice competence.

The Parent Institution

The parent institution has a geographic location, a history, a contemporary mission (which may differ greatly from its historical mission), restrictions based on funding sources and economics, a curriculum, a faculty, a student body, and all kinds of traditions, rituals, and codes of conduct among faculty and students that give the institution its ethos. What resources can be identified within this institutional framework that will enhance the attainment of social work practice competence? To what extent is the value orientation of the institutional milieu consistent with or different from professional social work values? To what extent and where within the institution is curriculum structured for integrative learning as contrasted with categorization of discrete knowledge areas? To what extent does the institution posit a service mission consistent with the service mandate of the social work profession? Positive answers to these questions suggest resources that are critical to a social work program that wishes to interact with the institutional fabric in order to develop practice competence in BSW practitioners.

Assessing resources within the institutional framework requires an attitude and a willingness on the part of social work educators to utilize the entire educational context. Such an attitude seeks out competence-developing learning opportunities wherever they may be located. No walls or arbitrary time periods separate the social work program from the general, liberal arts base or the entire educational experience. If inquiry is a required course for entering students, its relevance to social work practice will be explicated by social work faculty and further research competence will build on this foundation content. Similarly, if group discussion is included in a communications sequence, skills necessary for social work practice competence may be attained there. Course offerings such as social problems and public policy, sometimes enhanced by an interdisciplinary base, are resources for the attainment of analytical skills, social inquiry skills, skills in analysis of institutional economics and policies, knowledge of social change theory, and so on.

At the same time, it is important to note resources that the social work program brings to the institutional setting. These resources are too frequently overlooked or undersold. The social work program, with its separate accrediting process, lends prestige to the institution. The professional baccalaureate social work degree has wide appeal to diverse students and faculty. This appeal is useful during a period of declining student enrollment. The program's appeal to a diverse range of students impacts positively on institutional affirmative action programs. Some BSW programs meet the parent institution's need to prepare graduates for effective citizenship by offering various policy courses to students from many disciplines.

Social work faculty may provide counseling to students outside the program and/or serve as consultants to campus groups interested in providing human services on campus or in the community. If the institution posits a mission of service to the immediate region, the social work program may be in a position to provide a focus and leadership to this service effort.

The opportunities for the social work program and the parent institution to maximize, mobilize, and exchange resources are enormous. To the extent that these opportunities can be structured to enhance the attainment of practice competence for social work students, they are desirable and worth negotiating.

The Faculty Community

Program objectives must take account of the faculty resources existing in departments outside of social work. Objectives that require the mastery of foundation content need support by faculty who can and will teach such content. Attempts to develop knowledge, values, and skills related to critical thinking and self-direction must be supported by teaching/learning environments that provide the necessary opportunities. Efforts to impact on college or university activities, especially those pertaining to program support, are greatly enhanced when faculty throughout the school are knowledgeable about and supportive of the social work program. Finally, objectives related to the integration of liberal arts and professional knowledge, values, and skills are better achieved if there is an ongoing exchange of ideas and strategies between liberal arts and social work faculty members. In many ways, then, program objectives may be affected by non-social work faculty, and this resource should be used in program development efforts.

The Student Community

For the purpose of formulating program objectives, an assessment of diversity and resources in the student community is critical. Where do students come from? Where do they go to? Are they, as a group, disadvantaged? Elitest? Is there a broad spectrum of social, economic, and racial diversity among the student majors? among the student body as a whole? What is the median age of students? Do they commute? What do students see as the place and function of higher education in their lives? What are students interested in?

Social work students for the most part are service-oriented people operating out of humanitarian concern. This orientation can be most useful to a college or university community. Social work majors may initiate services such as human sexuality counseling, rape crisis counseling, suicide prevention programs, and any number of information and referral or volunteer community service programs on campus for the benefit of students, faculty, and local community residents. Social work majors planning and implementing these services have occasion to enhance a wide variety of practice knowledge, skills, and competencies.

In these situations the emerging practice competence of BSW students is recognized and employed as they engage in activities consistent with professional values and ethics. These activities doubtless constitute learning experiences. To the extent that they can be structured to enhance practice competence and/or reflected on for instructional purposes, the social work program has maximized a potent resource. A program objective can focus this interaction and facilitate resource utilization and exchange.

The Local Practice Community

The local practice community is an institution rich in diversity and resources. Historically, social work programs have been dependent on the local practice community to provide field instruction opportunities for social work students. Educators have been indebted to practitioners for their generosity. Other resources in the practice community may, however, have gone unnoticed or underdeveloped. If the outcome of undergraduate social work education is to prepare the entry level practitioner for practice, and if a cornerstone of effective practice means understanding the system in which one operates, then it follows that a program would want to involve that practice system in teaching practice skills. Such involvement would not be postponed until field instruction; practitioners can teach throughout the curriculum. They can facilitate observation and volunteer experiences for beginning students, serve as advisors to student service activities on campus, and serve on advisory committees to social work programs.

Social work educators and practitioners have been quicker to criticize each other than to ask what resources the educational program might mobilize to support the local practice community. Inquiry into the needs of local practitioners and social welfare agencies is past due. Do practitioners need and want continuing education opportunities? If so, in which form—degree-oriented or in-service? Do agencies need staff development resources? consultation? relief workers? future graduates?

Relationships between BSW programs and local practice communities must be strengthened. A high degree of reciprocity and exchange of resources between educators, students, and practitioners will increase practice competence for all participants.

Human Needs in the Service Area

Every social work program must concern itself with defining the community it intends to relate to and with analyzing human needs in that community. Community, here, is understood to mean either a geographic area or a community of interest that might be regional, national, or international in scope. However the community served is defined, the fact remains that human needs in the service area are probably the greatest single factor in program uniqueness, yet the most underutilized resource for attainment of practice competence.

How frequently is the collection and analysis of data on human needs in the service area employed when teaching skills of data collection and analysis? How many representative consumer groups have come to speak in class? What needs still await documentation? How does human diversity impact on human needs and service delivery in the community?

Taking seriously the human needs in the community served is not a call for narrowness or specialization at the undergraduate level. Rather, a program will utilize the community served as an arena in which basic skills are learned and then reflected on for application in a broader context.

A vast array of resources exist in any educational context. Many resources can be mobilized quickly and easily. Others require time to negotiate and some require special funding. Resources that reflect diversity in the environment and assist a program in achieving uniqueness while simultaneously developing competent entry level practitioners are resources worth structuring for program success.

INTERACTION WITH THE ENVIRONMENT
FOR INCLUSION AND RECIPROCITY

The social work program must accept responsibility and take the initiative for mobilizing resources within the environment that will positively impact on the social work program and the attainment of practice competence. A reactive, defensive, or passive posture on the part of the BSW program does not model the practice competencies the program's graduates are expected to achieve.

The social work program faculty must establish an open and ongoing process of inclusion and reciprocity between the program and representatives of all institutions and constituent groups with which the program will interact. The curriculum development project provides a model of such a participatory process resulting in a consensus report. Such participation must be desired and structured in order to become a reality. Faculty with particular strengths and interests may be assigned as liaison persons to various constituent groups.

Eventually, a forum is needed where program faculty and representatives of the constituent groups can come together to interact and to coordinate their various resources. Program advisory committees will serve this function in many programs. It seems advisable, insofar as possible, that membership on such a committee be consistent, as members must be willing to accept a primary role in insuring that the social work program functions to produce competent entry level practitioners.

Faculty in a developing program are encouraged to consider the formation of an advisory committee as a priority task to be accomplished prior to extensive program implementation. In an established program, if no advisory committee exists, field work supervisors serving as representatives of a constituent group may form a base from which to develop a more representative advisory committee in due time. Eventually, representation from the parent institution (faculty and administrators, in addition to social work faculty), students, practitioners, consumers, and funding sources are needed to make a truly integrative advisory committee.

An advisory committee of this nature can implement the process of resource exchange suggested earlier. However, to move from identification of resources and planning to implementation, this representative group must: 1) formulate action-oriented program objectives; 2) implement these objectives throughout the curriculum; and 3) periodically assess the extent to which social work program objectives are effective in developing practice competence in new entry level professionals.

FORMULATING PROGRAM OBJECTIVES

A social work faculty and representative advisory committee may deliberate for months before formulating initial program objectives. While all participants are aware of the basic practice competencies to be attained, the best means and structures for transmitting them may emerge very slowly.

Because the basis for program uniqueness is the situational diversity and resources available in the given educational context, program objectives chosen to maintain this uniqueness cannot be generalized. In this chapter an orientation for the forming of program objectives has been suggested. The major characteristics of this orientation are as follows:

1. Choose program objectives with the goal of fostering practice competence in beginning level professional practitioners.
2. Keep program objectives consistent with the values and ethics of the social work profession and related to the mission and goals of the parent institution.
3. Employ the diversity and resources located throughout the specific context to allow for program uniqueness.

4. Structure the interaction between the social work program and relevant institutions in the environment to ensure broad-based representation, participation, resource exchange, and ongoing reciprocity.
5. Involve students in assessing and utilizing the contextual situation for self-initiated learning experiences that are both analytical and interactional in nature.
6. Recognizing that competence is developed in many diverse arenas, structure mechanisms whereby competence-developing experiences that occur outside the social work program are integrated into the ongoing development of professional competence.
7. Design program objectives to allow for ongoing program development as well as ongoing program assessment.

A program objective is formulated when the orientation, values, and analytical and interactional skills of the social work faculty and advisory committee result in a statement of what the program intends to do, with whom, and for whom. While an action-oriented program objective points toward how the intended results will be accomplished, the statement itself is an objective, not a strategy, and therefore falls short of the details required for implementation. In this way, program objectives remain open-ended enough to allow for ongoing development and program growth without constant reformulation of objectives.

IMPLICATIONS FOR CURRICULUM

Program objectives that are specific and differential to an individual program can be enacted in many institutional formats. Assuming that the program faculty is in charge of curriculum development, the particular administrative auspices may themselves be a resource in operationalizing program objectives.

The curriculum is the conduit through which the BSW program transmits knowledge, skills, and entry level practice competence to students. Program objectives impact on the curriculum in a variety of ways. Curriculum content will be affected as faculty deem more explicit and relevant content as essential for practice competence. Program objectives will affect who teaches what content and when, in a class or practice setting, and so on. The resources identified earlier must be operationalized to allow constituent groups to participate in delivering curriculum. This broad-based participation has obvious implications for teaching and learning. No longer are content and classroom seen as the domain of faculty. Curriculum structures must be designed that incorporate all participants into a dynamic learning community. The analytical-interactional continuum necessary for effective practice must be modeled throughout the curriculum. A hallmark of curriculum becomes the extent to which both structure and content provide students with an integrated framework for professional social work practice.

The same resources that are utilized to deliver the curriculum can be utilized to assess practice competence in students. This assessment would ideally occur throughout the curriculum and would include peers, professional practitioners, and consumers as well as faculty. The work sample approach to assessment can be incorporated into the total curriculum, enabling a student to use volunteer experience, summer work experience, or experiential education as experiences in which developing competencies are demonstrated.

CONCLUSIONS

A new importance for program objectives is indicated by the report of the curriculum development project. While all programs will share a basic definition of the entry level professional and his or her competencies, programs will vary widely in objectives and curriculum structures that will produce this competent practitioner.

Program objectives, focusing on the interaction between the social work program and relevant institutions, publics, and constituent groups in the environment, will empower the program to structure for success and to use the diversity and resources throughout the educational context to develop competent entry level professional practitioners.

The context in which undergraduate social work education is offered must be thoroughly analyzed, leading to resource identification, exchange, and ongoing reciprocity. Interaction with representatives of various institutions in the environment must be structured to provide for broad-based participation in developing and implementing program objectives. Such interaction is also needed to deliver appropriate learning experiences, and to evaluate student competence and program accomplishment.

NOTES

1. Baer, Betty L. and Ronald Federico, *Educating the Baccalaureate Social Worker: Report of the Undergraduate Social Work Curriculum Development Project* (Cambridge, Mass.: Ballinger, 1979), pp. 88-89.

2. Ibid., p. 88.

REFERENCES AND BIBLIOGRAPHY

Argyris, C. *Interpersonal Competence and Organizational Effectiveness.* Homewood, Illinois: Irwin, 1962.

Barrett, J.H. *Individual Goals and Organizational Objectives: A Study of Integrating Mechanisms.* Ann Arbor: Institute for Social Research, 1970.

Beckhard, R. *Organizational Development—Strategies and Models.* Reading, Mass.: Addison-Wesley, 1969.

Burns, Richard W. "The Central Notion: Explicit Objectives." In Houston, W.R., and R.B. Howsam, eds., *Competency-based Teacher Education* (Chicago: Science Research Associates, 1972), pp. 101-3.

Carnegie Foundation for the Advancement of Teaching. *Missions of the College Curriculum: A Contemporary Review with Suggestions.* San Francisco: Jossey-Bass Publishers, 1977.

Cohen, Arthur M. *Behavioral Objectives in Curriculum Development, Selected Readings and Bibliography.* Englewood Cliffs, N.J.: Educational Technology Publishers, 1971.

Elden, J.M., R. Goldstone, and M.K. Brown. "The University as an Organizational Frontier." In W.H. Schmidt, ed., *Organizational Frontiers and Human Values* (Belmont, Ca.: Wadsworth, 1970), pp. 75-76.

Glick, Lester J., ed., *Undergraduate Social Work Education for Practice.* Washington, D.C.: U.S. Government Printing Office, 1970.

Hughes, Charles L. *Goal Setting: Key to Individual and Organizational Effectiveness.* New York: American Management Association, 1965.

Kapfer, Miriam B. *Behavioral Objectives in Curriculum Development.* Englewood Cliffs, N.J.: Educational Technology Publications, 1971.

Kibler, Robert J., Donald Cegala, Jr., David T. Miles, and Larry L. Barker. *Objectives of Instruction and Evaluation.* Boston: Allyn and Bacon, 1974.

Mager, Robert F. *Goal Analysis.* Belmont, Ca.: Fearson Publishers, 1972.

Pierce, Walter D., and Michael A. Lorber. *Objectives and Methods for Secondary Teaching.* Englewood Cliffs, N.J.: Prentice-Hall, 1977.

Ryan, Robert M., and Amy L. Reynolds, eds. *Issues in Planning for Social Welfare Education* and *Issues in Implementing Undergraduate Social Welfare Education Program*, 2 vols. Report of the Undergraduate Social Welfare Manpower Project. Atlanta: Southern Regional Education Board, 1970.

Undergraduate Programs in Social Work: Guidelines to Curriculum Content, Field Instruction and Organization. New York: Council on Social Work Education, 1971.

Chapter Six

Operationalizing Educational Outcomes in the Curriculum
Herbert H. Jarrett

INTRODUCTION

A major finding of the Undergraduate Social Work Curriculum Development Project is that curriculum development must be preceded by clearly conceptualized educational outcomes. Unless a program has a clear picture of the kind of entry level baccalaureate professional social worker that it wants to graduate, it is impossible to develop a curriculum to do so. Hopefully, the work of the project will help programs in their efforts to develop educational outcomes. The purpose of this chapter is to help persons involved with undergraduate social work programs to further develop their skill in formulating educational outcomes appropriate to their particular program. As educational outcomes become clearer and more precise, developing appropriate learning structures and content will be facilitated.

The first part of the chapter will discuss why we need to become more specific and systematic in developing curriculum. Next, the identification of expected educational outcomes or competencies will be examined as one vehicle for accomplishing that task. Curriculum strategies and possible approaches to the process will be explicated and a field illustration provided. Related assessment processes and design will be mentioned although not explored in depth. (Chapter 7 specifically addresses assessment strategies.) Then, implications for faculty, problems, issues, pitfalls, strengths, and rewards associated with this type of approach will be discussed, and the state of the art will be summarized.

EDUCATING FOR COMPETENCE

There are many ways to develop educational outcomes. Much of the educational literature on curriculum development during the last ten to fifteen years has gradually become more specific in defining what we expect our graduates to be able to do. Undergraduate social work has followed this trend in higher education. Before moving directly into examination of ways and means to achieve various educational outcomes, let us first examine the rationale of educating for competence.

Recent, relevant literature refers to this approach as competency-based education. That phrase, however, has become unclear in its meaning because it has been so overused. For this reason, this chapter will avoid using the phrase, wherever possible, to avoid the accompanying educational confusion. Instead, following the thrust of the curriculum development project, this chapter will speak in terms of educating for competency, that is, educating persons to be competent entry level baccalaureate professional social workers.

Historically, we as faculty have been more concerned with what we teach than with what students learn. We must constantly remind ourselves that there is no inherent relationship between what we teach and what students actually learn. The same point is made by other writers who say that we have focused for too long on "inputs." Perhaps a telling point needs to be made here regarding our selection of teaching materials, i.e., we tend to select concepts and theories to which we are committed and that we enjoy teaching. The selection of teaching materials should, however, be geared to students' learning needs, which in turn is related to the tasks they will need to perform after they graduate. This type of educational approach focuses on outcomes in the educational process. It uses precise learning objectives that are known in advance to the learner. It attempts to be objective in assessment and has behavioristic features.

Despite this, educating for competence remains an undeveloped educational process, not fully conceptualized or articulated. Gaps exist in defining what it is and how it can be understood, explained or measured. It has not been used widely in undergraduate education; most programs educating for competence have been located in professional and graduate education. However, a few schools are implementing it on a institution-wide basis.

There are multiple problems in developing educational strategies that are designed to produce competent practitioners. Pottinger specifies one fundamental difficulty associated with performance-based education: "Social pressures have led educators into attempting to clarify objectives, goals and outcomes without first establishing a strong methodological base from which to make reasoned decisions. Such decisions are being made from considerations which lack the vision, concepts and methods necessary to meet meaningful, long range assessment goals."[1] Another criticism of education for competence addresses the difficulty of adequately measuring and assessing outcomes. However, the potential benefits of a competency approach suggest that, even with the limitations and problems associated with becoming more specific regarding educational outcomes, and even in the face of incomplete research efforts, there is a need to move ahead with this approach.

The origins of education for competence are more than educational in nature. The historical roots have been evidenced by admission requirements on performance bases, public oral examinations, and more recent actions in holding business and government as well as education accountable for their actions in our society. Scott Briar says of social work and this trend that "the profession is moving into an age of accountability where little or nothing will be taken for granted."[2] This pervasive mood of accountability can be traced to earlier periods of our society as well.[3]

It is not the purpose of this chapter to argue that a competency approach is the only one possible in undergraduate social work education. Rather, it encourages educators to explore ways in which this approach can help build curricula that clearly identify the practice outcomes for their beginning level baccalaureate social worker graduates.

Curriculum designers should move cautiously in adopting this type of approach, because of the effort required to make it work. One of the major questions that should be asked is what is manageable or possible with the time, energy, and talent available from program faculty and field persons. With these blinking yellow caution lights in mind, let us proceed.

RATIONALE FOR DEFINING COMPETENCIES

Defining student competencies that must be achieved before graduation is important in that it lends order and clarity to what we expect our graduates to be able to do. This kind of expectation potentially provides coherence to our curricular offerings and some minimally defined standards that can be interpreted to future employers. It also lets the student know what is expected as a result of the teaching and learning interaction in our undergraduate social work programs.

THE PROCESS OF SELECTING
COMPETENCIES

The process of arriving at a set of competencies is a faculty responsibility. The statutes of most colleges and universities identify curriculum as the province and responsibility of the faculty. However, while faculty may appropriately provide leadership in curriculum development efforts, selecting and defining educational outcomes should not be limited to them alone. Rather, students, practitioners, alumni, field supervisors, and others such as clients or service consumers should play a vital role in the process of selecting and implementing competencies. In doing so collective wisdom may be obtained, and at the same time, these other constitutencies become identified with the faculty in determining educational policy. In addition, the implementation phase of curriculum building with the selected competencies becomes much easier if these groups have been an ongoing part of the selection process.

When involved in these efforts to define educational outcomes, one of the common problems or obstacles is that of "reinventing the wheel." At this point the curriculum development project seems especially valuable. In a three-year period the project has received considerable input from BSW practitioners, social work educators, the National Association of Social Workers (NASW), the American Public Welfare Association (APWA), minority groups, women, and various commissions of the Council on Social Work Education (CSWE). Based on this input, the project findings help to clarify what an entry level professional practitioner should be able to do upon exiting an undergraduate program.[4]

While the project material is helpful for all programs as a basic curriculum development resource, each program must retain its uniqueness. Hence, each program will need to arrive at its own distinctive, ethnic, regional, and other competencies that will be expected of its students. The educational outcomes or competencies selected by a program will probably change over time as teaching experience and practice developments dictate the need for better or different content.

While the range of program goals may lead to diverse outcomes, each outcome must be stated as precisely as possible so that proper assessment can be made. The political aspects of different constituencies arguing for adoption of their favorite areas of practice competence should not be overlooked. Finally, difficulties in knowing how to assess whether students have attained certain kinds of educational outcomes may influence the outcomes chosen, although greater skill in assessment through study and experience should reduce this problem.

CURRICULUM STRATEGIES

For educational objectives to be useful, the important task is to both formulate and implement the objectives in a way that fits in with the circumstances of individual programs. However, while the various ways of operationalizing educational objectives will result in different curriculum models,[5] all programs should have ongoing procedures to measure outcomes and a flexibility in designing learning strategies. One oft-cited complaint is that we do not really measure the student's competency until field experience. When we have questions about a student's ability to function as a social worker, we frequently say, "Let's wait and see if he or she makes it in the field." We must develop ways to assess each student's aptitudes and capacities much earlier in our programs.

Following are examples of how outcomes can be specified and measured at three different points in the social work program: at admission into the program, in classroom courses, and in field experience.

Admission

The first mechanism for specifying and measuring educational outcomes consists of admission procedures that test social work aptitudes, values, and potential. An example of this kind of test is the Strong Vocational Inventory, which deals with aptitude. Duehn and Mayadas's work on entrance and exit requirements appears to be a major contribution, although it concerns only graduate social work education. Values and social work are the subject of the work of McLeod and Meyer, Varley, and Koevin.[6] McClelland has shown in extensive research (1973) that people high in the need for achievement are practical, interested in efficiency, and are good decision-makers. They also make wise career decisions and regularly achieve greater success earlier in their careers.[7]

The references cited above may be useful to us in varying degrees. It is the opinion of this author that we should not be afraid of experimenting with our own mechanisms for evaluating aptitudes and potential for social work. In the absence of standardized tests we are forced to be creative in this process. The obvious danger would be to come to any conclusive decisions with limited data and unverified interpretations.

For many social work educators, serious screening at the BSW level may still be controversial. In many cases, this author contends, we may be able to identify quite early those students who are clearly not suited for social work. Several methods may be utilized. These could include close monitoring of student performance in introductory classes. It might also include an admission workshop type of atmosphere where simulations and various exercises could be employed in an effort to select the most appropriate students for admission into BSW programs. Whatever mechanisms are selected, it should be possible to develop them to assess a student's readiness to enter a social work program if the kinds of educational outcomes of the program have been identified.

Classroom Courses

One very tangible way to operationalize educational outcomes is to link them with specific courses. Table 6-1 is an attempt to outline in specific form how this might be accomplished, using the competencies as numbered in the curriculum development project. Naturally, each competency would be broken down into its component parts so that each course would cover certain parts of the specified competency(ies). When the total curriculum is completed, the student would be assured of having completed all of the competencies, while those students unable to master specific parts or competencies would be screened out at an appropriate point in the curriculum.

This kind of linkage accomplishes several important things. It takes some of the pressure off field experience to do "everything." It also makes instructors, who teach various courses in the curriculum, accountable to the program's ultimate educational outcomes. Further, this kind of flow chart provides students with information in

Table 6-1. Linking Competencies to Specific Courses

	Competency									
Course	*#1*	*#2*	*#3*	*#4*	*#5*	*#6*	*#7*	*#8*	*#9*	*#10*
SW 215						X			X	
SW 220				X		X				
SW 352	X		X			X				
SW 391A		X	X	X	X	X	X			
SW 470				X				X		
SW 441	X								X	
SW 560				X		X	X			
SW 391BCD		X	X			X	X	X		
SW 500								X	X	X

advance about what is expected. It also alerts faculty and field experience supervisors as to the nature and scope of their responsibilities.

The approach of linking educational outcomes to courses solves a few problems simultaneously. It addresses a specific behavior expected of the student within a framework or context that makes sense, i.e., a course. It also forces the professor to think through more clearly what it is that he or she wants students to gain from the given course. In attempting to measure educational outcomes in courses, social work educators have traditionally used examinations and required papers. Did the student know the examination material? Did the student's paper reflect the knowledge or insight required? Let's give ourselves credit for already engaging in this process.

An illustration of linking outcomes to courses would be a BSW program that has an educational outcome concerned with social work values. This outcome might be linked with a course such as "Social Welfare as a Social Institution." This outcome and course seem to go hand in hand; quite naturally, reading material and class discussion are going to revolve around value questions. Many conflicts about values and social work practice will arise for the beginning student, and the outcome is intended for the student to resolve or significantly modify these problems. This type of student assessment around values seems to occur in such a course, anyway; this linkage would merely formalize it and perhaps call for more specific means of assessing student progress. Later courses would then follow up on and expand this competence. One could envision a flow chart with all of the educational outcomes and their linkages with each course and field experience.

Field Experience

If we acknowledge that a person achieves competency in a gradual process, let us also note that assessment must take place throughout the social work curriculum. In the final analysis, our students must be able to function as practitioners. Why can't classroom courses be more geared to the application of theory and skill? Why doesn't each class have a community component? The key word here seems to be *application*. As practitioners, students must be able to apply what they have learned to real live situations. Therefore, a student's ability to apply knowledge in these situations is certainly a relevant educational outcome that can be assessed in each course. Papers using examples for theory application can be useful. Role play or simulation is also a helpful educational and assessment tool. The point is that identifying educational outcomes, specifying how each part of the curriculum contributes to their attainment, and assessing the student's appropriate level of competence in each course would make educating for competency a gradual, cumulative process versus a final "pass/fail" situation in field experience.

A Field Experience Illustration.   The following is a rather detailed illustration of how a program might specify and operationalize educational outcomes in the field experience part of the curriculum. This example will incorporate some of the current research that is being done in various social work programs. While few programs have implemented an education for competence approach to their classroom courses or other experiential opportunities, many have attempted to do so in their field experience component.

This illustration will use a work sample approach. Simply stated, we take a piece of student work from the field experience and assess performance according to the program's educational outcomes. The actual assessment will be conducted by a panel of judges, composed of a social work faculty member, a field supervisor, and the student. This group of people look at a work sample and assign it a qualitative judgment. The process is not unlike that of a panel of judges viewing a diving competition at a swim meet. The panel assessing the student's performance may choose from superior, good, fair, poor, or inadequate categories. To arrive at a final assessment, the student's score for each educational outcome is computed.

One of the most exciting aspects of helping students achieve educational outcomes is designing learning strategies. As not all learners need to take the same path, learning opportunities should be individualized. As long as the learning outcome is clearly specified, alternative ways to achieve it can be creatively explored taking available resources and opportunities into account.

It must also be recognized that students have different learning styles. Several questions can be asked of the learner. Do you learn best by experience? What do you have to do to make theory yours, to integrate it? Do you need structure from the teacher or do you provide your own? What helps you learn easily or quickly?[8]

A learning contract helps to relate educational outcomes to learning opportunities and strategies. For illustration purposes, table 6-2 is an attempt to operationalize the ten comptencies defined by the curriculum development project[9] in the form of a learning contract. This learning contract illustrates how the learning opportunities and strategies might occur and be measured. The form is adopted from a model established at the University of Georgia.[10]

It should be noted that at the beginning of the student's field

Table 6-2. Learning Contract

Competency	Learning Strategy	Evidence of Accomplishment
1. Identify and assess situations where the relationship between people and social institutions needs to be initiated, enhanced, restored, protected, or terminated.	1. Collect data on defined client population such as a predominantly black neighborhood. 2. Analyze above data into useable information. 3. Identify service or resources needed by neighborhood people.	1. Presents data analysis in written form for supervisor's critique. 2. Takes revised data analysis and discusses with neighborhood consumer. 3. Conceptualizes data collection and analysis through written or oral presentation highlighting student obstacles and successes in the process.
2. Develop and implement a plan for improving the well-being of people based on problem assessment and the exploration of obtainable goals and available options.	1. Meet with client population to discuss various ways to implement a plan. 2. Identify the various target groups and system components that must be considered in arriving at eventual plan. 3. Write plan.	1. Reviews plan with supervisor and revises where indicated. 2. Clarifies with supervisor the limitations, constraints, and strengths of the plan, including intended and unintended consequences.
3. Enhance the problem-solving, coping, and developmental capacities of people.	1. Direct interaction with client population around a perceived problem. 2. Reach definition with client population on course of action desired. 3. Assist client population in attaining the specified goal.	1. Process recording. 2. Videotape playback of interaction with client population. 3. Final written summary of intervention with or for client population.
4. Link people with systems that provide them with resources, services, and opportunities.	1. Initiate involvement with client population needing help. 2. Identify with client group the relevant systems and helping networks. 3. Assist in the decisionmaking process about what linkages client group desires.	1. Implements linkage plan in behalf of client group. 2. Reviews comprehensive written plan that takes into account the process and interaction necessary for client group linkage with resources to occur.

Table 6-2 continued

Competency	Learning Strategy	Evidence of Accomplishment
5. Intervene effectively on behalf of populations most vulnerable and discriminated against.	1. Engage in activity designed to focus on own attitudes regarding human diversity. 2. Do reading and other general data collection around a particular client group that is vulnerable. 3. Direct involvement with client group. 4. Identify unmet needs of client group. 5. Direct intervention to change policies that discriminate against client group.	1. Logs that detail involvement with client groups. 2. Reports or projects (written or oral) that deal with specific vulnerable client populations. 3. Audio or video recordings or process recordings that specify intervention strategy.
6. Promote the effective and humane operation of the systems that provide people with services, resources, and opportunities.	1. Obtain information about organization that would lead to maximum use of systems to help client groups. 2. Develop supportive networks among peers designed to humanize a particular part of daily agency operations. 3. Formally develop a particular strategy to change or modify existing policy.	1. Presentation of the strategy in written form, outlining strengths, constraints and consequences. 2. Detailing through logs, recordings, etc., the effort made with assessment of net gains and losses.
7. Actively participate with others in creating new, modified, or improved service, resource, opportunity systems that are more equitable, just, and responsive to consumers of services, and work with others to eliminate those systems that are unjust.	1. Engage in activity designed to examine own commitment to social justice. 2. Evaluate existing resource availability to particular group. 3. Research conclusions about adequacy of resource availability to consumer group. 4. If resources are inadequate or unjust, design action plan to change or modify existing situation. 5. Specify what part he or she will play in total strategy implementation.	1. Logs regarding involvement. 2. Written or oral presentation of own active participation including reasons for selection of strategies and various decision-making of group.

8. Evaluate the extent to which the objectives of the intervention plan were achieved.

1. Involve client population in determining if intervention objectives were achieved.
2. Renegotiate objectives or goals based upon client feedback.
3. Execute a particular research strategy.
4. Specify how failure or success will be measured

1. Performance of a research evaluation around a particular strategy.
2. Written assessment of the success or failure of a particular project with specification of appropriateness of the research design or the strategy used.

9. Continually evaluate one's own professional growth and development through assessment of practice behaviors and skills.

1. Develop feedback mechanism with client population being served regarding adequacy of worker performance.
2. Read current practice literature about the usefulness of certain intervention strategies.

1. Oral and written assessment of own strengths, limitations, unmet professional needs and areas of focus for professional development in next 12 months.

10. Contribute to the improvement of service delivery by adding to the knowledge base of the professions as appropriate and by supporting and upholding the standards and ethics of the profession.

1. Join NASW.
2. Write papers on ethical involvement of social workers regarding a particular case situation.
3. Organize a professional meeting on a topic of special interest.
4. Write position paper on a topic of own choice coming out of educational experiences.

1. Logs
2. Process recording of involvement.
3. Review tangible documents, e.g. papers, workshops and meeting programs.

experience the learning contract is blank, except for the left-hand column where competencies are listed. The student and agency field supervisor then negotiate the suitable learning strategies for column two. The student should be expected to play a major role here, with the agency supervisor delineating what is realistic, possible, and available.

The third element is the right-hand column, which contains evidence of the attainment of each competency. The faculty person may help determine how assessment should occur. While many of the illustrations in the third column use written work as evidence of accomplishment, the reader should not conclude that this is educationally preferable but rather a reflection of the state of the art. As much as possible, other sources should also be used, such as input from agency supervisors, seminar instructors, and clients, logs, process recordings, video- and audiotape recordings, behavior simulations, and seminar presentations.

This learning contract is intended to be an individualized, flexible, working document. Changes may be made as needed in order to meet individual learning needs.

ASSESSMENT

Any assessment procedure will raise a host of research issues and questions. The issue of precision is still being debated. Individual programs should not feel constrained about the development of their own assessment processes. The state of the art is quite limited and therefore open to considerable development. One suggestion would be to utilize a research person in the design phase of such assessment procedures.

IMPLICATIONS FOR FACULTY

There are several significant implications for faculty in the education for competency approach. Perhaps the major change would be the shift from a person who delivers content through such mechanisms as lectures and assignments to a facilitator of learning and a manager of educational resources.

This shift in faculty role generates a need for faculty development. The need becomes greater when one surveys the dramatic expansion of baccalaureate social work education, with many practitioners moving into the classroom as full-time faculty. What kind of responsibility does CSWE have in this area? What responsibility does the given college or university have for novice faculty members?

Professional socialization and learning opportunities for faculty, such as those provided in the late 1960s and early 1970s by the Southern Regional Educational Board, no longer exist. How will this currently unfulfilled need be met?

The curriculum illustrations provided here can partially help to meet this need. They recommend an educational atmosphere where students interact with faculty and practitioners in a way that encourages new approaches to curriculum development and teaching strategies. When related to the best efforts in social work education to identify educational outcomes, such as the recent Undergraduate Social Work Curriculum Development Project, the quality of teaching and practice will undoubtedly be improved.

PROBLEMS AND PITFALLS

One of the most serious criticisms of a competency approach in education is that it operates from a weak research base. Flanders cites three problem areas: (1) the difficulty of measuring educational outcomes; (2) the problems in analyzing the interactive patterns between teaching and learning; and (3) the difficulty in inventing more effective training procedures for adults who want to learn teaching skills.[11]

To engage in assessment of educational outcomes requires faculty time and energy. The overworked handful of faculty in many undergraduate programs do not want to bite off more than they can chew, nor should they. As in any planned change, a realistic assessment must be made to assure that the resources are adequate to meet the goals.

Perhaps the most discussed pitfall of a competency approach to education is the danger that it becomes too mechanistic and moves away from the humane interaction base that we treasure in social work. Monitoring and creativity are required to insure that this does not happen, that we are not reduced to tabulating numbers on a specific competency to see if the student "passes."

Finally, for a given student to achieve a set of specific competencies does not insure a liberally educated person, for the truly educated graduate will have synthesized and integrated all of the material and skills mastered into his or her unique personality. That is, the final product will not be a set of competencies, but rather a whole person who is much more than the sum of his or her parts.[12]

STRENGTHS AND REWARDS

This chapter has been deliberately cautious, outlining the problems and pitfalls of developing an approach that educates for competency ın BSW programs. However, let us recognize the strengths of such an approach.

Above all, perhaps, it gives both faculty and students an opportunity to design an educational plan with purpose and sequence. It lends coherence to the educational planning process. It provides checkpoints for monitoring and supervising competence attainment throughout the curriculum, while moving away from more subjective types of assessment. At the end of the program, the student feels a real sense of accomplishment that has been tangibly assessed. The process is in keeping with theories of teaching based on studies of adult learning, in that it creates both a mechanism and a climate for mutual planning and creativity in meeting student learning needs.

CONCLUSION

As the social work profession struggles to improve service delivery, efforts to more clearly define what social workers are competent to do have emerged. These practice competencies must be incorporated into educational programs in the form of educational outcomes that then help to shape curricula. In this chapter, some ways of approaching educational outcomes and curriculum development were explored, especially within the framework of the Undergraduate Social Work Curriculum Development Project. Implementation of classroom and field experience strategies for attaining social work practice competencies were explicated. Finally, the problems, pitfalls, and criticisms as well as the strengths and rewards of an approach that emphasizes education for competence were outlined.

NOTES

1. Pottinger, Paul S., "Competency Assessment at School and Work," *Social Policy* 8, 2 (September/October 1977):35-41.
2. Briar, Scott, "The Age of Accountability," *Social Work* 18, (January 1973):2.
3. Jarrett, H.H., "Implications of Implementing Competency-Based Education in the Liberal Arts," *Educational Technology* 17, 4 (April 1977):21-26.
4. Baer, B.L., and Ronald Federico, *Educating the Baccalaureate Social Worker: Report of the Undergraduate Social Work Curriculum Development Project* (Cambridge, Mass.: Ballinger 1978).
5. Jarrett, H.H., and F.W. Clark, "Variety in Competency-Based Education: A Program Comparison," *Journal of Non-Traditional Studies, Alternative Higher Education* 3, 2 (1978):104-113.
6. Duehn, W.D., and N.S. Mayadas, "Entrance and Exit Requirements of Professional Social Work Education," *Journal of Education for Social Work* 13, 2 (1977):22-29.

McLeod, D.L., and H.J. Meyer, "A Study of the Values of Social Workers," in Thomas, Edwin J., ed. *Behavioral Science for Social Workers* (New York: Free Press, 1967), pp. 401-16.

Varley, B., "Social Work Values: Changes in Value Commitments of Students from Admission to MSW Graduation," *Journal of Education for Social Work* 4 (Fall 1968):72-74.

Koevin, B., "Values in Social Work Education Implications for Baccalaureate Degree Programs," *Journal of Education for Social Work* 13, 2 (Spring 1977):84-90.

7. McClelland, D.C., "Testing for Competency Rather than Intelligence," *American Psychologist* 28 (1973):1-14.

8. Foeckler, M.M., "On Learning," paper presented to Society of Barnpsykiatriska Kuratorer, Stockholm, Sweden, September 1975, February 1976.

9. Baer and Federico, pp. 85-89.

10. Jarrett, H.H., A.C. Kilpatrick, and L.R. Pollane, eds., "Operationalizing Competency-Based BSW Field Experience," paper presented at Annual Program Meeting, Council on Social Work Education, Phoenix, Arizona, March 1977.

11. Flanders, N.A., "The Changing Base of Performance-Based Teaching," *Phi Delta Kappan* 55:312-15.

12. Jarrett, H.H., "Competency-Based Education in the Liberal Arts" (Ph.D. diss., University of Georgia, 1974), p. 108.

REFERENCES AND BIBLIOGRAPHY

Arkava, M.L., and E.C. Brennen, eds. *Competency-Based Education for Social Work: Evaluation and Curriculum Issues.* New York: Council on Social Work Education, 1976.

Bloom, B.S. "Affective Consequences of School Achievement." In J.H. Block, ed., *Mastery Learning: Theory and Practice.* (New York: Holt, Rinehart and Winston, 1971), pp. 47-48.

Clark, F.W. "Characteristics of the Competency-Based Curriculum." In Arkava and Brennen, eds., *Competency-Based Education for Social Work* (New York: Council on Social Work Education, 1976), pp. 23-46.

Cummins, D.E. "The Assessment Procedure." In Arkava and Brennen, eds., *Competency-Based Education for Social Work* (New York: Council on Social Work Education, 1976), pp. 62-81.

Dressell, P.L. *College and University Curriculum* 2nd ed. Berkeley, Ca.: McCutchan Publishing, 1971.

Houston, W.R., and R.B. Howsan, eds., *Competency-Based Education: Progress, Problems and Prospects.* Chicago: Science Research Associates, 1972.

Jarrett, H.H. "Implications of Implementing Competency-Based Education in the Liberal Arts." *Educational Technology* 17, 4 (April 1977):21-26.

Jarrett, H.H., A.C. Kilpatrick, and L.R. Pollane, eds. "Operationalizing Competency-Based BSW Field Experience." Paper presented at Annual Program Meeting, Council on Social Work Education, Phoenix, Arizona, March 1977.

Knowles, M. *The Adult Learner: A Neglected Species.* Houston: Gulf Publishing, 1973.

Kuhn, T.S. *The Structure of Scientific Revolutions.* In International Encyclopedia of Unified Science 2nd ed., vol. 2, no. 2. Chicago: University of Chicago Press, 1970.

Mager, R.F. *Preparing Instructional Objectives.* Palo Alto, Ca.: Fearon Publisher, 1962.

Maxwell, W.D. "PBTE: A Case of the Emperor's New Clothes." *Phi Delta Kappan* 55 (1974):306-31.

O'Connell, W.R., Jr., and W.E. Moomaw, eds. *A CBE Primer.* Atlanta: Southern Regional Education Board, 1975.

Sagen, H.B. "The Professions: A Neglected Model for Undergraduate Education." *Liberal Education* LIX, 4 (December 1973):507-19.

Spores, J.C., and M. Cummings. "Toward a Competency-Based Baccalaureate Social Work Curriculum." In Arkava and Brennen, eds., *Competency-Based Education for Social Work* (New York: Council on Social Work Education, 1976), pp. 95-124.

Tyler, R.W. *Basic Principles of Curriculum and Instruction: Syllabus for Education 305.* Chicago: University of Chicago Press, 1950.

Chapter Seven

A Faculty Guide to Educational Assessment

Ramon Valle

INTRODUCTION

The focus of this chapter is on the development of the social work program's self-assessment capabilities. The intent is to assist faculty in constructing comprehensive program-wide assessment systems tailored to local educational needs and designed to be used as tools for continued program and curriculum development. It should be noted that, as used here, the term assesssment indicates a systematic program review activity that builds a self-evaluative data base useful for decisionmaking around program progress and direction. Assessment sets the developmental rate for individual programs and is vital to the healthy as well as heterogeneous progress of social work education within overall accreditation standards.

An assumption of this chapter is that much more educational assessment regularly takes place than is recognized by educators themselves, and that this energy can be harnessed into a workable program-wide assessment system adapted to individual program requirements. Moreover, once an assessment system is in place, it can be maintained as a regular component of the program's curriculum development activity. In addition, it can serve to make external evaluative demands constantly impinging upon the program more intelligible and manageable. No claim is made here that an assessment system will make the work load implicit in educational accountability disappear, but rather that a program-wide system will ease the onerous features related to program monitoring, especially those concerned with allocating program resources and personnel time.

A further premise is that much more educational assessment will be required to take place over the next decade. The university and social work education in general are demanding more efficient uses of scarce educational resources. While social work has always had a built-in expectation of accountability, this generalized type of expectation is not enough. Educators must rise to meet the evaluative demands of the times with more technological sophistication. Such sophistication can be expressed through the development of a comprehensive program-wide assessment system.

EDUCATIONAL ASSESSMENT AS A NATURAL PROCESS IN CURRICULUM DEVELOPMENT

A decided advantage in meeting evaluative pressures and in constructing a program-wide assessment system is the fact that social work educators are presently engaged in assessment activity everywhere throughout their programs. This is particularly evident with regard to all accredited undergraduate social work programs, all of which have undertaken a series of evaluative reviews in preparation for accreditation within the current decade. A closer look at the field further indicates that this more formal type of educational evaluation activity takes place alongside more mundane day-to-day assessment. In this latter category, we can include (1) the continual reviews undertaken by curriculum committees; (2) the assessment processes related to faculty selection wherein a program's strengths and weaknesses are reviewed vis-à-vis the capabilities expected of potential faculty applicants; and (3) those overall program assessments that are made by faculty and students at the beginning and end of each academic year.

Institutional pressures also constitute a very constructive influence on programs to undertake self-assessment. These pressures come in the form of the many reporting requirements set by the parent institution based on the need to justify costs in the face of limited educational dollars. These pressures similarly confront program directors and faculty who find themselves making summary reports to community agencies; to potential employers of their graduates; and to other social work programs within their own regions. In a like manner, annual alumni meetings, seemingly removed from formal educational assessment, often serve the function of "state of the program" reviews—at least for the program administrator who has to assess his or her program prior to making the welcoming speech, and who has then to include such evaluative judgments in the body of the introductory remarks.

In effect, the ordinary operation of any social work educational program entails a considerable amount of program assessment activity. Perhaps the very normalcy as well as the ongoing necessity for such procedures hides their program-wide assessment system potential. Perhaps, also, the ordinariness of such activity masks the actual or potential faculty expertise. Social work programs can utilize such ongoing processes and expertise as starting points for the development of their own program-wide comprehensive assessment systems.

BARRIERS TO PROGRAM-WIDE ASSESSMENT

Difficulty of Transition

In the same breath that we admit to a certain normalcy regarding educational assessment procedures within social work education circles, we must recognize the fact that there are a number of barriers to developing program-wide assessment systems. First of all, the step from everyday assessment to a comprehensive system is not automatic. Throughout the field, much of the ongoing personnel assessment activity—including assessments conducted by students—is not consciously organized into program-wide systems. Most of the evaluative procedures have the quality of ad hoc activity performed to meet specific one-time-only program assessment needs, regardless of the fact that they are often repeated throughout the academic year as well as from year to year. The acts of designing new courses, hiring new faculty, or responding to program accountability requests from the host department, the university, and/or outside constituencies all contain elements to facilitate the development of program-wide assessment systems, but at present they are simply not handled as an integral part of educational planning.

Slow Integration of Technology

A second barrier is the fact that assessment-evaluation language and technology, particularly educational assessment technology, are not yet completely integrated within the repertoire of social work educators or practitioners. With few exceptions, most social work educators have acquired their program evaluation capabilities on the job after their professional training. This is not to say that the social work literature is devoid of its contribution to educational program evaluation.[1] The problem is that these contributions are not readily integrated into the visible technology of social work education as evidenced either in the curriculum or through the presence of comprehensive assessment systems in social work programs.

Demands on Personnel

A third set of barriers to initiating program-wide assessment systems are the multiple pressures affecting program personnel. The demands of teaching, the ongoing need to provide educational assistance to varied community constituencies, and the many institutional responsibilities to the department and to the university all constitute an inert force against systematization of assessment activity. Indeed, there are just so many hours in the work week or month. Current demands on personnel in other areas of the program can be seen as exceeding available time, leaving little for the redirection involved in building an assessment system.

Attitudinal Obstacles

We must also acknowledge the relatively formidable attitudinal difficulties that accompany the design and implementation of more accurate means of accounting for our teaching activity in terms of actual outcomes. At one extreme, controversy is rampant as to the appropriate configuration of variables that constitute accurate assessments of educational outcomes. As Huff indicates:

> Educators need to assume a more pragmatic stance. Undoubtedly, initial attempts to evaluate educational outcomes will be crude and justifiably subject to some suspicion. On the other hand, if we continue to be intimidated by the technical difficulties and political resistance surrounding the outcome evaluation task, we can only continue to suffer increasing public criticism and reaction to our failure to engage in self evaluation activity. Hopefully, we shall learn from the early attempt at evaluation and will be able to improve our measurement techniques over time in order to gain valid information concerning at least some outputs of higher education activities.[2]

Controversy is also present at the other attitudinal extreme. Here, a "causal property" is mistakenly attributed to educational assessment—an outlook perhaps stimulated by some of the literature itself, particularly the benefit-cost and efficiency oriented literature. This literature is misleading in indicating that cause and effect relationships will be uncovered through application of selected evaluation techniques. This overexpectation has taken hold, even though the greater portion of the writing on educational assessment and evaluation can be seen as more cautionary in nature. Nowhere among the serious writers are outcomes seen as the result of inputs on a strictly linear basis. Intervening and unintended elements are always taken into consideration. Unfortunately, the persistence of the "causal" mystique in social work educational circles generates resistance to comprehensive assessment approaches. For one, this attitude blocks the developmental approach so necessary to the design and implementation of comprehensive program-wide assessment systems. This attitude may also serve to turn off many faculty who have a more realistic perception of both the state of the art in educational assessment and the many subtle complexities at work in their own programs that defy establishing one-to-one causal relationships at any given evaluative moment.

Investment of Time and Personnel

Finally, apprehension about program personnel availability and possible attendant cost also create relatively formidable obstacles to the serious consideration of program-wide assessment systems. Admittedly, the start-up time investment of the approach suggested here would have to be taken into serious consideration by the administrator of a program where there are no clear concepts of assessment to begin with. This sort of apprehension, though, will quite possibly be present in all programs to some degree and may thereby inhibit progress toward full-fledged assessment capability under the guise of not wanting to overload either the system or its personnel. This type of apprehension, then, may be misplaced. As noted earlier, some assessment activity must normally take place within all social work educational settings just by the nature of the university milieu itself. Systemization of the effort can actually tend to offset the overload effect by making more efficient use of existing evaluative responsibilities to provide a more orderly use of program personnel time.

All in all, educator statements of a desire to attain educational excellence within social work programs need to be supported with evidence of how this excellence is to be attained and maintained, with regard not only to student outcomes but to the outcomes of the program as a whole. A step in this direction is the setting up of a planned self-monitoring system tailored to local educational formats that enables the program to obtain a holistic overview of itself in the process of meeting its specific objectives.

STEPS TOWARD A PROGRAM-WIDE
ASSESSMENT SYSTEM

To a great extent, the preceding chapters provide the overall framework of program efforts that constitute the basis for any program-wide assessment system. The university setting, the social work program's departmental home, its working relationships with other disciplines, the program's faculty and student composition, and its relationships with the practice community all furnish key assessment content inputs. The specific areas of the curriculum, the configuration of courses and the practicum, likewise furnish vital elements for any comprehensive self-monitoring system. How each program implements the different features of its overall curriculum in its own educational milieu then provides the custom-fitting aspects of the assessment system to be designed.

The development of a working program-wide assessment system requires the focusing of faculty, administrator, and student attitudes and energies along specific lines of evaluative activity. These include the following steps: (1) focusing program objectives and educational outcomes into assessable-measurable formats; (2) introducing a phasing approach to the design of any program-wide system; (3) conducting a thorough inventory of all current program assessment activity, however inconsequential such activity might appear; (4) gaining familiarity with available evaluative technology; and (5) acquiring the program-wide capability to make educationally centered evaluative judgments. Given this focusing activity, the program can readily move into its own tailor-made, comprehensive assessment system.

Specifying Program Objectives and Outcomes

As a definite principle of evaluative activity, educators need to recognize that an effective assessment system is dependent upon the scope and specificity of objectives. Assessment techniques are relatively meaningless unless the objectives of the program are clearly explicated. However difficult and time-intensive this undertaking might appear, the delineation of specific objectives forms the cornerstone of all subsequent evaluative activity. The reader should note that the overall assumption here is that a program's objectives will, in fact, reflect the ten core competencies as defined in the report of the Undergraduate Social Work Curriculum Development Project.[3] It is further assumed that both the curriculum and program-wide objectives expressing the competencies will be framed in terms of the unique features of each program and region that it serves.

Assessment techniques are also relatively meaningless if they are not tied to program outcomes. In the view of this author, a great deal of social work educational evaluative activity engages in what Tripodi terms assessment of "program efforts."[4] There is a tendency to focus evaluative attention on reviewing educational "process activities," giving less and less attention to assessing the "products" or accomplishments of the program.

Contrary to the somewhat popular opinion, program outcomes are quite documentable. During a given academic year a social work program sees and records various achievements in terms of its currently enrolled and graduating students; in terms of the courses provided; and in terms of recordable interaction between the educational milieu and its actors. These achievements are all recordable and usually available in any of several program documents, such as the end-of-the-year report to the program's constituencies. It should be noted that the outcome focus being discussed here is broader than student competency outcomes alone. Unquestionably, the raison d'être for programs is the student component. At the same time, however, programs have many other levels of operation besides the classroom and the field instruction process. Any program-wide assessment system must, therefore, look to all these other facets that also produce educational results of varying types.

Developing a "Phased"
Assessment Strategy

The careful timing of assessment events becomes a second key element of the overall assessment system to be developed. Figure 7-1 summarizes the concept behind the phasing approach suggested here. As a rule of thumb, an academic year can be seen as the most convenient unit of time for the design of any given segment of a program-wide assessment system, as well as for its subsequent implementation. The premise underlying the phasing concept has already been expressed above, namely, that despite many constant pressures for ad hoc short-term evaluative reports, programs will gain more by moving toward planned development of a comprehensive system.

In interpreting figure 7-1, a word of caution is in order. While the notion of sequencing activity over time is the critical element, the steps as outlined should not be rigidly interpreted. Some programs may find themselves in more advanced stages than those suggested in Phase I. For example, they may already be well into the actual implementation of a complete assessment system. Similarly, some programs may find that their Phase I activity can be compressed into a very brief time frame with a minimum of effort. The phasing concept as expressed here is offered only as a guide; there is no one fixed rate of progress for all programs. Each program, therefore,

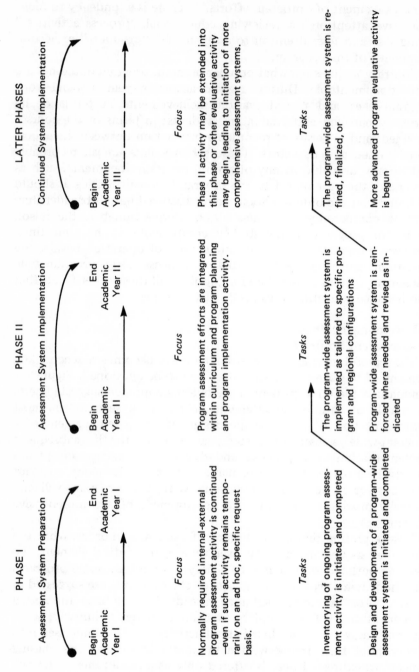

Figure 7-1. Planned Development of a Program-Wide Assessment System.

should proceed toward the development of a comprehensive assessment system at its own pace.

Evaluative activity beyond Phase II is not delineated, as the chapter focus is on the initiation of program-wide assessment systems. At the same time, forward or long-range planning is an important feature of sound curriculum development within the phasing concept. The implementation of a fully comprehensive assessment system needs to be seen in terms of a possible five-year cycle.[5] This is not to deny the fact that a relatively extensive and comprehensive system can be put in place within the figure 7-1 two- to three-year phasing period.

Inventorying Current Assessment Activity

The systematic inventorying of the program's current assessment activity in order to determine current assessment strengths and weaknesses serves as a third vital step toward building a program-wide assessment system. Actually conducting such an inventory may well surprise most programs in that much more evaluative activity may be in process than faculty and students might suspect.

In taking the inventory, educators should note that the form of the current assessment activity does not matter. It is also important that educators suspend for the moment their judgments as to the quality of the evaluative efforts being documented. The point of the inventory is to record any types of assessments that may be occurring within the program. Personnel are, therefore, encouraged to look thoroughly at all aspects of the program where some assessment is taking place or is projected to take place.

Table 7-1 carries out the suggested inventory schema in miniature. As seen here, the inventory takes the following sequential steps:

1. The programs where assessments are currently being conducted are listed by category and level.
2. The frequency of the specific category and level of assessment activity as well as the time in the academic year when the assessment takes place is recorded.
3. The type(s) of assessment instrument(s) utilized for each specific activity, such as a questionnaire and summative committee reports, are listed and described briefly.
4. The principal criteria used to make the varied assessments are documented. (This criteria list becomes crucial to the development of the program's assessment judgment capability. The criteria used in the program's ongoing assessment activity can be the basis for developing more advanced criteria for verifying progress or lack of

Table 7-1. Current Assessment Activity Inventory Form

1. List the element or category and level of the program where assessment activity currently takes place (The categories listed below are for illustrative purposes only.)	2. Note frequency and time in academic year when assessment takes place, for example, annually, quarterly.	3. Indicate and briefly describe type of assessment instrument used, e.g., questionnaire, annual report, summative committee assessment, minutes of a specific committee.	4. Delineate principal criteria employed in the assessment activity, e.g., cost data, student performance competencies, student faculty ratios, levels of content (knowledge and skills contained in courses).
Budget or Resources			
Institutional Support			
Departmental Support			
Program Administrative Support			
Program Priorities			
Faculty Competencies			
Student Performance in Process, e.g., Comprehensive Exam, etc.			
Student Exit Competencies			
Courses			
A			
B			
C			
etc.			
Practicum Program and Resources			
Other Categories			

Note: This form is intended to be illustrative, not exhaustive, of potential levels or frequencies. Each program is encouraged to develop its own individualized assessment inventory format.

it at various levels of program performance, once the comprehensive assessment system is in place.)

The information gathered through the inventory will be invaluable for determining the actual program-wide assessment system starting points as well as for highlighting evaluative capabilities already existing within the program itself. It should be noted that assessment activity conducted in previous years can be included in the "current" assessment activity category if pertinent. At the same time, the emphasis should be on mapping present and ongoing evaluative measures. One can become stalled if the inventorying activity attempts to be historically exhaustive. The intent of the inventory process is to build the ground floor of what will eventually become the program's overall assessment system.

Familiarity With Available
Evaluative Technology

Gaining familiarity with evaluative technology is a necessary further preparatory step in the overall sequence of designing a program-wide assessment system. This, in turn, entails three related steps: (1) becoming familiar with a series of key definitions; (2) recognizing the hierarchical nature of evaluative terms and tasks; and (3) becoming familiar with the range of key evaluative instruments critical to developing well-rounded assessment systems.

There is no clear substitute for gaining familiarity with the technological features of assessment. Unfortunately, as Baizerman indicates, until recently evaluative technology has not been a part of the human services—or by extension, of those social work educational systems that prepare professionals to enter the human services.[6] Educators need to see, however, that acquiring the technology and using evaluative language do not in any way compromise social work values. On the contrary, educational assessment speaks directly to the value of accountability. Moreover, the educator's command of available instrumentation adds humanistic perspectives to what can become a very mechanistic process.

In addition, if it has not already done so, educational assessment technology will strike a familiar chord with educators in terms of similarities to research techniques. For example, the evaluative activity makes use of questionnaires, observation techniques, informed judgment procedures, and case-by-case analysis, all of which are already known to social work educators in the research format. At the same time, though, an important distinction is in order. Information gathering in a research context is primarily geared to

knowledge gains with respect to the research question itself. Information gathering under the assessment rubric must be subsumed under
curriculum and program development objectives.

   Assessment Terminology and Definitions.   As indicated, the development of a program-wide assessment system is facilitated only if
educators attain a working knowledge of evaluative terms and
definitions. Faculty and student resistance must be met head-on.
Unfortunately, resistance may be aided and abetted by the contro-
versies that appear in the literature itself. For example, it is certain
that educators will encounter considerable semantic controversy over
evaluative language, particularly in educational circles.

   The discussion here suggests an alternative to such controversy.
Educators have the option of proceeding directly to the core notions
implicit in any of the current evaluative language, and of tailoring
that language to their home systems. The intent here, then, is to
provide a descriptive context for the concepts under discussion. For
example, the nature of educational objectives is described in a variety
of texts (from Mager[7] onward). Granger, though, has succinctly
captured the core notion of objectives, namely that they are the aims
of action.[8] These aims in turn can be seen as either general or
specific along a process continuum. The terminology below follows
this same core notion/descriptor approach. The reader should note
that the assortment of terms selected for discussion encompasses
concepts considered absolutely essential to all program-wide assessment systems. The various reference documents cited in the text as
well as in the bibliographical section can serve to provide educators
with a more than ample evaluative vocabulary.

   1. *Assessment*—As used here, assessment indicates a systematic
activity that builds the information/data base for making decisions
about program development and direction. Assessment activity sets
the developmental rate for individual programs in pursuit of their
general and specific aims. It is important here to be clear on the
purpose and limitations of assessment. As *Social Work Education:
Planning and Assessment Systems* suggests, assessment must not be
confused with evaluation research. The latter's intent is to make
judgments between programs and of the field as a whole. In contrast,
assessment provides limited generalization and this *only* to the
program itself. As the *Handbook* further states, assessment permits
(1) generalizing from experiences to date (within the program) to
expectations for the future, and (2) generalizing from a sample of the
program to the entire program.[9] Assessment is the correct strategy
for initiating a system of educational accountability because it

facilitates the development of indexes in terms intelligible to specific programs.

2. *Appropriateness*—As employed here, appropriateness refers to the goodness of fit between the educational program outcomes, the target populations, and the educational milieu. Appropriateness issues focus on the mesh between the program and its educational targets. For example, a program may decide to implement a course sequence that applies to a region other than its own. Using this measure, educators can look to the manner in which their curriculum and program supports match and interact with the complex of culturally diverse unique features of their own region.

3. *Adequacy*—As utilized within educational assessment, adequacy refers to the correspondence between the amount and extent of program offerings and the actual educational goods available to the program's targets. For example, a program in the Southwest may be very appropriately geared to serving Latino/Mexicano/Hispanic population groups. At the same time, it may be completely understaffed or lack sufficient courses for this purpose. Here the question is not goodness of fit, but rather the extent of that fit.

4. *Effectiveness*—As employed here, effectiveness refers to the correspondence between stated objectives and actual program outcomes as attained through program inputs. Effectiveness measures are central to all assessment strategies. They include all those types of evaluative activities that in some manner measure the educational goods of the program against its actual deliverable products. A program may have an excellent fit with its regional and target groups. It may also have sufficient curriculum and faculty power to deliver the diversity encountered in this region. At the same time, after a year's activity not much may happen educationally. It is here that effectiveness assessments enter the picture. All of the program inputs in terms of its institutional supports, budgetary resources, faculty capabilities, and curriculum content are assembled together and reviewed against results attained.

"Efficiency measures" usually follow effectiveness assessments. Measuring efficiency refers to evaluating the educational products attained in terms of the cost of resources.[10] Explication of this range of evaluative activity is not included in this chapter; efficiency evaluations exceed the domain of assessment measures. As indicated in 1970 in *The Cost and Output of Graduate Social Work Education*, there is no question that cost-effective measures are more and more in vogue in both the educational sphere and the human service program sector. As seen here, however, there is a current strategic need to first define the social work education accountability parameters in assessment terms, so that efficiency measures may be appropriately applied at a later stage.

The Hierarchy of Assessment Terms and Tasks. The development of a program-wide assessment system is facilitated if evaluative processes and terminology are understood to operate in a relatively hierarchical order.[11] First, evaluative language demonstrates this hierarchical notion in terminology that moves from the general to the specific. It is more usual to set general goals or objectives and then proceed to detail the more measurable aims of action. Second, evaluative events tend to exhibit an hierarchical process over time. Some evaluative acts must precede others in order to allow assessment to take place. Simply put, in any assessment system, objectives precede outcomes. Third, the hierarchical tendency of evaluative processes is also evident in the fact that educational assessment activity generally proceeds through several levels of varying depth and complexity in some sequential or stepwise manner. For example, appropriateness, adequacy, and effectiveness assessments each imply successively more comprehensive overviews of the processes under scrutiny. Here the hierarchical order, however, is somewhat reversed. In contrast to the delineation of objectives, the less comprehensive measures of appropriateness and adequacy tend to precede the more comprehensive measures of effectiveness and efficiency. Again, a word of caution is in order. While evaluative language and processes are relatively hierarchical and sequential in nature, it must be understood that once a system is in place, the measures can be applied simultaneously, particularly since a program will be moving along several dimensions at once.

Figure 7-2 encapsulates the overall concept. In essence, any assessment system is seen as a series of program steps moving along an educational continuum, proceeding from the general to the specific with regard to objectives, tasks, and outcomes, and proceeding from the specific to the comprehensive in terms of evaluative levels of analysis. This theme will appear in the remainder of the chapter's examples.

Assessment Instruments and Techniques. A comprehensive assessment system becomes a reality only if program personnel attain command over evaluative instruments and techniques. As described in the publication *Social Work Education: Planning and Assessment Systems,* assessment information gathering techniques can be classified into several major categories for use in designing a program-wide assessment system:[12]

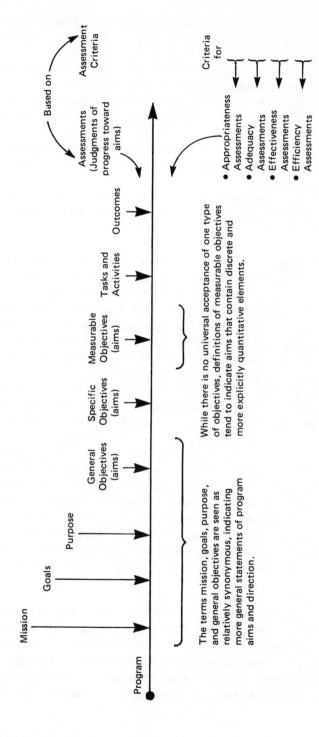

Figure 7-2. Hierarchy of Evaluative Terms and Tasks.

1. *Retrospection techniques*—These include a review of the accumulated experiences of the program, including past records as well as recollections and reconstructions of past program events.
2. *Review and inspection techniques*—These include a review of the variety of current written program products and records.
3. *Observation techniques*—Included here are data-gathering approaches based on a variety of open-ended and closed viewing techniques.
4. *Testing techniques*—Periodic readings of performance, primarily oriented to student performance and including pre- and post-assessment approaches.
5. *Interview and questionnaire techniques*—These include data gathering by means of structured schedules soliciting responses from individuals and groups.

Each of these categories of assessment contains a relatively wide range of specific instruments that are available to the educator but that need to be tailored to the overall evaluative process. As indicated above, program personnel will find a similarity between evaluative techniques and research methodology. Moreover, they may well find many assessment techniques already used in the program's ongoing evaluative activity. Many of these techniques will have surfaced during the program inventory activity.

It should be noted that each of the five categories of assessment has its own inherent technical limitations, so that a holistic assessment of the program generally requires the use of several methods collectively. If used in this manner and tailored appropriately, the above assessment techniques can provide the evidence of program performance needed to permit the social work program to document its strengths and weaknesses in a comprehensive manner for program development purposes. It is also recognized that the very richness of available evaluative instruments can serve to overwhelm as well as aid educators. This is all the more reason for developing a phasing approach within any program-wide assessment system. Time, technique, and process can therefore work together in the overall effort.

Making Assessment Judgments

The capability to make evaluative judgments with regard to all aspects of assessment constitutes the critical fifth step in the development of a program-wide system. This rests on the ability to establish operational or performance criteria related to the program objectives and processes. As used here, criteria are the basis for deciding on the appropriateness, adequacy, and effectiveness of program events. They are the specific performance indexes that show levels attainment with respect to program objectives as well as overall program operations.[13]

Table 7-2 suggests a basic format for building a judgment capability within program-wide assessment systems. In following through the table, the assessor first proceeds to sort out the program element to be assessed. Judgments are made as to the level of progress or attainment over a given period of time. They may be scaled from high/excellent to low/poor performance or attainment. It is critical that each judgment meet the criteria illustrating the level of performance attained.

As noted before, it is to be expected that a goodly portion of the assessment criteria will emerge from the program-wide inventory of current assessment activity. Ideally, such criteria are established prior to conducting any assessment. At the same time, it is recognized that some criteria will emerge during the actual process of assessment, particularly in the early stages of initiating a program-wide system. In actual fact, the phasing approach suggested here allows for the gradual refinement of all aspects of the assessment system, including the refinement of performance criteria over time. It is important that such developmental indexes are not denigrated. Programs have to begin somewhere, and as Enthoven indicates, educational programs stand to gain more from being roughly right than entirely wrong, with regard to their overall self-appraisal.[14] Eventually, however, criteria at all levels of the assessment system need to become a before-the-fact reality—even if they remain relatively crude indexes.

It is well beyond the scope of this present chapter to detail all of the judgment situations and combinations of criteria possible within any given program. There are a variety of assessment/evaluation manuals available to the educator that contain more than enough examples to cover the evaluative needs of most social work programs. Several examples are annotated at the end of this chapter.

SUMMARY

The focus here has been on the development of the social work program's self-accounting capabilities with the intent of assisting educators to implement program-wide assessment systems reflecting local educational priorities. The strategy of assessment has been carefully selected as the one most appropriate to social work education at this point in time, in terms of the current evaluative state of the art. From the individual program perspective, the assessment approach offers the most flexibility in permitting each

Table 7-2.   Basic Assessment Judgment Schema

Program Elements to be Reviewed/Assessed	Judgment of Level of Attainment or Performance			Criteria for Judgments
	High/ Excellent	Medium/ Moderate	Low/ Poor	
The program element to be reviewed/ assessed is listed.	Judgments of high to low performance are based on comparing the progress over time of the specific program elements being reviewed/assessed against its performance criteria.			These criteria which may take the form of a simple checklist or more extensive statements must be linked to performance variables that become explanatory indicators or evidence for the judgment made. The presence of criteria is critically important as this type of evidence provides the program personnel with the context in which to alter or enhance current inputs and their educational direction.
The objectives applicable to this aspect of the program are listed.				
Assessors may encompass more than one program element at once, although each one needs to be assessed on its own criteria.	*Note:* Only a three-point judgment scale has been indicated here. Some assessors prefer five-point and even seven-point scales, to provide more latitude for intermediate judgments between high or low performance.			
The objectives for the program element must be clearly specified.				

individual program to formulate and then explicate its own indexes of performance within the general performance standards of the field. The principal limitation of the assessment strategy is that it ties all evaluative generalizations to the program itself. At the same time this may also be a strength, in that assessment findings can be incorporated immediately into the program's own curriculum development efforts.

A properly constructed assessment system permeates the entire program. It includes all the components that sustain the curriculum. Educational outcomes are, therefore, only one part of the assessment picture. Perhaps because the teaching/learning relationship between students and faculty is so central to our programs, it is easier to focus most of our evaluative activities in that direction only. However, the totality of the program needs to be incorporated into the assessment system.

The social work program operates within a complex milieu that includes inputs not only from central university administration but also, in most cases, from departmental and other organized inter-departmental auspices. The interplay of the program within this institutional fabric has a bearing on budget and personnel allocations. Such allocations can, in the real world of everyday program operations, be translated into sufficient secretarial services to support teaching efforts; sufficient funds to bring adjunct and/or consultative assistance to the programs; into conference travel to upgrade faculty skills; and access to necessary equipment and supplies. The curriculum and the educational milieu are therefore intertwined. A comprehensive assessment system permits program personnel to track their efforts within the milieu in an organized manner.

The sequential nature of the preceding discussion is based primarily on an expository rather than a lock-step actual implementation strategy. It is expected that each social work program will have its own unique configuration, which in turn will dictate differential utilization of any specific feature of the assessment technology presented here or contained in any of the cited assessment sources. In keeping with this theme, the chapter closes with figure 7-3, which summarizes the program-wide assessment process in several specific areas. It should be recognized that the figure itself is narrower in scope than the actual extent of educational activities within a given program. At the same time, however, it is illustrative of the process of assessment with the selected aspects of the program.

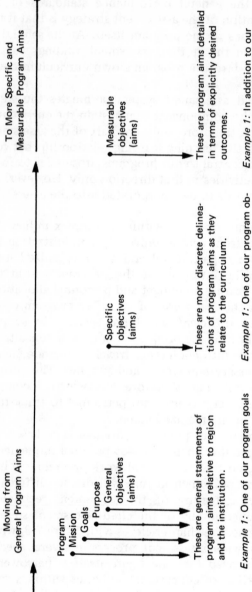

The Program's Educational Continuum

Moving from General Program Aims → To More Specific and Measurable Program Aims

Program
Mission
Goals
Purpose
General objectives (aims)

These are general statements of program aims relative to region and the institution.

Example 1: One of our program goals is to serve the culturally diverse populations of our region, which include primarily Latinos and Blacks.

• Specific objectives (aims)

These are more discrete delineations of program aims as they relate to the curriculum.

Example 1: One of our program objectives is to prepare individuals for practice with the two principle minorities of color in our region.

• Measurable objectives (aims)

These are program aims detailed in terms of explicitly desired outcomes.

Example 1: In addition to our other content, our program will offer minority practice content in work with Latinos and Blacks in all practice courses and settings for all students enrolled in our program and currently in the field. The *primary* objective will be to prepare students for practice in these communities. The *secondary* objective will be to sensitize them to work with these populations.

Example 2: As our mission, the program will provide social work personnel for service in the rural communities of the state.

Example 2: Our program objectives will focus on (1) developing a curriculum emphasis in rural social work practice (the initial curriculum supports to be elective in nature), and (2) developing a linkage liaison network with agencies and community organizations throughout the state's rural regions.

Example 2: Our program will offer a two-semester elective Rural Practice course for selected seniors in our program. In addition, we will provide a specific number of placements in rural agencies to support the practice courses.

During the first half of the present academic year the program, through selected personnel, will participate in the Rural Agency Coordinating Task Force as an active planning partner with specific responsibility for assisting in developing the Task Force's "forward plan."

Moving to Specific Implementation Actions

● Tasks and Activities

These are work assignments that support the general, specific, and measurable objectives.

To Actual Results

● Outcomes

These are the specific results of the preceding aims and actions.

To a Review of Program Aims, Actions, and Results

● Assessments

These are the judgments of program progress based on pre-established criteria (evidence) that serve to indicate how the program objectives and tasks have been carried through to outcomes.

Example 1: Content on Latinos and Blacks will be provided by both campus-based and practicum-based faculty. Content will include assignments "a, b, c, and d," and media presentations and discussions by community representatives who, at the end of the term, will also act as a hiring panel simulating a screening experience for students as if the students were being hired by agencies serving Latino and Black populations.

Example 1: The majority of students enrolled in the program demonstrated competency vis-à-vis the secondary objective, sensitivity to the minority populations based on assignments "a, b, c, and d," as well as their panel ratings.

The rest of the students demonstrated competency for immediate practice with Latino and Black populations based on assignments "a, b, c, and d" as well as their panel ratings.

Example 1 of Appropriateness Assessment: The content in the practice courses utilized current research on Latinos and Blacks, current literature, etc.

Example 1 of Adequacy Assessment: The faculty were knowledgeable, the library holdings were sufficient, the practice content was supported in the practicum, the screening panels were composed of Latinos and Blacks, etc.

Example 1 of Effectiveness Assessments: On the level of the secondary measurable objective, the majority of students were "sensitized" to Latinos and Blacks, as demonstrated in their semester work, conferences, community input, and screening panel ratings. On the level of the primary measurable objective, the rest of the students were able to attain practice proficiency in work with Latino and Black populations, as demonstrated in their semester work, conferences, community input, and screening panel ratings.

Example 2: Rural Practice course syllabi will be developed for both courses. Key students will be selected for the program. The necessary rural placements will be developed for the students with this emphasis.

The program director will serve as a voting member of the Rural Coordinating Task Force.

Example 2: During the academic year, "X" number of students took the two sequenced Rural Practice courses. These students also were placed in rural practicum experiences.

Linkage was maintained throughout the year on a regular basis through the Rural Agency Coordinating Task Force. Linkage was reinforced through the social work program director's assumption of the chair of the rural task force the next year. During the present year she served as the research planning coordinator for the task force.

Example 2 of Appropriateness Assessment: The course content in Rural Practice was seen as relevant to the state's rural needs. For example, case situations were drawn from the area examples. The placements as developed were centered in the state's rural human service establishment.

The Rural Agency Coordinating Task Force was composed primarily of agency and community organization heads. The participation by the program director was seen as appropriate.

Example 2 of Adequacy Assessment: The course content, while rural in emphasis, was insufficient vis-à-vis providing supporting rural theory. The practicum settings, while appropriate to the region, failed to provide much direct service contact with rural consumers of services; most was in the planning arena.

The rural liaison-linkage function was stretched thin in that the social work program director was the only program person assigned to the rural task force.

Example 2 of Effectiveness Assessments: The newness of the courses and the weaknesses in the rural theory notwithstanding, the students participating in the program were able to be certified as having a minor in social work practice in rural settings, having passed this segment of the end-of-the-year comprehensive examinations.

The program's input to the rural task force, despite the lack of personnel resources assigned from the program (other than the director), was significant, the research planning function was carried out in terms of providing the task force with a three-year "forward" plan of action to include an expanded role for the social work program.

Figure 7-3.   Hierarchy of Program Assessment Terms.

NOTES

1. Two recent examples are: Department of Health, Education, and Welfare, *Social Work Education: Planning and Assessment Systems* (Washington, D.C.: U.S. Government Printing Office (SRS 76-05418), 1976). McGrath, Frances, David O'Hara, and Thomas Duane, *Instructional Manual and Evaluation Guide: Graduate Social Work Education in the University-Affiliated Facility* (Washington, D.C.: U.S. Government Printing Office (HEW Publication HSA 18-5226), 1978). Other works are annotated in the bibliography at the end of this chapter.

2. Huff, Robert, *Inventory of Educational Outcomes and Activities*, Technical Report 15 (Boulder, Colo.: Western Interstate Commission for Higher Education, 1971), p. 4.

3. Baer, Betty L., and Ronald Federico, *Educating the Baccalaureate Social Worker: Report of the Undergraduate Social Work Curriculum Development Project* (Cambridge, Mass.: Ballinger, 1978), pp. 85-89.

4. Tripodi, Tony, Phillip Fellin, and Irwin Epstein, *Social Program Evaluation* (Itasca, Ill.: F.E. Peacock, 1971), pp. 45-47.

5. Lewy, Arieh, ed., *Handbook of Curriculum Evaluation* (New York: Longman, 1977), p. 15.

6. Baizerman, Michael, "Evaluation Research and Evaluation: Scientific Social Reform Movement and Ideology," *Journal of Sociology and Social Welfare* (supplement) 2, 2 (Winter 1974):282.

7. Mager, Robert F., *Preparing Instructional Objectives* (Palo Alto, Calif.: Fearman, 1962).

8. Granger, Charles H., "The Hierarchy of Objectives," in Zaltman, Gerald, Philip Cutler, and Ira Kaufman, eds., *Creating Social Change* (New York: Holt, Rinehart, and Winston, 1972).

9. Department of Health, Education and Welfare (HEW), *Social Work Education Planning and Assessment System* (Washington, D.C.: U.S. Government Printing Office [SRS 76-05418], 1976), pp. 15-16.

10. Deniston, O.L., I.M. Rosenstock, and V.A. Getting, "Evaluation of Program Effectiveness," *Public Health Reports* 8314 (April 1968):323-34.

11. Wholey, Joseph F., John W. Scanlon, Hugh D. Duffy, James S. Fukumoto, and Leona Vogt, *Federal Evaluation Policy* (Washington, D.C.: Urban Institute, 1971), p. 93.

12. HEW, p. 43.

13. Ibid., p. 61.

14. Enthover, Alain C., "Measures of the Outputs of Higher Education: Some Practical Suggestions for Their Development and Use," in *The Outputs of Higher Education: Their Identification, Measurement, and Evaluation* (Boulder, Colo.: Western Interstate Commission for Higher Education, 1970), p. 53.

ANNOTATED BIBLIOGRAPHY

Department of Health, Education and Welfare, *Social Work Education: Planning and Assessment Systems.* Washington, D.C.: U.S. Government Printing Office (SRS 76-05418), 1976.

This publication focuses specifically on social work program assessment. It can serve as an excellent guide to strategy for a comprehensive assessment system tailored to local needs. The publication provides direct access to the technology of assessment from the standpoint of beginning as well as advanced system capabilities.

Isaac, Stephen, and William B. Michael. *Handbook in Research and Evaluation.* San Diego, Calif.: EDITS Publishers, 1971.

This document contains most of the key evaluative instruments in current use in program assessment and evaluation circles. Most or all of the instruments can be adapted to educational assessment needs.

Lewy, Arieh, ed. *Handbook of Curriculum Evaluation.* New York: Longman, 1977.

This text offers a comprehensive overview to educational assessment and evaluation strategies. Its focus is primarily on primary and secondary educational systems in an international (UNESCO) context. The principles outlined, nonetheless, with slight modifications have considerable applicability to educational assessment at the university level.

McGrath, Frances C., David O'Hara, and Duane Thomas. *Instructional Manual and Evaluation Guide: Graduate Social Work Education in the University-Affiliated Facility.* Washington, D.C.: U.S. Government Printing Office (HEW Publication No. (HSA) 18-5226), 1978.

This publication encapsulates evaluative technology in current terminology and with current applicability to graduate social work programs. An overall evaluative schema for assessing student performance is presented. Special emphasis is given to the human behavior aspects of the social work curriculum.

REFERENCES

Baer, Betty L., and Ronald Federico. *Educating the Baccalaureate Social Worker.* Cambridge, Mass.: Ballinger, 1978.

Baizerman, Michael. "Evaluation Research and Evaluation: Scientific Social Reform Movement and Ideology." *Journal of Sociology and Social Welfare* (supplement) 2, 2 (Winter 1974):277-88.

Department of Health, Education and Welfare. *The Cost and Output of Graduate Social Work Education: An Exploratory Study.* Washington, D.C.: U.S. Government Printing Office (SRS 69-11), 1970.

Deniston, O.L., I.M. Rosenstock, and V.A. Getting. "Evaluation of Program Effectiveness." *Public Health Reports* 8314 (April 1968):323-34.

Enthoven, Alain C. "Measures of the Outputs of Higher Education: Some Practical Suggestions for Their Development and Use." In *The Outputs of Higher Education: Their Identification, Measurement, and Evaluation.* (Boulder, Colo.: Western Interstate Commission for Higher Education, 1970), pp. 51-58.

Flanagan, John, Robert F. Mager, and William Shanner. *Behavioral Objectives: A Guide to Individualized Learning.* Palo Alto, Calif.: Westinghouse Learning Press, 1971.

Goldstein, Howard K., and Rachel Dedmon. "A Computer-Assisted Analysis of Input, Process, and Output of a Social Work Education Program." *Journal of Education for Social Work*, 12, 2 (1976):17-20.

Granger, Charles H. "The Hierarchy of Objectives." In Zaltman, Gerald, Philip Cutler, and Ira Kaufman, *Creating Social Change* (New York: Holt, Rinehart, and Winston, 1972), pp. 528-541.

Harper, Dean, and Haroutun Babigian. "Three Evaluations of Social Welfare Programs." *Journal of Sociology and Social Welfare* (supplement) 2, 2 (Winter 1974):271-76.

Hoshino, George. "Social Service, The Problem of Accountability." *Social Services Review* (September 1973):373-83.

Hudson, Barclay. "Domains of Evaluations." *Social Policy* 6, 2 (September/ October 1975):79-89.

Huff, Robert. *Inventory of Educational Outcomes and Activities* (Technical Report 15). Boulder, Colo.: Western Interstate Commission for Higher Education, 1971.

Kirsuk, Thomas, "Goal Attainment Scaling at a Community Mental Health Service." *Evaluation* Special Monograph No. 1 (1973):12-18.

Laughton, C.W. "Multiple Objectives in Undergraduate Social Work Programs: Problems and Issues." *Journal of Education for Social Work* 4, 2 (1968):43-51.

Mager, Robert F. *Preparing Instructional Objectives.* Palo Alto, Calif.: Fearman Publishers, 1962.

Newman, Emanuel, and William Wilsmark. "Measurements of Effectiveness of Social Services." *Public Welfare* (January 1970):80-85.

Toward More Effective Management: The Role of Objective-Setting and Monitoring. Washington, D.C.: U.S. Government Printing Office (HEW Publication 76-20203), 1975.

Tripodi, Tony, Phillip Fellin, and Irwin Epstein. *Social Program Evaluation.* Itasca, Ill.: F.E. Peacock, 1971.

Wholey, Joseph F., John W. Scanlon, Hugh D. Duffy, James S. Fukumoto, and Leona Vogt. *Federal Evaluation Policy.* Washington, D.C.: The Urban Institute, 1971.

IV. Curriculum Content

Chapter Eight

Social Work Practice
Betty L. Baer

INTRODUCTION

The Undergraduate Social Work Curriculum Development Project has placed its emphasis on practice outcomes, on the competencies that graduates of baccalaureate programs should hold as they leave the educational program and enter practice. The emphasis is on what the baccalaureate social worker (BSW) should be able to do at the beginning level of professional practice toward the achievement of the profession's purposes.

As the purposes of social work are achieved through practice,[a] mastery of the expected practice competencies becomes the overriding objective of the professional curriculum. (There are, of course, other objectives, such as the education of enlightened citizens, but these do not conflict with the development of the competent social work practitioner.) In this way, the curriculum components called "methods," "practice," or "field instruction" must serve to direct all of the relevant parts of curriculum content toward application and practice. In other words, the knowledge content indicated by the curriculum development project as critical to the development of practice competence becomes almost irrelevant unless the BSW is able to draw upon it as he or she confronts situations. Research, social policy, human growth and development, and other required foundation content areas are not at all separate from practice even though they may be taught as separate entities.

[a]Practice, as it is used here, includes theories and methods of intervention, as well as their application.

The practice competencies identified by the project as essential to the achievement of the purposes of social work demand that the worker be able to move back and forth easily, from carrying out practice tasks that are conceptual and analytical in nature (the "what" and "why" of practice) to those that are implementing and intervening in nature (the "how to").[1] Both types of practice tasks, the analytical and the interactional, must have their foundation in appropriate knowledge. Their application in specific practice situations is always guided by the values and the ethics of the profession as well. Because every practice situation demands effective use of both sets of skills, they will be treated together in this chapter. Their application, which may take place in a variety of ways and a variety of places throughout the curricula, including the traditional field experience, will be discussed.

CHAPTER OBJECTIVES

This discussion of social work practice, including methods of intervention and their application, will begin with an analysis of some of the major implications of project findings. Second, the chapter will delineate some of the practice principles that flow from the competencies. These principles, in turn, should guide workers' tasks and activities in every practice situation if the profession's purposes of helping people, as these have been designed by the project, are to be achieved. Third, some of the major issues that surround the conceptualization of practice in educational programs will be raised. What model or framework of practice will be utilized by the educational program to achieve the outcomes sought? While the project does not wish to specify any particular model for a given program, project findings appear to support some directions more than others. Finally, the chapter will briefly consider some issues in the area of application that includes the field experience.

It is important to note that this chapter, like all others, does not intend to indicate number of methods/practice courses, their arrangement within the curriculum or the hours spent in the field. Nor does it aim to indicate specific methods/practice content. Rather, it is our intent, through the discussions which follow, to point as clearly as possible to the directions indicated for the organization and content of practice by Project findings. The bibliography at the end includes material which seems especially supportive of the Project thrust. It is by no means exhaustive; faculty and others are urged to add particular materials they have found useful as well as remain conscious of the fact that additional material is constantly being developed.

PROJECT IMPLICATIONS FOR PRACTICE

The major implications of project findings for practice, toward the development of the competencies, are as follows:

1. *The social worker must be able to carry various modes of intervention simultaneously and sequentially.*
   The competencies or practice capabilities defined by the project clearly point to a beginning social worker who has the ability to confront situations, whether they involve individuals, families, groups or persons, community groups, or organizations. Problem concerns of people are understood in their many dimensions, with interventions developed that will best serve to modify and/or change the situation. The worker's interventive repertoire consists of both "people helping" and "system changing," and is applicable to a wide range of problems and settings. Finally, "people helping" and "system changing" are not viewed as dichotomous actions but rather as interventions that, in some measure, go together in each situation or practice event. The beginning social worker, for example, may frequently attend to the immediate pain and discomfort resulting from a particular situation, but simultaneously be aware of and consider ways to intervene in the conditions that support and perpetuate the problems in the person's institutional, environmental milieu. To do less is to negate that which makes social work unique in its purposes. The project's definition of social work is as follows:

   > Social work is concerned and involved with the interactions between people and the institutions of society that affect the ability of people to accomplish life tasks, realize aspirations and values, and alleviate distress. These interactions between people and the social institutions in which people function occur within the context of the larger societal good. Therefore, three major purposes of social work may be identified: (a) To enhance the problem-solving, coping, and developmental capacities of people; (b) to promote the effective and humane operation of the systems that provide people with resources and services; and (c) to link people with systems that provide them with resources, services, and opportunities.[2]

2. *The worker's perspective must be holistic insofar as this is possible. This is necessary in order to understand, identify, and implement the interventive modes most appropriate to the situation at hand.*
   Clearly, the identification and choice of interventions most appropriate to the resolution of the situation is predicated on the

worker's capacity to understand and assess the situation within its broadest context. The situation and the other systems within the environment that interrelate with and influence the client's situation must be understood to the fullest extent possible. This is, of course, no small task. A particular way of thinking is needed, one that becomes an orientation to practice. This way of thinking encourages analytic and conceptual thinking coupled with the appreciation that seldom does anyone understand everything about a situation. The push to reduce the complex and the complicated to the simple is obviously a pressure to be avoided. Instead, what appears important is a humility that supports an ongoing struggle and sharpening of skill to learn and understand more about the situation, even as the worker must act with the best comprehension he or she has at the time.

There is also a second significant aspect to this issue. It is doubtful that a holistic orientation to practice can be developed as a practice component alone. There seems to be no question about the capacity of undergraduate students to develop such an orientation to problem solving. Less certain, however, is the likelihood of its occurrence, unless the orientation is pervasive throughout the curriculum. The approach taken by the liberal and foundation content must support this orientation, and all social work faculty must nurture it by consistently demonstrating such a holistic perspective in their approach to all content and to students as well.

There is a final but no less significant aspect to this project implication. Students must have well-developed skill in the use of a cognitive, conceptual tool, one that provides a framework for the conduct of holistic assessment. Fortunately, such frameworks are available;[3] skill in using them will most likely develop only if, again, there is a pervasive drill in their use throughout the curriculum.

This way of thinking about practice and about skill in the use of conceptual frameworks that support a holistic perspective and assessment appears to be very fundamental to the skills of the entry level professional social work practitioner. Moreover, this perspective lends itself to practice in a social scene where the issues, problems, and concerns of people (including organizations and communities) are shifting rapidly.

3. *The interventions taught and the practice experience in the educational program should be consistent with and supportive of the competencies, as these reflect activities appropriate for the beginning level social worker that lead to the achievement of the profession's purposes.*

As noted earlier, the competencies reflect a view of the social worker as one concerned with the interactions between people and social institutions. Concerns and problems for people arise when the relationship between the two breaks down, or otherwise fails to support and enhance human well-being. People develop differing strategies for adapting to their environment and coping with life crises because they have differing abilities. In general, however, most people have the capacity to learn behaviors that will help them face future situations more effectively. Knowing this, and understanding that organizations and institutions serve many societal purposes, the social worker is persistently concerned with the ways in which these organizations and institutions can help people cope and provide greater opportunities and more effective services to them.

The above suggests that the interventions taught must reflect human behaviors as essentially normal rather than pathological responses to environmental circumstances. Understanding ways in which people learn, as well as developing an interventive repertoire that includes teaching skills, may need to replace much of the current emphasis on interventions as a treatment and therapeutic approach to what are often viewed as pathological, deviant behaviors.

Interventions relevant for the beginning worker at the institutional and organizational level are developed, as indicated by the competencies, out of the worker's case load. There must be an understanding that, at the institutional level, interventions are not necessarily interpersonal in nature. Such learning cannot happen unless the worker has a repertoire of knowledge about individual, group, community, organizational, and interorganizational processes for which interventions consistent with the competencies are developed.

4. *There is the expectation that as much assessment knowledge and skill that can be developed at the baccalaureate level will be taught. However, the beginning level social worker is not expected to carry out all of the intervention roles and tasks necessary to achieve the purposes of the profession.*

The first volume on project findings calls for a worker who, at the beginning level, has the capacity to carry out and assess activities. In addition, heavy emphasis is placed on the ability of the worker to identify, verbalize, and manipulate resources as well as to teach people how they may be secured and used more effectively. Thus, roles related to teaching, resource mobilization, brokering and enabling are emphasized as well as the caregiver role in instances where persons may be in maximum need of societal resources, sustenance, and maintenance. These are roles carried out with groups of people as well as individuals. Pervasive throughout the performance of such roles is the capacity to help people maximize their own strengths and capabilities. Within the institutional/ organizational arena, there is the expectation that the worker will be skillful in collecting and summarizing data for the service assignment that will contribute to the improvement of policy and practice. Moreover, the worker is able to analyze policy and practice as it affects his or her client/consumer groups and collaborate with others, including colleagues in the profession, in efforts to influence change or improvements in policy and practice. He or she is able to carry out the range of roles simultaneously and sequentially, using and giving consultation along the way. Finally, the worker is able to practice with autonomy,[a] making professional judgments and decisions appropriate to the level of practice and assignment.

The above does not cover the entire range of roles expected of a beginning level social worker; it merely indicates some level of expectation. The BSW's work will, hopefully, be supplemented by others within the profession who will assume responsibility for roles and tasks both qualitatively and quantitatively different in their complexity and in their purpose.

5. *The competence to practice through mastery of the competencies can be demonstrated only in practice, thereby creating the necessity for a close working relationship between education and practice.*

The need for a new practice-education relationship was deemed critical enough to devote a full chapter to it (see Chapter 2). Therefore, only one aspect of the issue will be addressed here.

Clearly, the end result of the methods-practice component of the curriculum is demonstration of the competence to practice. The curriculum development project has consistently emphasized that educators cannot and should not attempt to assess such competence on their own. What is indicated is not a decrease in the responsibility educators carry for the educational preparation of the social worker, but rather a greater accountability to others. Students want assurance that their program will prepare them for competent practice, and the profession and society-at-large want

---

[a]Autonomy is used throughout this chapter to indicate self-directedness, a hallmark of every profession. The size of assignment and scope of responsibility is seen as the critical variable. That is, the responsibility assigned to a beginning level social worker will usually be far less than that assigned to an experienced MSW or DSW. Within that responsibility, however, it is expected that the entry level worker will be self-directed and make professional judgments.

similar assurance.[4] The implication is that faculty, students, practicing professionals, and others will together develop ways to assess students' readiness to enter practice prior to their leaving the educational program.

6. *The practice component of the curriculum should be organized and taught in such a way that there is maximum emphasis on the teaching of principles that will serve to guide behaviors and situations as they are confronted.*

Principles, or "rules and guides for actions," should serve to pull together knowledge, values, and skills in a more coherent approach to problem solving.[5] This clearly goes far beyond the mere teaching of "how-to" techniques and skills, although the competent baccalaureate social worker must also have specific intervention skills. It is equally clear that the practice competencies defined by the project demand that students have some principles to guide them. Otherwise, a program cannot develop in students an emphasis on holistic perspectives in assessment and problem solving. Being able to select from a range of interventions, which requires having some notion of the "what" and "why" of the situation, as well as being able to assess the effectiveness of the effort to be helpful demand that students have some principles to guide them. Random techniques and methods will be of little use to students in confronting and working through complex situations. What students really need are some principles that are transferable and helpful in formulating their actions, in whatever situation they may confront.

PRACTICE PRINCIPLES

The purpose of this section is to identify some of the specific principles, or action guidelines, that emerge from project findings. These should guide the actions of every practice event in which the worker is involved, if the competencies are to be utilized to achieve the purposes of social work. The competencies reflect the ultimate outcomes of the educational program and do not, in that sense, provide guides for specific interventions. They do, however, indicate some principles that should guide interventive, practice actions. These principles are stated broadly here, and may serve as a useful starting point for faculty. There are, of course, many other more specific practice principles that could be subsumed under them.[6]

The identification of the principles will be followed by illustrations of both the analytical and the interactional tasks that flow from each one. By "analytical" tasks is meant the thinking, analytical, intellectual work involved in problem solving. These are the tasks the practitioner must perform in order to decide *what* will be done, when, and how. Carrying out analytical tasks requires ongoing analysis of the situation, the specific problem, and the objectives sought. "Interactional" tasks are those actions taken by the practitioner in relationship with others, including the client, in carrying out the intervention activities. The interactional tasks are always guided by the practitioner's analysis.[a] Action in turn provides the material for ongoing analysis. Thus, the interrelationship is an ongoing one.

Finally, some of the knowledge content that undergirds the principles is summarized. There is, as has been our persistent stance, no effort to be exhaustive—to imply that the knowledge indicated is the *only* knowledge content. Rather, the intent is to show how practice does indeed draw upon other content from throughout the curriculum.

As outlined above, the approach to the development of the practice component has several benefits. First, it clearly emphasizes the need for equal emphasis on analytical and interactional content as essential components of every practice event. It eliminates the traditional dichotomy between the "class" (where students learn the cognitive, intellectual content) and the "field" (where students "do"). In the realities of practice both sets of tasks must occur simultaneously. Therefore, they should also occur simultaneously during the student experience in the range of settings where the student learns how to be a competent practitioner. Second, carrying out both sets of tasks toward purposeful problem solving and intervention requires the use of foundation as well as other program content. Thus, it serves to show faculty, students, field personnel, faculty from other disciplines, and others involved in the educational program how all content is integrated into an organized, coherent approach to practice.

Major Practice Principles

1. *The assessment of any situation, whether experienced by an individual, group, community, or organization, demands continuous examination and reexamination to arrive at the fullest possible understanding of the problem.*
   a. *Illustrative Analytical Tasks*—using a conceptual framework for study; analyzing and assessing the situation in its

[a]The practitioner's analysis includes, in addition to the client/consumer situation and goals, such areas as worker and organizational resources, limitations, and options.

broadest dimensions (identifying other systems, such as mutual support systems and/or formal organizations that are relevant to understanding the situation); collecting relevant data, including information on client system strengths and resources, and pertinent institutional policies and practices; recording, analyzing, and interpreting the meaning of the data; reviewing literature for information on similar situations; summarizing where people-institutional relationships have broken down; understanding and assessing one's own values, ethical stance, and resources with regard to client situations; making professional judgments.

b. *Illustrative Interactional Tasks*—observing and interviewing clients and others who impact on the problem situation; involving the client and others in the data collection and analysis; interpreting to the client the reasons for necessary data; learning from the client about the significance of the situation; consulting with colleagues and others; checking out professional judgments with others.

ILLUSTRATIVE KNOWLEDGE INDICATED: research methodology, including problem formulation, data collection, and data analysis; systems theory; principles of group dynamics; life cycle developmental stages and patterns; community structure; the causes of social problems and their impact on human behavior; communication theory.

2. *The definition of the situation and formulation of an intervention plan must reflect a holistic assessment of the problem situation, so that the immediate discomfort is attended to as well as the conditions that support and perpetuate the problem.*

a. *Illustrative Analytical Tasks*—defining both short- and long-range objectives within the context of time, resources, client strengths and resources, options available, and political and other constraints; identifying areas of change readiness and resistance in institutional network involved; analyzing one's own agency/organizational base; identifying the resources available and the politics involved; developing a change plan to achieve the objectives; summarizing data that identifies sources of distress and/or malfunctioning.

b. *Illustrative Interactional Tasks*—involving client to fullest extent possible in development of intervention plan and objectives; assisting client with identification and articulation of strengths, client resources, desires, realities, and constraints; discussing and collaborating with others relevant to the immediate change effort; presenting data relevant to the conditions that perpetuate the problem to the profession, legislators, and appropriate others; participating and collaborating with others concerned with the problem.

ILLUSTRATIVE KNOWLEDGE INDICATED: strategies of planning and problem solving; research findings concerning the effectiveness of various intervention strategies; theories of social work practice; community resources, including organized social welfare resources and more informal and/or non-social welfare resources.

3. *Every intervention effort must take into account the fact that there may be institutional policies and practices that discriminate against particular persons and/or groups of people.*

   a. *Illustrative Analytical Tasks*—observing agency clientele; studying service region for information regarding vulnerable groups; studying, collecting, and summarizing data on discriminatory policies and procedures; assessing agency policies and procedures against knowledge about vulnerable persons and groups; developing strategies for interventions to overcome discriminatory policies and practices; studying and identifying of legal rights, entitlements, benefits, and resources available; assessing agency policies and procedures against the profession's code of ethics.

   b. *Illustrative Interactional Tasks*—interpreting legal rights, or arranging for interpretation of legal rights, benefits, resources, and entitlements to client; involving client to the fullest extent possible in development of plans for intervention and/or change of discriminatory policies and practices; presenting data regarding discriminatory policies to appropriate individuals and groups; advocating for client's rights; following up with client to assure that services and resources were received.

   ILLUSTRATIVE KNOWLEDGE INDICATED: existing social policies and their effects on people's lives; social stratification and the creation of minority groups; minority life chances and lifestyles; social structure and functions of social institutions; culture, values, norms, and roles; processes of social policy development and change; NASW Code of Ethics; program application, administration, and benefit characteristics; legal basis of policies, programs, and social work roles; theories of conflict and oppression; methods to demonstrate unmet needs in ways that are effective for specified audiences.

4. *Every intervention effort must recognize human and group diversity as a resource to be evaluated for use in interventive activities.*
   a. *Illustrative Analytical Tasks*—studying the heritage, culture, and lifestyle of individuals and groups; analyzing values held and ways in which individual and group differences are expressed; assessing own strengths as well as "blind spots," prejudices, and intolerances, and developing plans to deal with them when they interfere with professional functioning; identifying uniqueness, strengths, and other resources emerging from assessment of individual and group diversity, and developing plans to utilize and maximize them in the development and implementation of an intervention plan.
   b. *Illustrative Interactional Tasks*—observing, interacting with, listening to, and learning from individuals and groups about their heritage, lifestyle, culture, and life experiences; developing plans to support and encourage expressions of individual and group strengths; involving client to the fullest extent possible in development and implementation of intervention plans that utilize client strengths as a major resource; interpreting client uniqueness to appropriate peers, supervisors, and others when necessary.
   ILLUSTRATIVE KNOWLEDGE INDICATED: conceptual framework to understand the biological, social, and cultural bases of human diversity; common human needs; the meaning of difference for people; the uses of difference by majority groups for political, economic, and social purposes; diversity within and between groups; diverse group membership and its impact on self-concept, lifestyles, and life chances; natural helping networks.
5. *Every intervention effort must recognize that people cope with and adapt to life's circumstances in a variety of ways, and that people have the capacity to learn how to utilize services, resources, and opportunities more effectively.*
   a. *Illustrative Analytical Tasks*—understanding client life experiences, aspirations, and circumstances, and identifying and assessing the particular ways the client responds to them (coping and adapting behaviors); assessing client's coping and adapting strengths as well as areas of limitation, and inappropriateness; understanding and assessing when coping behavior is inadequate in terms of its personal consequences as opposed to when it is labeled inadequate

because a traditional collective standard or norm is violated; identifying ways in which hurtful aspects of labeling can be minimized; developing a teaching/learning strategy appropriate to the client's learning needs; assessing services, resources, and opportunities, including those of significance to the client, e.g., mutual helping networks to identify those that will most effectively meet client needs; identifying inadequacies in services and resources vis-à-vis client need.

b.   *Illustrative Interactional Tasks*—observing, listening to, discussing and learning from the client the meaning of client behaviors and actions; assisting client with identification, assessment, and articulation of client resources and client access to resources; involving client in development and implementation of intervention plan that mobilizes and maximizes client resources; assisting client with interpreting his or her needs to those with relevant services, resources, and opportunities; teaching, counseling, and coaching client in areas where more effective coping and adapting skills are indicated; mobilizing resource systems as needed by client.

ILLUSTRATIVE KNOWLEDGE INDICATED: the meaning and functions of coping and adapting; theories of teaching/learning; crisis intervention; self-help; the differential impact of social institutions on diverse groups; personality development; functional and dysfunctional behavior.

6.   *Every change plan must recognize that organizations, including the worker's own, are in a constant state of change and can become more responsive to human need.*

a.   *Illustrative Analytical Tasks*—studying and assessing agency organizational setting, including organizational resources and access to resources, structure, policies and practices, informal and formal networks, leadership, power, conflict, decisionmaking processes, and other internal and external organizational processes; identifying points of tension and organizational vulnerability; identifying support system(s) within organizations; identifying and assessing ways to gain access and acceptance within organizations; identifying and assessing organizations, agencies, groups, and individuals in the external environment that have influence with one's own organization; identifying and assessing areas where organization is responsive as well as unresponsive to human need; assessing potential for change; identifying person(s) within organization concerned about similar issues; developing plan for modifying and/or changing dysfunctional policies and practices; studying own work assignment; developing work plan and priorities.

b. *Illustrative Interactional Tasks*—carrying out own work assignment responsibly and creatively; presenting and interpreting work assignment needs, satisfactions, successes, and problem areas to appropriate individuals and groups; implementing plan for development of support system, both internal and external to organization; consulting with and involving appropriate others in development of plans to improve use of agency services and resources; modifying and/or changing dysfunctional agency policies and procedures; seeking feedback from peers and appropriate others on ways to improve one's own professional functioning within agency/organizational structure.

ILLUSTRATIVE KNOWLEDGE INDICATED: organizational theory; organizational policies and decisionmaking processes; professional roles in organizations, including strategies for collaboration, teamwork, and autonomy; organizational change processes.

7. *Every intervention effort should recognize that there are ethical issues involved in the effort that should be identified and assessed against the stated ethics of the profession.*

a. *Illustrative Analytical Tasks*—identifying and assessing value conflicts and ethical issues and dilemmas posed by the situation and the development of the intervention plan; continuously assessing one's own values as they relate to the ethics of the profession; identifying and assessing the range of options and alternatives that most nearly meet client needs and the demands of the ethics of the profession.

b. *Illustrative Interactional Tasks*—interpreting to client when situations arise where professional ethics do not permit carrying out client wishes; explaining and supporting the profession and its ethics to clients and others; seeking support from and consulting with colleagues on ethical issues; helping clients find whatever resources are available in situations where professional ethics make continued social work intervention inappropriate; explaining to clients and others why ethical issues prohibit social work intervention in certain situations.

ILLUSTRATIVE KNOWLEDGE INDICATED: NASW Code of Ethics; societal values and major value systems; professional organizations and their grievance and social action procedures; one's own values and priorities.

8. *Every intervention effort should attempt to build upon a critical use of existing knowledge and experience.*

   a. *Illustrative Analytical Tasks—*studying and critically evaluating research findings and personal practice experiences pertinent to the situation at hand; identifying others knowledgeable in the particular practice area; developing hypotheses regarding an intervention plan and its presumed effectiveness in achieving intervention objectives.

   b. *Illustrative Interactional Tasks—*conferring and consulting with peers and other colleagues to expand access to knowledge and to test ideas; using knowledge storage facilities (libraries, research centers, computer terminals, etc.) to obtain needed information, and conferring with staff at such facilities as needed.

   ILLUSTRATIVE KNOWLEDGE INDICATED: major sources of relevant knowledge; professional roles and their interrelationships; methods to systematically organize data for practice purposes; basic statistical tools to assess the significance of data; basic research methods tools to assess the appropriateness of data collection and analysis strategies; communication strategies appropriate to various purposes and situations; vocabulary adequate for professional purposes (including specialized practice vocabularies needed in particular agency settings).

9. *The objectives of every intervention effort should be sufficiently clear, with criteria for continuous assessment of progress and the achievement of objectives.*

   a. *Illustrative Analytical Tasks—*identifying assessment criteria that are relevant to intervention objectives; recording observations and information pertinent to progress of interventive plan; using data collected to evaluate intervention outcomes; developing and using various methods for securing direct client feedback on services and resources received.

   b. *Illustrative Interactional Tasks—*involving client in developing intervention objectives and criteria for assessment of progress and achievement of objectives; discussing and reviewing progress periodically with client; conferring and consulting with colleagues and supervisors to discuss assessment procedures and better ways to achieve objectives.

   ILLUSTRATIVE KNOWLEDGE INDICATED: reporting and accountability procedures in one's own agency; record keeping strategies and purposes; the purposes and appropriate use of practice objectives; assessment terminology and strategies; the purposes of contracting; setting objectives; characteristics of diverse client groups relevant to the setting of objectives and criteria for assessment; social work process.

10. *Every intervention effort should include recognition of the worker's resources, including his or her access to them.*

    a. *Illustrative Analytical Tasks*—identifying and assessing the worker's own competence to carry out intervention plan; identifying areas where assistance, including consultation, might be needed; identifying and assessing resources needed and the worker's access to them; identifying others who can assist worker in gaining access to needed resources; analyzing agency resources available for achieving intervention goals.

    b. *Illustrative Interactional Tasks*—conferring and consulting with peers and other colleagues in identifying resources; using supervision to increase knowledge of resources and to clarify procedures; discussing with client the worker's resources that are most compatible with client's needs and goals.

ILLUSTRATIVE KNOWLEDGE INDICATED: one's own strengths, weaknesses, and priorities; agency structure and resources; community resources (formal and informal); use of consultation.

CONCEPTUALIZATION OF PRACTICE IN EDUCATIONAL PROGRAMS

This section will explore some of the difficult issues concerning the conceptualization of practice, which have confronted social work educators for some time.[7] Unless there is some coherence in the way that practice is conceptualized within the curriculum, the desired outcomes—even if these are clearly stated—are seldom achieved. There is always *some* conceptualization, whether it be covert or overt, or stated differently by each faculty member. In these instances, the educational outcomes sought tend to be vague and of little practical use as a curriculum guide and assessment tool. Most confused of all are the students, who have little sense of what they are being prepared to do or of how the curriculum organization and design, including the way that practice is conceptualized, is relevant to whatever the program's objectives might be.

A major reason for the difficulty in conceptualizing practice is a duality perceived in the profession's concern. One aspect is concerned with attending to immediate needs and discomforts, while the other is concerned with changing the institutions through which services and resources are made available to people. The labels change—clinical versus social change agents, direct versus indirect, micro versus macro, and so on—but the basic problem remains.

A related problem concerns the lack of consensus on the profession's purposes. Carol Meyer addresses this issue as follows:

> The harsh fact of the matter is that social workers do not agree as to their professional purposes; therefore it continues to be very difficult to develop general practice modalities, to build a necessary knowledge base through research, and to teach students what social work is. Without agreement about purpose, practitioners in social work find it difficult to sort out their work from other disciplines, but more seriously, they sidestep the implications of their professional purpose and become preoccupied with methodology as if it were all there was to practice.[8]

Others have made a similar point.[9]

The above suggests that the first order of business for the profession as a whole is a consensus on a definition for social work and on professional purposes. This is not a task for social work education alone, but it affects social work education in its efforts to conceptualize practice. The curriculum development project developed a definition of social work and its purposes so that its charge could be fulfilled. This definition is consistent with that of the Council on Social Work Education (CSWE) and other professional groups. According to this definition, the beginning level professional social worker must be able to intervene in a variety of situations, utilizing interventive mode(s) that are most appropriate to the particular situation. In short, the definition calls for a generalist even though the project has elected to use the term "social worker" rather than "generalist."

As noted earlier, the way in which practice is conceptualized within the curriculum does affect the outcomes. Let us now look at the five major ways that practice seems to be conceptualized in current curricula.

1. *The traditional methods of casework, group work, and community organization.*
This conceptualization of practice focuses on the development of specialized knowledge in a particular method, or methods. There have been, over the years, many efforts to try to identify the

knowledge base underpinning all of the methods in a "generic" approach to practice.[10] At least a few persons in the field believe that it cannot be done. Each of the methods is seen to be based on very different kinds of assumptions and thus cannot be integrated into one whole.[11]

2. *The generalist approach.*

All efforts in the generalist, unitary approach to practice are based on the premise that all of a person's needs involve a variety of systems and that the social worker functions at the interface of people and social systems or societal institutions. Social systems theory is the basis for all efforts to explicate the generalist approach to practice.[12]

3. *Focus on problems and/or population groups.*

In this approach practice is conceptualized around the development of specialists in particular areas (such as housing, income maintenance, and health) or with particular groups (children, the aged, alcoholics, and so on). In one sense, the effort is toward a generalist-specialist, in that the worker attempts to look at all aspects of a situation (generalist) as they affect, for example, a specialized population group.

4. *Direct-Indirect (or micro-macro) approach.*

In this approach practice is conceptualized around the provision of direct services to individuals and groups who are in need of it, or the provision of indirect services that focus on a variety of activities (such as administration, policymaking, and planning) aimed at improving or changing the social welfare system.

5. *Combination of methods.*

In many baccalaureate programs at the present time there seems to be an effort to "plug" the traditional methods or micro-macro with a unitary, generalist conceptualization of practice.

For purposes of conceptualizing practice in order to achieve the outcomes sought for the beginning level social work practitioner, each of the above methods appears to have some limitations. For example, the preoccupation of the traditional methods with methodology, with much less emphasis on and concern with the interacting systems that create problems for people, is clearly at odds with the definition and purposes of social work proposed by the project. The generalist or unitary conceptualization, with its emphasis on systems and their interactions, appears to be the approach that best helps the student to understand situations from a holistic perspective. Yet once there is some understanding of the situation, this approach seems to lack enough specific guides for action. Perhaps this is why one sees the effort to utilize the traditional methods or direct-indirect along with the generalist conceptualization, despite what would appear to be blatant contradictions between them. The specializations by problem and/or population group would appear to be inappropriate for the beginning level social worker, except for elective concentration—an activity already occurring in many baccalaureate programs. Finally, the direct-indirect approach, which suggests that the knowledge for interventions with individuals differs substantially from the knowledge required for interventions at the institutional level, also has its limitations. It seems to do violence to the notion that, if social workers really are to be helpful to people in their relationships with societal institutions, the choice of intervention must be based upon a holistic assessment.

The findings of the curriculum development project are most supportive of a generalist conceptualization, since they emphasize holistic assessment and intervention at the levels of both people and systems. However, the difficulty of operationalizing this conceptualization in terms of action guidelines remains, although the project's identification of basic knowledge, values, and skills for the competent baccalaureate social worker should help in this effort. Nevertheless, each faculty must make its own choice of a conceptualization, based upon its collective knowledge and the interest of its members to experiment with and contribute to the further development of this aspect of the curriculum. At the very least, however, each faculty should be clear about the choices made, and have a rationale that is understood by other faculty, students, and field personnel and that explains how the particular conceptualization chosen supports the intended educational outcomes.

PRACTICE APPLICATION AND FIELD LEARNING

The ultimate test of the student's competence to practice must occur in the field. The development of skills and the application of his or her knowledge toward the achievement of professional purposes, then, become a critical part of curriculum.

Several implications emerge from project findings for the ways in which students develop skills and learn to translate values into ethical practice behaviors. Long before the curriculum development project came into being, however, many undergraduate programs were already experimenting with different patterns of experiential field learning, in efforts to help students develop greater mastery of the needed skills. Some of this was undoubtedly the result of the influence of liberal education. Many liberal educators, concerned with finding ways to help students understand the usefulness of knowledge in real life situations, had begun to experiment with off-campus activities in which the students could apply classroom-learned concepts to real problems and issues. Thus, there have been and continue to be departures from some of the more traditional social work educational patterns of helping students develop skills in application.

In social work, the major burden for the development of application skills has been assumed by field instruction. That is, the student learns a great deal of knowledge and values as well as some techniques and skills in the classroom. The real integration and application of all this learning is presumed to take place in the field practicum as the students work with clients. This was where it all "came together" for the student. There are, of course, undergraduate programs that continue to follow this pattern. After all required course work is completed, the student is assigned to field practicum to apply and "integrate." As we shall see, project findings recommend a somewhat different arrangement.

Project Implications for Skill in Application

1. To assure the practice competence sought, opportunities for application need to be continuous and pervasive throughout the curriculum, with learning experiences to provide such opportunities sequenced throughout the entire professional curriculum.

   There is a great deal to be mastered. When opportunities are maximized for students to acquire and test out knowledge concurrently, skill in practice can be developed all along the way. Application, as we use it here, encompasses a range of learning experiences, all designed and sequenced to help students build toward the practice competencies sought. Such learning experiences include simulated activities, role playing, and field assignments from the "mini" short term to the long term, agency- or organization-based field practicum.

   Understanding the processes of problem solving, for example, should begin early in the educational experience, hopefully in the liberal foundation courses. If there are not opportunities along the way to apply this understanding through some type of simulated or other experiential activity, it is highly doubtful that the knowledge gained of problem solving will have meaning or that the student will have solid skill in its use when application is demanded in helping clients with the resolution of their problems or concerns.

   Structured, sequential application opportunities also allow students as well as faculty to assess whether the appropriate knowledge and skills are being mastered along the way. This is not to suggest that all students will be at the same place at the same time. However, if students are expected to demonstrate the application of the skill and processes of problem solving before entering senior practicum, for example, then an assessment must take place. In this way the student is helped to integrate what he or she knows, by understanding and applying it concurrently and sequentially throughout the curriculum.

2. Developing learning experiences, including the field practicum, that insure a variety of opportunities for students to develop skills in application over time is a responsibility that must be shared by faculty and practitioners. Assessment criteria must also be a shared responsibility, to assure that students have indeed mastered the required skills in application and are competent to practice when they leave the educational program.

3. Since the outcome of the educational program is a competent practitioner, and since the development of skills in application should occur concurrently and sequentially throughout the curriculum, it appears critical that all social work faculty responsible for the curriculum "think practice." That is, each faculty member needs to develop opportunities for the application of the content for which he or she is responsible. Moreover, faculty together need to understand how all parts of the curriculum content reinforce each other so that fragmentation does not occur. For example, each of the competencies can be divided into subcontent parts, with the designation of particular content to be mastered sequentially (e.g., at the completion of x courses, the student should be able to understand and apply a conceptual framework to a situation assessment). All faculty, whether they are teaching social welfare institutions content, a methods course, or other content, should consider ways in which they can support and reinforce students' mastery of the content, including its applicability to practice.

4. The competencies indicate a beginning level professional practitioner who can be self-evaluative and make professional judgments within an appropriate area of responsibility and level of activity. These behaviors must be encouraged by opportunities to develop such skills throughout the curriculum, culminating in their demonstration in actual practice. This suggests that the practicum should be as real as possible. The student should not be unnecessarily coddled and protected from the realities of practice. Developing skills and dealing with the frustrations that are an everyday part of

practice are critical to the development of appropriate practice behaviors. Consistently asking students "what" and "why" questions as they are engaged in practice activities forces them to become more articulate about the kinds of professional judgments they are making, just as expecting students to be a central part of the continuous assessment process assures some measure of objectivity in students' evaluation of their own professional functioning.

5. The extent to which education—and the competencies—direct practice should be given much thought. Otherwise, the competencies could become the method idolatry of the future. It is one thing to negotiate an appropriate service assignment for a student with the expectation that he or she, following assessment, will select the most appropriate interventions. It is quite another to negotiate placements around the competencies. The former method is to be desired, so that the student's focus is on the client's needs and concerns and not on the competencies. In working through the client situation, there is the assumption that the competencies altogether will constitute the necessary practice skills. This, however, has not yet been tested in actual practice. Faculty and practitioners, working together, need to evaluate the extent to which the competencies do indeed represent the skills essential to the effective beginning level professional practitioner in social work.

These project implications for the development of skills and their application will hopefully stimulate discussion, leading to a strengthening of curriculum's ultimate function as a place where students demonstrate whether they can, indeed, "cut the mustard."

NOTES

1. This concept of analytical and interactional tasks is developed by Robert Perlman and Arnold Gurin in *Community Organization and Social Planning* (New York: Wiley, 1972). The concept is also used by Max Siporin in *Introduction to Social Work Practice* (New York: Macmillan, 1975). Argyris and Schoen use a similar concept although they call the tasks "interpersonal" and "technical" skills. See Chris Argyris and Donald B. Schoen, *Theory in Practice: Increasing Professional Effectiveness* (San Francisco: Jossey-Bass, 1974).

2. Baer, Betty L., and Ronald Federico, *Educating the Baccalaureate Social Worker: Report of the Undergraduate Social Work Curriculum Development Project* (Cambridge, Mass.: Ballinger, 1978), p. 61.

3. Pincus, Allen, and Anne Minahan, *Social Work Practice: Model and Method* (Itasca, Ill.: F.E. Peacock, 1973), and Warren, Roland, *Social Change and Human Purpose* (Chicago: Rand McNally, 1977).

4. The project is aware that there are very mixed reactions within social work education on this issue. Some educators, for example, see education for competence merely as a political response to the current push for greater accountability. The project stance is otherwise. One can regard the possibility that 7000 seniors in New York City high schools may not graduate this May because they are unable to pass the externally developed State Board of Regents minimum competency tests in reading and mathematics as some kind of political gimmick, or regard it as one illustration, to be taken seriously, that New York City public schools are preparing their students less well than they should—for whatever reasons. See *New York Times*, 12 January 1979, pp. B 1-3.

5. Goldstein, Howard, "A Unitary Approach: Implications for Education and Practice," in Ainsworth, Frank, and Joan Hunter, eds., *A Unitary Approach to Social Work Practice—Implications for Education and Organisation* (Dundee, Scotland: School of Social Administration, University of Dundee, 1975), pp. 41-42.

6. See particularly Siporin.

7. As attested to by the fact that an entire issue of *Social Work* was recently devoted to the subject: *Social Work*, "Special Issue on Conceptual Framework," 22, 5 (September 1977).

8. Meyer, Carol H., *Social Work Practice: The Changing Landscape* (New York: The Free Press, 1976), p. 40.

9. See, for example, Scott Briar's editorial in *Social Work* 21, 4 (July 1976):262, 341.

10. Such as Harriett M. Bartlett, *The Common Base of Social Work Practice* (Washington, D.C.: National Association of Social Workers, 1970).

11. Goldstein, Howard, "A Unitary Approach: Its Rationale and Structure," in Ainsworth, Frank, and Joan Hunter, eds., *A Unitary Approach to Social Work Practice* (Dundee, Scotland: School of Social Administration, University of Dundee, 1975, pp. 17-31).

12. See, for example, Howard Goldstein, *Social Work Practice: A Unitary Approach* (Columbia, S.C.: University of South Carolina Press, 1973); Pincus and Minahan; and Sipovin.

REFERENCES AND BIBLIOGRAPHY

Argyris, Chris, and Donald B. Schoen. *Theory in Practice: Increasing Professional Effectiveness.* San Francisco: Jossey-Bass, 1974.

Atherton, Charles L., Sandra T. Mitchell, and Edna B. Schein. "Locating Points for Intervention." *Social Casework* 52 (1971):131-41.

Bisno, Herbert. "A Theoretical Framework for Teaching Social Work Methods and Skills." *Journal of Education for Social Work* 5, 1 (1969):5-18.

Briar, Scott. "Effective Social Work Intervention in Direct Practice, Implications for Education." In *Facing the Challenge* (New York: Council on Social Work Education, 1973), pp. 17-30.

Chin, Robert. "The Utility of Systems Models and Developmental Models for Practitioners." In Bennis, Benne, and Chin, eds., *The Planning of Change* 3rd ed. (New York: Holt, Rinehart, & Winston, 1976), pp. 90-102.

Germain, Carol B. "An Ecological Perspective in Casework Practice." *Social Casework* 54 (1973):323-30.

Germain, Carol B. "General Systems Theory and Ego Psychology: An Ecological Perspective." *Social Service Review* 52, 4 (December 1978):535-50.

Goldstein, Howard. *Social Work Practice: A Unitary Approach.* (Columbia, S.C.: University of South Carolina Press, 1973).

Goldstein, Howard. "A Unitary Approach: Its Rationale and Structure." In Ainsworth, Frank, and Joan Hunter, eds., *A Unitary Approach to Social Work Practice—Implications for Education and Organisation.* (Dundee, Scotland: School of Social Administration, University of Dundee, 1975), pp. 17-31.

Goldstein, Howard. "A Unitary Approach—Implications for Education and Practice." In Ainsworth and Hunter, eds. (Dundee, Scotland: School of Social Administration, University of Dundee, 1975), pp. 33-46.

Hearn, Gordon, ed. *The General Systems Approach: Contributions Toward An Holistic Conception of Social Work.* New York: Council on Social Work Education, 1969.

Lippitt, Ronald, Jeane Watson, and Bruce Westley. *The Dynamics of Planned Change.* New York: Harcourt, Brace, 1958.

Middleman, Ruth, and Gale Goldberg. *Social Service Delivery: A Structural Approach to Social Work Practice.* New York: Columbia University Press, 1974.

Perlman, Robert, and Arnold Gurin. *Community Organization and Social Planning.* New York: Wiley, 1972.

Pincus, Allen, and Anne Minahan. *Social Work Practice: Model and Method.* Itasca, Ill.: F.E. Peacock, 1973.

Rothman, Jack. "Development of a Profession: Field Instruction Correlates." *Social Service Review* 51, 2 (June 1977):289-310.

Siporin, Max. *Introduction to Social Work Practice.* New York: Macmillan, 1975.

Spergel, Irving S. *Community Problem-Solving.* Chicago: University of Chicago Press, 1969.

Spitzer, Kurt, and Betty Welsh. "A Problem Focused Model of Practice." *Social Casework* 50 (June 1969):323-29.

Teare, Robert J., and Harold McPheeters. *Manpower Utilization in Social Welfare.* Atlanta: Southern Regional Education Board, 1970.

Warren, Roland. *Social Change and Human Purpose: Toward Understanding and Action.* Chicago: Rand McNally, 1977.

Westbury, Ian, Bernece K. Simon, and John Korbelik, eds. "The Generalist Program: Description and Evaluation." Chicago: University of Chicago, School of Social Service Administration, 1973.

Schwartz, Edward E. "Macro Social Work: A Practice in Search of Some Theory." *Social Service Review* 51, 2 (June 1977):207-27.

Chapter Nine

Research and the Process of Social Inquiry
Katherine Hooper Briar

INTRODUCTION

Being able to pose researchable questions and to understand what is required to answer them is essential to the baccalaureate social worker's (BSW's) achievement of practice competence. For a numer of years there has been ambiguity over the role and utility of research methods at the undergraduate level. While BSW's have been expected to be consumers of others' research, to what extent they should be prepared to conduct their own research has been unclear. This chapter will address such issues by suggesting the scope of knowledge and skills that the BSW should require through his or her undergraduate education.

The undergraduate social work curriculum must foster attitudinal, conceptual, and skill-building opportunities that ensure effective mastery of beginning research methods. Such opportunities should stimulate in students an appetite for and confidence in the process of problem formulation and information gathering, so that mastery of formal research methods is viewed as a logical extension of this inquiring process. In the past, research methods may have been seen as alien to or inconsistent with the tasks of the practitioner rather than as central to practice competence. More recent perspectives on practice suggest that research is critical to BSW competence and effectiveness. In fact, social work practice draws on the very skills and concepts of research.

Many of the tasks of the BSW practitioner involve information gathering for purposes of problem formulation and problem solving.

The practitioner gathers information presumably because of its utility to the helping process. Inability to gather information could result in an inappropriate analysis of the problem, limited assessment, ineffective interventions, and an inability to evaluate one's practice effectiveness. Scientific methods applied to information gathering may fortify this process by providing the practitioner with additional tools and evaluative criteria. Even more compelling may be the fact that research knowledge and skills may enable BSW practitioners to evaluate their own practice as well as to assess the specific knowledge bases of their practice interventions. Research tools may also strengthen the ability of the practitioner to discern specific obstacles to effective functioning and unmet needs of an individual, group, or community. Moreover, practitioners are increasingly being asked to participate in research projects that seek to evaluate agency or program effectiveness, or that attempt to describe or explain the dynamics of clients' problems. Effective participation in both the design and implementation of such projects requires that the BSW practitioner be knowledgeable and skilled in research methods.

The helping process itself, based in part on the testing and refinement of assumptions, inferences, and hypotheses throughout problem formulation, assessment, and intervention, parallels several of the processes of scientific inquiry. The need for evidence and verification, central to appropriate problem analysis, assessment, and intervention, can also help pinpoint when "the facts aren't in." Such recognition may result in a new regard for practice. Practice will not as frequently be seen as a series of tested, effective methods but instead as a series of trial-and-error approaches similar to those found in experiments.

Dissemination of information regarding practice successes is a necessary component of the practice process. Yet, for others to replicate successful interventions, there must be specificity as to the interventions that worked as well as the conditions and the groups for which such interventions were found to be effective. Dissemination and replication of these successes depend on the extent to which practice interventions can be described in nonambiguous, observable terms. Thus, the BSW who might find that instruction in assertiveness assists the unemployed client with job seeking must be able to specify what is meant by "instruction in assertiveness." While such broad concepts guide everyday practice, replication requires that these concepts be presented in operational terms. Operational definitions and specificity as to what was said and done with the client will reduce the need for interpretation and inference, and may prevent inaccurate attempts at replication.

It should come as no surprise to learn that only a fraction of the social work profession is engaged in formal research.[1] This must be changed so that practitioners are able to systematically organize their daily contact with people, in order to contribute to an increased understanding of the dynamics that lead clients to seek help, and the social, psychological, economic, physical, institutional, and health care contingencies that impede effective functioning. Baccalaureate practitioners must play their part in this effort by knowing how to collaborate with others to improve the knowledge base for practice. Moreover, once empirical inquiry becomes a practice tool, it may be hoped that practice activities will redress the stereotypical attitudes and invalid assumptions that may be held by the public or by decisionmakers, through the marshalling of data-based, empirically supported arguments.

The fact that social work knowledge is vastly incomplete should not be conveyed to the student as a source of embarrassment but instead as an appeal for practitioners to contribute to the knowledge base. It is possible to imagine a time in future social work practice when there will not be a need to base so many practice interventions on untested or empirically unvalidated methods.

This chapter proposes that the baccalaureate social work curriculum promote the following three learning outcomes for students through its research component: 1) a penchant for empirical inquiry so that questioning, testing, and validating become a foundation for the development of practice competence; 2) knowledge of scientific methods and research skills to ensure that the baccalaureate social worker can critically evaluate the utility of research findings of others; 3) skills in the use of research methods for practice. This chapter will suggest ways in which each part of the curriculum can fortify these attitudinal, conceptual, and skill-related objectives.

INTEGRATION FOUNDATION CONTENT INTO CURRICULUM

Both conceptual and skill development of BSW's in the scientific methods of social inquiry may have occurred prior to formal course work within their social work baccalaureate program. For this reason it is important for baccalaureate social work faculty to evaluate and build upon the scope of formal research-related content by reintroducing, applying, and integrating it within the social work curriculum. Of utmost importance, however, is the extent to which earlier course work has shaped students' proclivity for appreciating, mastering, and applying beginning scientific methods of social inquiry. If they have acquired a dislike for quantitative methods or for research prior to their formal courses in social work, they will undoubtedly require help in overcoming such aversion. Social work faculty must share in the effort to promote an understanding of the importance of empirical inquiry. To leave such a task solely to the faculty who teach research methods courses discounts the critical relevance of empirical inquiry to all courses and student learning. The following section will cite ways in which the spirit of empirical inquiry along with basic scientific concepts can be infused throughout the baccalaureate social work curriculum.

Scientific Inquiry in Foundation Content and Social Work Beliefs

Of central importance to social work faculty is the fact that before students engage in social work courses, they may be exposed to a variety of perspectives on methods in "knowing" and the way in which knowledge develops. The fact that scientific methods contribute to the establishment of stable belief systems has pressing relevance for the BSW who will hopefully contribute to and advance professionally with developments in social work knowledge. Yet the significance of scientific methods to the field of social work may not be immediately clear to the student. Consequently, undergraduate social work faculty may have to ensure that the implications of such content are integrated into students' professional learning. Course work in formal logic, philosophy, religion, the sciences, mathematics, and statistics may all contribute to students' understanding of the nature of sources of knowledge and the meaning of proof, causality, and correlation. However, under what circumstances they should rely on "gut level" feelings or intuition as alternative ways of "knowing" may need to be clarified during their professional development in social work.

Even more important may be the need for the social work curriculum to deal directly with whatever has been unclear in the formal foundation and liberal arts courses. Students who have been confused or frustrated by such content may need to have these previous learning experiences interpreted for them. In fact, baccalaureate social work faculty may need to clarify the linkage between that part of foundation content pertaining to the processes of social inquiry and the world of practice. Students questioning the relevance of probability theory or of scientific methods studied in a biology course may wonder what it all has to do with helping a client or improving the services to a group of clients. Faculty may need to counter feelings of frustration toward "irrelevant" content by explicitly addressing its implications for social work practice and for the research-related attitudinal, conceptual, and skill development objectives of the curriculum.

Appreciation of Empirical Inquiry

Students need to understand that much knowledge in social work is not based on unswerving truths or even proven causal relationships but instead on probabilities or correlations. Faculty may need to help students understand that where there appear to be linkages between variables, these may be mere associations and not causal relationships. For example, does child abuse "cause delinquency" or is it "merely associated with delinquency"? Consideration of content reality with the nature of proof may enable faculty and students to call into question the stability of some of our social work beliefs. For instance, just because poverty is assumed to be caused by income inequality and insufficiency at the present time does not guarantee that such relationships will persist. It may be, for example, that one hundred years from now, access to energy resources may be as powerfully linked to poverty as income inequality. Scientific methods enable the social work profession to recast ideas not as truisms but as probabilities that may hold true under certain contexts for certain groups and at certain points in time.

Concepts mastered in the acquisition of foundation content, such as validity and reliability, may not always seem relevant to professional social work practice. Undergraduate faculty may want to reintroduce such terms in an interviewing class or in a social policy class to enable students to more readily see their utility. Students' sensitivity to labels and to measures that may be harmful to clients, such as the way IQ tests have hurt Spanish-speaking children and the way psychiatric labels have been applied to gay persons, may increase the likelihood of their understanding the relevance of such concepts to social work practice.

Students also should have derived from their liberal arts and foundation content an appreciation for the complexity of social welfare problems and social work interventions. The limitations of research in solving these problems must also be clear. For example, income inequality may be cited with increasing frequency as the cause of poverty yet the implications of such findings may not impel society to redistribute or to equalize economic resources. While the role of research in solving some of these problems needs to be made clear, misuse of research as well as the negative consequences of research must also be cited. Constructive discounting of statistical abstractions of human problems, and distrust of the scientific process because of its negative technological consequences are not inconsistent with becoming skilled in the assessment and utilization of research. Social workers need to marshal all sources of support, especially those scientifically derived findings that advance the social welfare perspective and understanding of human problems. The validity of such a perspective rests with our ability to prove its accuracy in shaping the way society should approach human problems. For example, if social workers can prove that the human, social, and economic costs of unemployment to its victims and society at large outweigh the costs of inflation, there might be less frequent use of the unemployed as instruments to fight inflation.[2]

Students will have undoubtedly mastered such concepts as deductive reasoning (specific assumptions and hypotheses derived from general principles) and inductive reasoning (more general principles developed from specific observations) in foundation and liberal arts course work. Social work faculty may want to assist them in understanding how such concepts relate to social work learning. Faculty may cite examples of such reasoning as they help students to isolate topics for term papers or to review how they reason through questions on exams. In fact, the benefits and pitfalls of both processes of reasoning as they apply to social work knowledge may need to be woven into several of the social work courses.

Similarly, there should be some attempt to make clear the utility of explanatory versus prescriptive or intervention levels of research. For example, students may attempt to translate explanatory levels of knowledge about social problems into prescriptions as to how one should intervene. If "anomie" or "alienation" were found to be related to depression, implications of these findings for the alleviation of depression may leave much to professional interpretation, inference, and possible oversimplification. As another example, knowing that labeling may lead to delinquency may not provide the professional with prescriptive knowledge of how to help the client to get in control of his or her behavior. Theories and research are needed at both explanatory and intervention levels; knowing the dynamics or causes of a problem may not suggest effective strategies for dealing with it. Moreover, extrapolation from interventions to explanations for the problems may also be inappropriate. Students need to be able to appreciate the utility of both levels and to refrain from artificially forcing one level to answer questions related to the other level.

Scientific Methods and Social
Work Values

It is expected that students will have derived an appreciation for cultural and human diversity from liberal arts and foundation content. Appreciation of cultural and cross-cultural differences and human diversity is essential to the development of research values, knowledge, and skills. Research that does not respect the diversity in ethnicity, culture, and lifestyle of those studied may utilize invalid assumptions and, even worse, generate inaccurate findings. Atrocities abound of research endeavors that have discounted diversity or attributed pathology to groups whose cultural and economic status deviated from the prevailing norms of the middle-class-white society.[3] Student sensitivity to different cultural groups and human diversity must be linked to ethical and practice considerations in addition to research. Moreover, the commitment to understanding the phenomenology of the experiences of others through their eyes will shape students' ability to assess the research of others, as well as to carry out their own. Biased findings derived from middle-class-white premises, assumptions, and questions have damaged entire groups of people. The social problem focus of the social work profession may reinforce the ease with which pathology rather than strengths are identified within certain groups and individuals.

Social work educators must help students guard against the imposition of stereotypic assumptions and explanations for human diversity. The processes of social inquiry may offset some of these stereotypic responses by calling into question the assumptions and premises upon which research endeavors are based and by posing the possibility of alternative perspectives. Some social science knowledge may be dated by the way in which pathology or deviance is attributed to persons or groups such as the black family, the single-parent family, or the gay family.

Clearly, assessment of others and implementation of one's own research do not occur in a value-free, dispassionate context. Social work ethics and values are threaded throughout our assumptions. Research that advances social welfare knowledge cannot be separated from the values of the social work profession. Consequently, the burden may be even greater on the social work professional to safeguard against bias in the way answers are sought through the use of research methods. Becoming emotionally involved with one's research is normal; social workers would probably not conduct their own research if they did not think that it would in some way make a difference. However, the tools that enable the researcher to distance his or her "burning" questions from the process of answering such questions are derived from scientific methods.

Students may need help in understanding how social work values not only guide research but also prevent us from engaging in certain kinds of research that might be harmful to our clients or to the social welfare of groups of people. Even so, societal values and ideologies influence social work values, and what may be acceptable lines of questions and assumptions at one point in time may be viewed as inappropriate or harmful later. Social work knowledge may be intricately linked to the belief systems of the larger society at different points in time. As these belief systems shift, so will social work knowledge. For example, assumptions about women embedded in previous psychoanalytic thought are now found to be dated and erroneous.[4]

RESEARCH METHODS

Students may acquire formal knowledge of research methods from a variety of sources, including research projects, social work research or social inquiry courses, self-paced instruction, and social science research experiences and course work.[5] Beginning competencies in research methods assume the ability to conceptualize and to formulate researchable problems and questions. Translating a difficulty into nonambiguous researchable questions requires a creative and rigorous thinking process that may be prompted in students long before they learn formal research methods, but that may need to be refined in reserch methods courses. methods, but that may need to be refined in research methods courses. methods of posing and answering questions will be applied. Students should recognize how essential it is to acquire assistance from colleagues in the refinement of problem statements, and in the development of hypotheses or questions. Isolation of the researcher even in the earliest stages of research may result in a less effective or inappropriate problem selection process.

Once students have demonstrated confidence and competence in problem formulation and specification, they must address the issue of whether activities such as empirical data collection, secondary data analysis, gathering stories, engaging in library research and bibliographical analysis, or conceptual model building can best facilitate the problem-solving process. Hopefully, social work students will have been encouraged during previous educational activities to turn to the community and not just the library as an alternative source of information and answers to questions.[7] Ideally, the choice of how to proceed to study the research problem at hand will not constitute a departure from the kinds of decisions students have encountered in other social work learning experiences.

Conceptualizing and Operationalizing

How to operationalize concepts and to generate both abstract and empirical referents to the concepts under study are skills that, again, may be acquired or reinforced through other learning experiences. For example, depression is a concept that is widely used in social work practice—but its empirical referents are not necessarily agreed upon nor are they always observable. In operationalizing terms, the rich imagery resulting from their ambiguity and generality may be lost. Conversely, the specificity and clarity of empirical referents may be lost as more general, encompassing terms are sought. Students undoubtedly will have had the opportunity to engage in both processes of conceptualization before they learn formal research methods. The challenge to operationalize concepts and to generate valid and reliable measures of them must be viewed as a creative, rigorous process that lacks predetermined, standardized guidelines.

Students may find that developing acceptable, relatively accurate, and reliable measures for concepts and variables under study is not possible. Consequently, the research focus may shift, or the limits of measures employed may be spelled out beforehand. Many productive research questions may never be studied because of problems in generating appropriate nonbiased data, problems with measurement, or potential risks to the human subjects.

Library research and literature reviews, characteristic of many student learning activities, will accompany the early phases of problem selection and formulation and will usually precede the development of the methodology. Knowledge of how to use abstracts and data-based journals will normally be acquired early in the baccalaurate program.

Research Design

The design of the research sets forth the plan. Students' knowledge of designs and types may include experimental, exploratory, and qualitative and quantitative research, single-subject designs, program evaluation, impact analysis, theoretical model building, operations research, cost-benefit analysis, and so forth. The choice of design is determined by many factors. Students' familiarity with these various kinds of designs and approaches may vary. Experimental research designs may be understood due to previous course work in psychology or the natural sciences. Single-subject design or program evaluation may be new to the student. In fact, single-subject design and evaluative research may not be covered in the research courses currently taught. This can be attributed to the applied nature of such methods and the fact that some social scientists are less well acquainted with applied research. However, these evaluative tools build on the experimental model of research and are important for the baccalaureate practitioner to understand, since much of the literature deals with the evaluation of programs and/or intervention efforts. Also, baccalaureate practitioners will need to understand the ways in which these research strategies can be helpful in evaluating their own practice efforts. Inappropriate generalizations occur every day,[8] so concern over bias in sampling or in data collection techniques should be a natural outgrowth of a sensitivity inherent in the undergraduate social work student. Learning formal sampling techniques and their limitations may help students to assess the appropriateness of others' studies and findings, in addition to providing students with skills useful for gathering data in their own practice.

Bias may occur as well in the way questions are posed and answers are sought. "Loaded" questions, which presuppose or predetermine certain responses, are all too frequently a part of everyday life. Prevention of bias and the development of valid, reliable, and systematic measures to acquire data may be enhanced if the student actually learns how to develop an instrument. Development of an instrument to record system or client change or to survey an entire community may familiarize the student with ways to handle large classes of data or events. In addition, students will become familiar with classification systems or typologies, and with issues of validity, reliability, operationalization of concepts, assessing the relationship between two variables, and so forth.

Data Analysis:

The choice of how to analyze data depends on the reasons for its collection and on the audience to which it is directed. Complex statistical analyses may not be necessary in most of the systematic inquiry that baccalaureate practitioners conduct. However, it is essential that the student know how to connect the data analysis to the questions or hypotheses posed. The challenge of the data analysis process rests primarily with the creative abilities of the researcher. Finding commonalities and patterns, discerning a linkage between one variable and others, and being able to organize data into subgroups for purposes of comparison often requires more creativity, perseverance, and rigor than the application of highly codified data analysis procedures data. Statistics that describe or provide a profile regarding a population or a sample may be sufficient in exploratory research. The appropriateness of the use of statistics will vary according to the sample size and the kind of measures used to acquire data. Students should be encouraged not to shy away from data analysis just because they are unsure about the use of statistics.

Instead, the basic question of what one wants the data to do should shape the kind of analysis undertaken. For example, if the baccalaureate social worker wanted to convey to community officials the importance of natural helping systems to the functioning of the single-parent ethnic minority family, observations from the findings that are presented in statistical terms may detract from the impact of the study findings. Instead, data might be more appropriately reported in a way that reflected the phenomenology of the experiences of these families.

Faculty must assess the research content required as part of the social work curriculum to ensure that a broad range of research tools are offered to the social work student.[9] Research courses that discount the relevance of exploratory or quantitative research need to be revised to reflect the empirical realities of some social problem content. Social work students' animosity to research may easily be reinforced by a course that focuses more heavily on statistics than on research methods.

APPLICATION CONTENT

Students should be able to demonstrate that they have achieved certain minimal competencies that ensure their ability to utilize research knowledge in their own practice. They should exhibit confidence and skill in the critiquing of others' research. It should be possible for them to develop their own framework for critiquing others' research. This framework may be derived from that used in a formal research course or it can be tailored to the particular questions and concerns of each student. Such a framework may guide students in the assessment and evaluation of research studies and their relevance for students' practice. This framework may address 1) how well the research problem is conceptualized; 2) the degree of conceptual purity, simplicity, relevance, and completeness of the hypotheses;[10] 3) the extent to which operationalization of concepts is empirically sound; 4) the validity and reliability of measures; 5) the correctness of assumptions; 6) the appropriateness of the design and the data base used; 7) the extent to which the generated data shed light on questions or hypotheses posed; and 8) the implications for understanding client problems and prescriptions for intervention.

Students should be able to recast practice problems into empirical questions. Such an empirical edge to practice inquiry may encourage the student to view practice events as experiments where interventions are independent variables and practice outcomes are dependent variables. Furthermore, students should be able to see that certain interventions may be more effective when timed to occur under certain conditions and not others. In addition, students should demonstrate an ability to use the literature as one source of conceptual and empirical knowledge on the use and timing of various interventions.

The ability to gather data through a modest data collection effort should be promoted through projects associated with the baccalaureate social work curriculum. Students may demonstrate such abilities within their field work experience where they can evaluate their own practice effectiveness. Faculty may want to join students in these research projects. Demonstration projects are particularly useful in this regard, as service and evaluation can be combined. Moreover, if such a project is ineffective, it can be easily dismantled when implemented under the auspices of the social work program. Such demonstration projects may especially appeal to students when little is known about a community problem or about how to best serve the needs of its victims. In one student-faculty project, students delivered social services to battered women who sought divorce and restraining orders in a legal services office.[11] Students working on the project were practitioners and evaluators at the same time. Program evaluation assessed whether the provision of a social worker and social services resulted in a wider range of choices for the battered woman, and whether they helped her to meet immediate needs more effectively than did delayed divorce services.

Other projects that link students to the study of client needs and to methods of intervention might include the provision of job-seeking skills to a group of single parents or displaced homemakers. School faculty involvement in such projects may increase the likelihood that field work faculty will also become involved in the process and even offer supervisory help to the students. Some research projects can be aimed at the analysis of policy in social or governmental agencies, private industry, or legislatures. Family impact analysis is an example of policy-related research that estimates or evaluates the impact of policy decisions on the functioning of certain groups of people. There are many other research models as well that could inform policies and decisions. Needs assessments, trend analysis, and the collection of anecdotal or case studies all may be used to shape or inform such decisionmaking processes. All are information gathering efforts that can be carried out by the baccalaureate social work practitioner.

Students must demonstrate the ability to tailor research designs to the practicalities of the practice setting. Consequently, they may need to show that they can differentiate between research methodology that meets all criteria of acceptable and most desirable designs and the one most appropriate—given limited time and resources—to the practice setting. Some research designs will not only be impractical but also unacceptable because of the risks to human subjects. Such risks, and the process by which safeguards against those risks must be developed (including acquiring informed consent from clients), must be understood by the student. Moreover, students should be able to identify when research projects need to be cleared through human rights review committees and should know how to prepare proposals for such committees.

Many of the inferences derived during practice constitute tentative assumptions that guide and should be guided by information and observations generated during the practice event. Empirically based practice should not limit the ability of the student to distinguish between the roles of researcher and practitioner. Students should be able to give practice considerations priority throughout the practice event. However, it should be possible for the baccalaureate practitioner to view practice as a series of empirical events that corroborate, compound, or counter inferences, hypotheses, and assumptions.

The baccalaureate practitioner should be able to demonstrate the ability to include the client or client group wherever feasible as a partner in the evaluative-practice exercise. Thus, the choice of interventions and of the measures of change and practice outcomes can be conceptualized jointly. Even more pressing is the need to exhibit sensitivity to the cultural variations and diversity within the client group. In fact, the student should be able to demonstrate an awareness of the way in which human diversity may actually shape practice decisions, including problem definition, choice of interventions, and measures of change. Students must show that they can conduct research that takes into account the diversity of cultural contexts in which clients' problems are most appropriately defined and alleviated.

Of utmost importance to the student is the educational process, which not only fosters such competencies but also ensures continuing access to sources of advice and expertise on all facets of the practitioner-researcher endeavor.

STRATEGIES FOR IMPLEMENTATION OF RESEARCH CONTENT

Earlier in this chapter the point has been made that the value of scientific inquiry must pervade the entire learning environment.

Some social work faculty may feel uncomfortable with the details of research methods as taught in research courses, but hopefully all faculty would be able to mode systematic problem solving through the orderly use of information gathering, situational assessment, decisionmaking, and planning. In confronting research content, the problem is often minimized for social work faculty by the fact that much of the specific research content discussed in here is often taught in courses outside of the social work program, or by non-social work faculty. This removes some of the pressure from social work faculty members who may not feel comfortable teaching this content.

Nevertheless, the social work faculty is responsible for insuring the integration of research content into the curriculum. This suggests that research can serve to stimulate the development of linkages with other programs and faculty. Social work faculty will need to discuss the research content and methods of its presentation with non-social work faculty who teach in this area, so that they can most effectively meet student and program needs. Social work faculty members may also decide to team teach research content with non-social work faculty, in order to affect what is taught and to expand their own knowledge.

There are, then, a number of ways in which research content can enrich a baccalaureate social work program. In addition to its practice value for students, it provides a focus for the integration of much of the liberal arts and foundation content that students learn. It also provides opportunities for dialogue with non-social work faculty members and with other programs/departments in those instances where research content is not taught by social work faculty or in the social work program. Finally, it offers opportunities for social work faculty to collaborate with others to enrich both curriculum content and their own professional growth. When seen from these perspectives, the anxiety that research content sometimes raises for social work faculty members can be viewed instead as a vast opportunity for program and faculty enrichment.

NOTES

1. "Research in Social Work," *Encyclopedia of Social Work*, Sixteenth Issue, 2 (1971):1099. Also see Stuart Kirk, Michael J. Osmalov, and Joel Fisher, "Social Workers' Involvement in Research," *Social Work* (March 1976):121-25.

2. This idea has been developed by Michael Borrero, Associate Professor, School of Social Work, University of Connecticut.

3. Montiel, Miguel, "The Chicano Family: A Review of the Research,"

Social Work 18, 2 (March 1973):22-31. Scott, Patricia Bell, "Sex-Roles Research and Black Families: Some Comments on the Literature," *Journal of Afro-American Issues* 4, 3 and 4 (Summer/Fall 1976):349-61.

4. See Women's Issue of *Social Work*, 21, 6 (November 1976).

5. It is possible to imagine an undergraduate social work curriculum where knowledge and skill development in research methods can be acquired from policy, practice, social problems, or human growth in social environment courses, rather than set aside in a separate course. Research methods have been integrated with practice courses at the graduate level at the University of Washington School of Social Work. See Scott Briar, "Incorporating Research into Education for Clinical Practice in Social Work: Toward A Clinical Service in Social Work," presented at the conference on Research Utilization in Social Work Education, New Orleans, October 1977.

6. Ripple, Lillian, "Problem Identification and Formulation," in Polansky, Norman, ed., *Social Work Research*, 1st ed. (Chicago: University of Chicago, 1960), pp. 24-77.

7. This may be necessitated when little is known about an issue, or when the literature is dated. Battered women and the human costs of unemployment are examples of content areas with limited or dated coverage in the literature.

8. Students complain that even the titles of research articles themselves may misrepresent the actual study by overgeneralizing in the selection of the title.

9. Research courses that exclude exploratory, qualitative, descriptive, or survey research methods may need to be revised. Research courses that focus entirely on explanatory levels of research to the exclusion of intervention levels may also need to be examined. Social work students need to be familiar with research methods that include single-subject design and program evaluation. The following may be useful supplements to such courses: Thomas, Edwin J., "Uses of Research Methods in Interpersonal Practice," in Polansky, ed., *Social Work Research*, 2nd ed. (Chicago: University of Chicago, 1975), pp. 254-83; Gottman, John M., and Sandra R. Leiblum, *How to Do Psychotherapy and How to Evaluate It* (New York: Holt, Rinehart and Winston, 1974); Levy, Rona, "Single-Subject Experimental Designs in Social Work Education," prepared for Council on Social Work Education Annual Program Meeting, Phoenix, 1977. Dr. Levy is also the author of a book on single-subject design, soon to be published by Columbia University Press. Carol Weiss, *Evaluation Research* (Englewood Cliffs, N.J.: Prentice-Hall, 1972), may be a useful introduction to program evaluation.

10. These are explicated in Harris K. Goldstein's *Research Standards and Methods for Social Workers* (Wheeling, Ill.: Whitewall, 1969), pp. 48-66.

11. This was conducted through the Family and Work Policy Study Group at Pacific Lutheran University.

ANNOTATED BIBLIOGRAPHY

Babbie, Earl R. *The Practice of Social Research*. Belmont, Calif.: Wadsworth, 1975. A sociology research text accompanied by a practice manual. Does not include material on single-subject research but the practice manual is a resource.

Birnbrauer, Jay S., Christa R. Peterson, and Jay V. Solknick. "Design and Interpretation of Studies of Single Subjects." *American Journal of Mental Deficiency* 79, 2 (1974):191-203. An excellent description of examples of single-subject research, showing the differences among various designs including reversals and multiple baseline.

Bronowski, J. *Science and Human Values.* New York: Harper & Row, 1965. The first several chapters are particularly helpful in dispelling the myth that science is mechanistic. Bronowski compellingly describes the commonalities in creativity required for artistic as well as scientific endeavors.

Cambell, Donald T. "Reforms as Experiments." *American Psychologist* 24, 4 (April 1969):409-29. An excellent discussion and description of the methods of assessing and evaluating the effectiveness of interventions in social systems. Provides useful tools for program evaluation.

Goldstein, Harris K. *Research Standards and Methods for Social Workers.* Wheeling, Ill.: Whitewall, 1969. An easy-to-read introduction to research with some useful practice questions. It does not include material on single subject design or statistics.

Gottman, John M. and Sandra R. Leiblum. *How to Do Psychotherapy and How to Evaluate It.* New York: Holt, Rinehart and Winston, 1974. An introductory resource for the clinician-scientist. Demonstrates the way in which practice questions can be studied empirically utilizing single-subject designs.

Kaplan, Abraham. *The Conduct of Inquiry.* San Francisco: Chandler, 1964. A theoretical discussion of the processes of social inquiry and the role of scientific methods.

Kerlinger, F. *Foundations of Behavioral Research.* New York: Holt, Rinehart and Winston, 1964. A basic text on research methods.

Krathwohl, David R. "How to Prepare a Research Proposal." Syracuse, N.Y.: Syracuse University (bookstore), 1977. A pragmatic, step-by-step guide to developing a competitive research proposal.

Levy, Rona. "Single-Subject Experimental Designs in Social Work Education." Prepared for Council on Social Work Education Annual Program Meeting, Phoenix, 1977. This article provides excellent examples of the use of single-subject research. Dr. Levy is the coauthor of a book on single-subject research soon to be published by Columbia University Press.

Polansky, Norman, ed. *Social Work Research.* Chicago: University of Chicago, 1975. This text contains some useful chapters, including Thomas' article on single-subject design.

Thomas, Edwin J. "Uses of Research Methods in Interpersonal Practice." In Polansky, pp. 254-83. This article provides an excellent foundation for conceptual and skill development in single-subject research.

Tripodi, Tony. *Uses and Abuses of Social Research in Social Work.* New York: Columbia University Press, 1974. An analysis of the problems and consequences of inappropriate research as well as the benefits of research for the social work profession.

Tripodi, Tony, Phillip Fellin, and Henry J. Meyer. *The Assessment of Social Research,* Itasca, Ill.: F.E. Peacock, 1969. A critical analysis of various research designs and methods by which actual research articles can be evaluated.

Weiss, Carol. *Evaluation Research.* Englewood Cliffs, N.J.: Prentice-Hall, 1972. An easy-to-read discussion of methods and problems in evaluative research. Contains extensive bibliography.

REFERENCES

Babbie, Earl R. *The Practice of Social Research.* Belmont, Calif.: Wadsworth, 1975.

Billingsley, Andrew. *Black Families in White America.* Englewood Cliffs, N.J.: Prentice-Hall, 1968.

Birnbrauer, Jay S., Christa R. Peterson, and Jay V. Solknick. "Design and Interpretation of Studies of Single Subjects." *American Journal of Mental Deficiency* 79, 2 (1974):191-203.

Briar, Scott. "Incorporating Research into Education for Clinical Practice in Social Work: Toward a Clinical Service in Social Work." Presented to the Conference on Research Utilization in Social Work Education, New Orleans, October 1977.

Bronowski, J. *Science and Human Values.* New York: Harper & Row, 1965.

Brown, Caree Rozen, and Marilyn Levett Helinger. "Therapists' Attitudes Toward Women." *Social Work* 20, 4 (July 1975):266-77.

Cambell, Donald T. "Reforms as Experiments." *American Psychologist* 24, 4 (April 1969):409-29.

Chafetz, Janet S., Patricia Sampson, Paul Beck, and Joyce West. "A Study of Homosexual Women." *Social Work* 19, 6 (November 1974):714-23.

Chommie, Peter W., and Joe Hudson. "Evaluation of Outcome and Process." *Social Work* (November 1974):682-87.

Cohen, Morris R., and Ernest Nagel. *An Introduction to Logic and Scientific Method.* New York: Harcourt, Brace, 1939.

Evaluating Social Programs. Edited by Peter H. Rossi and Walter Williams. New York: Seminar Press, 1972.

Family Impact Seminar. Washington, D.C.: George Washington University Institute for Educational Leadership, 1978.

Fischer, Joel. "Is Casework Effective?" *Social Work* (January 1973):5-20.

Freeman, Howard E., and Clarence C. Sherwood. *Social Research and Social Policy.* Englewood Cliffs, N.J.: Prentice-Hall, 1970.

Glaser, Barney G., and Anselm L. Strauss. *The Discovery of Grounded Theory.* Chicago: Aldine, 1967.

Golden, M. Patricia, ed. *The Research Experience.* Itasca, Ill.: F.E. Peacock, 1976.

Goldstein, Harris K. *Research Standards and Methods for Social Workers.* Wheeling, Ill.: Whitewall, 1969.

Gottman, John M., and Sandra R. Leiblum. *How to Do Psychotherapy and How to Evaluate It.* New York: Holt, Rinehart and Winston, 1974.

Ho, Man Keung. "Evaluation: A Means of Treatment." *Social Work* (January 1976):16-23.

Howe, Michael. "Using Clients' Observations in Research." *Social Work* (January 1976):24-27.

Kaplan, Abraham. *The Conduct of Inquiry.* San Francisco: Chandler, 1964.

Kerlinger, F. *Foundations of Behavioral Research.* New York: Holt, Rinehart and Winston, 1964.

Kirk, Stuart, Michael J. Osmalov, and Joel Fischer. "Social Workers' Involvement in Research." *Social Work* (March 1976):121-25.

Krathwohl, David R. "How to Prepare a Research Proposal." Syracuse, N.Y.: Syracuse University (bookstore), 1977.

Levy, Rona. "Single-Subject Experimental Designs in Social Work Education." Prepared for Council on Social Work Education Annual Program Meeting, Phoenix, 1977.

Montiel, Miguel. "The Chicano Family: A Review of the Research." *Social Work* (March 1973):22-31.

Myrdal, Gunnar. *Objectivity in Social Research.* London: Duckworth, 1970.

Polansky, Norman, ed. *Social Work Research*, 2nd ed. Chicago: University of Chicago, 1975.

"Research in Social Work." *Encyclopedia of Social Work*, Sixteenth Issue, 2 (1971).

"Research in Social Work." *Encyclopedia of Social Work*, Seventeenth Issue, 2 (1977).

Ripple, Lillian. "Problem Identification and Formulation." In Polansky, pp. 24-77.

Scott, Patricia Bell. "Sex-Roles Research and Black Families: Some Comments on the Literature." *Journal of Afro-American Issues*, 4, 3 and 4, (Summer/Fall 1976):349-61.

Thomas, Edwin J. "Uses of Research Methods in Interpersonal Practice." In Polansky, pp. 254-83.

Tripodi, Tony. *Uses and Abuses of Social Research in Social Work.* New York: Columbia University Press, 1974.

Tripodi, Tony, Phillip Fellin, and Henry J. Meyer. *The Assessment of Social Research.* Itasca, Ill.: F.E. Peacock, 1969.

Women's Issue. *Social Work* 21, 6 (November 1976).

Chapter Ten

Human Behavior and the Social Environment within a Human Diversity Framework

Ronald C. Federico

INTRODUCTION

The Undergraduate Social Work Curriculum Development Project report contains a number of implications for curriculum content on human behavior and the social environment in baccalaureate social work programs. These may be summarized as follows:

1. The baccalaureate social worker must have analyiical and interactional skills, for use with the many different types of people with whom he or she will work. These skills must be used in a way that is consistent with the profession's ethical imperatives to respect and value each individual's and group's uniqueness and right to self-determination.
2. The psychologically-based model of normative human development through the life cycle is by itself inadequate to develop the necessary analytical and interactional skills needed to understand human difference in all its richness and practice potential. Seeing only one "normal" pattern ignores the cultural, social, and genetic factors that lead to multiple views of appropriate life goals and multiple resource and behavioral networks to achieve them. Therefore, human behavior must be understood as resulting from the interplay of equally important psychological, social, cutural, and biological factors.
3. There has tended to be an overemphasis in social work education on individual development and family functioning, to the relative

neglect of other types of groups, formal organizations, and the economic and political institutions of society. A better balance must be achieved if human behavior in the social environment content is to support social work practice.

4. The major purpose of curriculum content is to facilitate the attainment of basic practice competence as a baccalaureate social worker. This competence requires the ability to function at the interface of people and social institutions. Curriculum content in human behavior and the social environment must be adequate in scope, integration, and focus to facilitate such practice competence.

In seeking to operationalize the need for an expanded and more practice-focused approach to human behavior and the social environment curriculum content, project staff developed a human diversity framework within which this content could be conceptually organized and taught.[a] This approach is, of course, only one of many possible approaches to thinking about and teaching this content, but it is one that is directly supportive of project findings. It differs in scope and focus from most of the approaches currently used, yet it shares a number of important features with them. These include the following:

1. While the focus is on diversity, it is recognized that human differences are expressed by efforts to satisfy common human needs.
2. The life cycle is incorporated into the approach to human behavior and the social environment.
3. Each person's uniqueness always cuts across the diverse group memberships that he or she has, and it must be nurtured and respected.
4. While rejecting rigid and universally applied concepts of normalcy, it is recognized that some behaviors are more socially acceptable and rewarded than others. There is also recognition that social workers often carry societal mandates to support and enforce behaviors defined as socially acceptable. However, a focus on diversity goes beyond this to look at reasons why behaviors are considered socially acceptable, the costs of such definitions to

[a]The definition of human diversity developed by the curriculum development project is the following: "The notion of diverse groups has to be understood in a complex and developmental context that can include both ascribed and self-designated categories that are neither mutually exclusive (e.g., age and ethnicity) nor necessarily interchangeable (e.g., ethnic and cultural groups). Diversity is to be understood as on a continuum."

members of diverse groups, and appropriate professional activities vis-à-vis such behaviors as they are displayed by members of diverse groups.

The project approach to human behavior and the social environment directly confronts the dilemma of social science knowledge that attempts to be value-free and the uses of it that serve value-based objectives. Generating truly value-free knowledge in the social sciences is an extraordinarily difficult task, due to the ethnocentrism of researchers and the fact that social science research is itself accountable to those who support it.[1] Here, as in all parts of the societal structure, those persons and groups with greatest access to resources can influence events. In the world of social science research, this often means the ability to influence what is studied, how it is studied, and how the information is interpreted and used.[2] Further deviations from the value-free ideal are introduced by persons and groups that use existing knowledge for their own purposes. This chapter is an example, since it explicitly attempts to utilize social science knowledge in a way that emphasizes the need to understand, value, respect, and build upon human diversity. The author believes this approach to be consistent with the values and ethics of the profession that support human equality, social justice, and self-determination.

Other persons and groups that are not committed to such values may use social science knowledge quite differently, in order to achieve their own objectives. To the extent that those who control knowledge dissemination and social policy decisionmaking do not support professional social work values, knowledge may be used to justify concepts of "normal" and "deviant" that are unfavorable to members of selected groups. It is precisely this use of social science knowledge that the approach discussed in this chapter seeks to expose and avoid. Since this is obviously a value-based issue, readers will want to draw their own conclusions about the utility of this approach. This is only one of many possible approaches, but it is believed that this one strongly supports the profession of social work as well as the findings of the project.

ORGANIZATION OF THIS CHAPTER

The main body of this chapter examines human development as the result of three equally important types of factors: genetic, cultural, and social. The individual is seen in constant interaction with cultural groups and social institutions. Personality development and life cycle experiences occur within such a context rather than themselves serving as the context for human growth and development. This approach emphasizes difference rather than normalcy, showing how the divergent objectives and social patterns that characterize diverse groups affect human development throughout the life cycle. Difference is seen within a perspective of cultural relativity, in which the distinctive activities and characteristics of diverse groups are all equally valid attempts to perform life tasks. Majority and minority group relations as structured through social institutions are used to explain ethnocentric definitions of normal and abnormal that serve to advantage some groups and disadvantage others.

The second part of the chapter addresses some basic issues in teaching the content developed in the first part. A baccalaureate social work program may choose from a variety of curriculum strategies to teach human behavior and the social environment content. Whichever strategy is chosen must accommodate the need to cover a broad range of social and biological science content, to sequence that knowledge in a cumulative, minimally repetitive way, and to integrate it so that the interacting biological, cultural, and social forces that create and maintain the conditions that influence people's behavior are identified. This approach attempts to develop a way of analyzing human behavior and the social environment, rather than simply charting "normal" development through the life cycle.

THE FOUNDATIONS OF SOCIAL BEHAVIOR

Social behavior results from the complex and continuous interaction of three forces.

Genetic Inheritance

Biological uniqueness as well as common human needs are the legacy of one's genetic inheritance. Each person inherits a uniquely distinctive gene pool that establishes the potential and ultimate limits of his or her individual development. The realization of this potential and the ability to develop close to one's genetic limits depend on the satisfaction of common human needs for sustenance, nurturance, protection, stimulation, and supportive interaction. These come from the individual's environment, and their provision or absence will determine the degree to which the individual's uniqueness as defined genetically can be attained. Similar environments can result in quite dissimilar individuals, since both the biological potential and the way in which environmental input is processed vary from person to person. On the other hand, environments that are either unusually enriching and supportive or primarily stressful and depriving are likely to have fairly predictable results for the average individual. Human differences, then, result from the fact that each individual is genetically distinctive as well as from the way in which common human needs are met through the unique interplay of the social environment and genetically determined characteristics. Since genetic factors may be affected during pregnancy, the impact of the social environment on the mother can also affect the developing human being. For example, nutrition, the use of drugs and medications, physical and mental traumas, and other factors may have an effect on the offspring.

Cultural Influences

The culture into which an individual is socialized provides the context in which biologically transmitted potential will be operationalized. It establishes concepts of desirable and appropriate life goals, behavior patterns, and resource utilization. This serves as a framework for the selective perception of events, and motivates people to act in certain ways (as well as to resist other types of behavior). Cultural socialization also influences the development of self-concept, with resulting effects on attitudes and behaviors.

Social Influences

People's lives are organized by the social structures and social processes that surround them. These social realities facilitate certain kinds of behavior and serve to inhibit others. For example, early socialization into sex roles by social institutions such as the family, religion, and education makes it increasingly unlikely and difficult for men and women to choose other than "appropriate" behaviors. Social structures include the whole social institutional structure within which people live, including the creation of systems of socialization, social control, social stratification, and social change. They also include the dynamics of interaction that govern various structures, such as bureaucracies and families.

These three sources of behavior interact in complex ways to create the environment in which people act. They must be understood individually and in interaction if human behavior as it occurs in its social environment is to be comprehended in ways that support practice activities. Learning about behavior occurs through the mastery of knowledge generated from scientific, experiential, and artistic data sources. Large-scale statistical data, individual life history information, life experiences as filtered through the artist's sensibilities, and carefully aggregated data from practice experience are all useful in understanding genetic, cultural, and social factors that influence human behavior.

THE MEANING OF HUMAN DIVERSITY

Although each person is a unique combination of genetic and environmental characteristics and experiences, people are grouped according to particular characteristics that they possess in common with others. Since each person has many characteristics, each of which are shared with a set of other people, he or she may be grouped in any number of ways. Characteristics and group memberships may be biologically determined and therefore ascribed, such as race and gender. Other characteristics are culturally and socially created and are more likely to be achieved, such as religious affiliation and marital standing. Still others, such as ethnicity, are partly ascribed and partly achieved. As life goals and situations change, some characteristics and resulting group memberships may change, or their significance in a person's life may be altered. In general, ascribed characteristics are less likely to change than those that are achieved, although the socially defined meaning and importance of an ascribed characteristic may change.

Since each individual possesses many characteristics, the composition of a group based on any one characteristic will include a wide range of people with respect to other characteristics. The "women" group includes the rich and the poor, the lesbian and the heterosexual, the physically handicapped and those not handicapped, and the Black, the Oriental, and the Caucasian. Therefore, a group that is different from others with respect to a particular characteristic (for example, Puerto Ricans as an ethnic group contrasted with Chicanos as an ethnic group[3]) will itself have a wide range of internal diversity (among Puerto Ricans, racial mixtures, socioeconomic differences, gender differences, etc.). Therefore, there is as much difference within a group as between groups, except with respect to the defining group characteristic and factors that are directly related to it, such as ethnicity. In addition, any group may change over time, as exemplified by the increased willingness of the physically handicapped to fight for the opportunity to engage in activities from which they were frequently excluded in the past.

While people become members of groups due to a wide range of characteristics (tennis skill, left-handedness, avocational interests, etc.), groups based on certain characteristics become especially important in people's lives. These groups affect the way their members relate to the institutions of society, to other people, to other groups, to other members of their own group, and to themselves. Groups that transmit cultural values to their members (such as ethnic groups), groups that significantly affect the assumptions made by society regarding the typical behaviors of their members (such as homosexuals), or groups whose members are limited in their ability to act in expected ways in social situations (such as the poor and the handicapped) are of particular importance in influencing the life experiences of their members. It is those groups that are usually of most concern to social workers.

Groups have roles assigned to their members by society. These roles are frequently based on stereotypes about biological or cultural characteristics, for example, the elderly are forgetful and cannot be trusted with important tasks, or Hispanics cannot speak English and are only suited to farm labor or factory work. These roles can become significant barriers to members of diverse groups since role definitions become part of the socialization performed by social institutions. This socialization may serve to perpetuate stereotypes and become self-fulfilling prophesies by denying members of diverse groups opportunities to act differently. Socialization may also encourage the internalization of negative self-concepts and group concepts. Furthermore, people occupy many roles at once—ethnicity, religion, race, and sex roles, for example. The particular combination of roles that people have will affect the way they interact in given situations. A wealthy gay[4] politician may be less hurt socially and economically in a situation of police entrapment than a gay person with fewer influential friends and fewer financial resources.

The diversity of groups such as these leads to social arrangements being differentially experienced. The concept of normalcy may differ according to cultural values, lifestyle preference, or physical ability. Differences between a group's and society's definition of normalcy may lead to conflict and attempts to control or disadvantage members of diverse groups. Once "normal" is defined, alternative behaviors are "abnormal" or *deviant*, leading to a process of *stigmatization* that gradually tends to define the person so *labeled* as outside the acceptable bounds of social behavior. This easily becomes a self-fulfilling prophesy that makes it increasingly difficult for the stigmatized individual to be seen and treated as anything other than deviant and therefore unacceptable. For example, the concept of the intact nuclear family may be imposed on racial and ethnic groups as a condition of receiving financial assistance even though it violates cultural and social patterns in those groups. The interaction between group members and society is constantly shifting as the group itself changes and as societal values change.

To understand the behavior of people from a diverse group, a dual perspective is needed.[5] It consists of the views held by those who belong to the group as to what behavior is appropriate and normal, and the views held by outsiders who evaluate the behavior of members of the group according to their own perceptions and standards. Knowing both views is necessary for understanding the behaviors of oneself and others in social situations. All behavior must then be seen within the general societal concern of whether a specific behavior is harmful to others. However, like all societal values, this one becomes politicized so that the activities of certain groups are considered normal and acceptable even though there is evidence that they are harmful to certain other groups.

Social workers face a major problem when confronting human diversity and societal definitions of normalcy and deviance. The structures within which social workers practice and the societal values that support them generally reflect society's dominant majority group(s). Neither social workers nor the persons whom they attempt to assist can afford to disregard these dominant-group definitions of reality and acceptability, unless they are willing to risk censure through the existing social control mechanisms (loss of financial aid, loss of employment, arrest, etc.). While working for systemic change to redefine prevailing ethnocentric and disadvantaging standards of normalcy and acceptability, the social worker must help the client to avoid direct confrontation with structures and processes that he or she cannot hope to challenge successfully at that particular time. To accomplish this, the social worker must clearly understand the prevailing strengths of the group to which the client belongs, and use these as resources to enable the person to obtain as much help as possible from within the group as well as from outside the group. The social worker must also know how to utilize the structure of services as effectively as possible to obtain needed resources while simultaneously avoiding destructive confrontation. Throughout this process, the social worker's commitment to greater social equity, social justice, and self-determination requires continuous efforts to effect systemic changes to attain these goals.

BASES OF DIVERSITY

Differences between people are both biologically founded and created by cultural and social definitions. Diversity appears to be functional both biologically and culturally, in that it provides maximum adaptive flexibility, but it nevertheless can create difficulties for the establishment of social arrangements (difficulties described at greater length later in the chapter).

Biological Characteristics

Inherited at birth, biological characteristics provide the most fundamental type of diversity within the human species (although humans are, of course, more similar to each other than to members of other species). A review of basic genetics demonstrates this point, showing how the 23 chromosomes inherited from each parent have genes that carry a mixture of traits from previous generations. Through one's genetic inheritance, several externally visible characteristics are given to individuals that distinguish them from others:

1. *Race*—People inherit externally visible, racially related characteristics such as hair texture; head, nose, and eye shape; stature; and skin color. Other racially related characteristics, such as blood type and certain kinds of food intolerance, are also inherited but are not visible. While racially related characteristics generally do create visible differences between people, and hence can be used to group people into racial categories, there is no scientifically respectable evidence to link racial differences to genetically caused significant behavioral differences or abilities. Indeed, scientists increasingly question the concept of race as a meaningful biological concept, since interbreeding has eliminated whatever traces of "pure" racial differences may have existed in the past. A racial continuum rather than discrete racial groups is a more accurate way of looking at current racial realities.

2. *Gender*—Human gender differences also consist of those that are visible, such as external genitalia and secondary sex characteristics, and those that are not visible, such as differences in growth rates. As with race, there is little evidence to support assertions of genetically determined significant behavioral differences or capability, other than the female's ability to bear and nurse children and the male's more extensive musculature.

3. *Age*—Each person's genetic inheritance includes an aging "clock" that determines the rate at which aging processes occur. There is considerable variation in this rate. From birth to death, the human organism undergoes maturational and degenerative processes. These affect behavioral capacity, although social arrangements and definitions can greatly exaggerate the relationship between behavioral capacity and chronological age.

4. *Physical appearance; physical and mental ability*—People vary considerably in appearance features, such as hair and eye color, facial appearance, stature, and so on. They also vary with respect to mental and physical ability along a continuum ranging from extreme handicap (mental retardation, severe palsy, profound

deafness, total blindness, etc.) to exceptional gifts (creativity, high intelligence, good physical coordination, etc.).

In addition to genetically inherited visible characteristics, people vary with respect to nonvisible characteristics. People's circulatory and other systems vary in size and capacity with relatively little effect on behavior in most cases. However, people also vary in their ability to tolerate stresses of various kinds, and organisms have distinctive responses to stressful conditions. These differences seem to be important determinants of behavior under such conditions.

Although biological factors are an important source of diversity, most behavior and behavioral capacity is not genetically determined (except within broad limits). Thus, biological characteristics become most meaningful for behavior when they are elaborated through cultural role definitions related to biological diversity. Often these cultural definitions are quite far removed from biological reality. Sex role differences and differences based on racial roles assume biologically based limitations that either do not exist or are greatly exaggerated. Age, while affecting behavior, is used to create age roles that greatly distort the relationship between age and behavioral ability. Similarly, physical appearance and ability are used to create roles that often relate poorly to behavioral capacity. Social and cultural roles, then, while based on biological diversity, may function to exaggerate biological limits and to prevent the attainment of full biological potential. Examples of this are sex roles that deny men opportunities to express feelings and to nurture others, racial roles that block aspirations, and age roles that prevent the participation of youth and the elderly in productive, independent activities.

Nonbiological Characteristics

Nonbiological characteristics may also be used as a basis for grouping people. Religious affiliation is used in this way, as are sexual preference (homosexuality and heterosexuality) and socioeconomic standing (social class). A particularly significant nonbiological differentiating factor is ethnicity. While ethnicity is basically culturally defined, it is often confused with nationality, race, and even religion. However, societal definitions of diversity, whether based on biological or nonbiological criteria and regardless of their accuracy, become social reality. If Jews or Italians are defined as members of races, they will be treated as such even though neither is, in fact, a race. Similarly, if poor people are defined as unable to make rational economic choices, they will be deprived of opportunities to do so regardless of their actual abilities.

EFFECTS OF DIVERSITY ON
INDIVIDUAL DEVELOPMENT

The process and experience of individual growth and development is a function of diversity. The maturational sequence that individuals inherit genetically creates a pattern of biological and cognitive development that social conditions either reinforce and operationalize, or inhibit and frustrate. Optimal periods of development broadly affect the likelihood that full biological potential will be attained, but there is considerable flexibility in each organism's ability to be deprived and to catch up later when the deprivation is removed. Of course, the entire genetic inheritance can be altered by conditions during gestation and fetal development, and these conditions are themselves related to the culture and the social conditions in which diverse groups exist.

The Life Cycle

Human growth and development have traditionally been viewed in the context of the life cycle. This is a process by which age and related biological abilities are associated with social needs, structures, and processes. The life cycle is essentially defined by periods with chronological age boundaries that bring together social expectations, resources to help fulfill them, and obstacles to their fulfillment. In western industrialized societies, there have been a number of influential theories positing life cycle stages, age-defined periods during which certain social expectations are realized. At each stage, certain resources—biological, cultural, and social—are available. For example, in infancy (a chronologically defined period), developing a sense of basic trust has been posited as the major social expectation. There are biological resources (physical dependency and certain clinging responses), cultural resources (adults caring about and loving infants), and social resources (the family). However, there may also be biological, cultural, and social obstacles that make attaining the social expectation problematic. The infant may be ill and need surgical procedures that may remove him or her from a stable, loving environment, or the infant may be unwanted and either abandoned or abused.

Even in conceptions of the life cycle built around stages, a particular individual's progression may be far from typical. Yet people do grow and develop into adequately functioning human beings in spite of atypical experiences. In addition, comparative anthropological and other research has made it clear that the stage theories western industrial societies take for granted are not accepted in many other societies. In the latter, the whole developmental experience may be conceptualized and hence structured in very different ways. Again, however, people grow into functioning human beings.

The life cycle, then, seems to be a particular society's way of structuring both the tasks that must be accomplished in that society (the social expectations) and the resources available to prepare people to accomplish them. Societies also face some common as well as some different obstacles to the fulfillment of social expectations, which also become part of the conception of the life cycle. The fact that the biological capacity of an individual is so basic to his or her ability to act and to meet social expectations explains why the life cycle is tied in some way to chronological age in all societies.

Even within one society, and especially one as pluralistic as our own, the way in which the life cycle is conceptualized varies considerably between diverse groups. The definition of significant biological characteristics and capacities, and of desirable values, social skills, and knowledge, is different for different groups. Some emphasize certain physical features, such as stature and speech fluency, while others do not. Some emphasize individual achievement; others value cultural awareness and generational respect. Some expect group members to remain within a defined geographical area; others expect their members to move at will.

The significant group contexts and ritualized activities that mark movement through the life cycle also differ among diverse groups. In this sense, human growth and development are different experiences for members of different groups in terms of cultural learning, social structures encountered, learned ways of dealing with people and situations, access to resources, and learned ways of using resources. For example, children raised in culturally or economically created ghettos frequently have little contact with formal organizations, and learn to be suspicious of those they do encounter. This limits their ability to use the many societal resources that are provided in such organizational structures. These differences take place within the broadly defined basic needs of the organism for sustenance, nurturance, socialization, and protection.

Three group contexts are of particular importance in defining social expectations and creating resources and/or obstacles for diverse groups throughout the life cycle. The significance of the *family and kin* as agents of socialization, sources of interpersonal relationships, and sources of support varies between groups. There is also a variety of alternative family-like structures that some groups use, such as friendship and lover networks among gay and lesbian people. Differences exist in the use of indigenous self-help networks and formal organizations. Some groups strongly value interpersonal and self-help relationships, and are suspicious of formal organizations, seeing them as arbitrary, impersonal, and demeaning. This is especially true where there are major value, behavior, and language differences, such as often exist between ethnic groups and welfare structures. Mexican Americans, for instance, have different norms than do Anglos in defining the importance of the family and kin networks, along with appropriate patterns of interaction between family members. These may interfere with welfare regulations that focus on financial data rather than social patterns and cultural beliefs. Where such differences are less, as between middle-income women and the public schools or elderly whites and social security offices, relationships with formal organizations are likely to generate less conflict and miscommunication, and thus be seen as more acceptable and useful.

Life cycle experiences are also shaped by the relationships that diverse group members have with *social institutions.* For example, migration is a common fact of life for groups that experience economic and social oppression, discrimination, and exploitation. Such migration often imposes strains on group members that interfere with the group's usual types of parenting, family relationships, socialization processes, and interaction with outsiders. Children may be left on their own or in the care of other children while parents work or seek resources. Traditional authority patterns between parents and children as well as between spouses may be disrupted. While diverse groups are generally very resourceful in adapting to such strains, age-related developmental roles may be altered, compressed, or even eliminated in the process.

The *economic realities* that many diverse groups face also have an impact on role relationships, expectations, and performance throughout the life cycle. Poverty inevitably affects the availability of resources for nurturing and the achievement of biological potential. It erodes self-confidence and often forces others to assume roles for which they are barely prepared in developmental terms, either physically (such as having to work) or emotionally (having to nurture others, for example). Poverty and other forms of oppression and exploitation experienced also tend to create social isolation, so group members do not learn skills needed to participate effectively in the formal organizations through which decisions are made and resources are delivered. The result in many cases is greatly reduced social power.

Personality Development
The different ways in which diverse group members experience the life cycle naturally affect personality development. Different groups have different cultural definitions of appropriate and desirable

personality characteristics, and these are transmitted and reinforced through the life cycle. Every group seeks to preserve its boundaries and socialize its members to a strong group identity, although they vary in the degree to which they also incorporate outside values. Women experience strong socialization about male as well as female roles, while American Indians may be socialized more exclusively to their own group's values. In situations where diverse groups are subject to powerful external hostility and imposed disadvantage, their members may experience considerable conflict as they struggle with a self-concept partially reinforced and partially denigrated. Different groups have different ways of coping with such difficulties, so personality characteristics that relate to individual identity, development of a sense of well-being, patterns of relating to others, and strategies for dealing with situations in productive ways will vary. Among many Blacks, for example, pride has replaced internalized feelings of inferiority. This has facilitated active life direction rather than reactions to ascribed roles, as well as greater readiness to organize as a group to resist exploitation and disadvantage.

Erratic socialization, role demands that strain the individual's ability to function, incorporating definitions of minority standing imposed by majority groups, and social isolation may all result from social structural arrangements defined by the dominant groups in society. These are not patterns of functioning preferred by the nondominant groups. The life cycle for members of these groups, while different from the usual stereotyped conceptions of "normal," still functions to promote individual development and the performance of needed activities in the group. Indeed, the strategies of adaptation that members of diverse groups develop reflect the strength frequently developed by people who experience institutionalized disadvantage in order to survive and thrive. Social workers must be able to recognize and mobilize these strengths, as well as to respect the anger and hostility that may result from the destructive and often demeaning experiences that members of diverse groups undergo within many of the structures of society. As in all of social work, the strengths must be used fully and the potentially dysfunctional behaviors rechanneled, while the worker must try, at the same time, to change the systems that breed frustration and hostility.

EFFECTS OF DIVERSITY ON INSTITUTIONAL ARRANGEMENTS

The preceding sections of this chapter have concentrated on the definition of human diversity, the biological, cultural, and social bases of it, and socialization processes that perpetuate it. This section turns to an analysis of the social structural arrangements that impact on diverse groups. A three-part framework is used: 1) social institutions and their interactive effects on human diversity; 2) social differentiation and stratification as these social processes relate to diversity; and 3) social control mechanisms that impact on human diversity.

Social Institutions and Their Interactive Effects

The family socializes people to values and roles, both of which are basic to the development of functional self-concepts and patterns of interacting with others. Culturally diverse groups transmit and maintain their differences through such socialization. Members of many diverse groups learn how to manage their differences through family-based socialization. For generations black parents have taught their children how to survive in a predominantly white America. Other groups utilize different socializing mechanisms such as friendship groups and informal organizations. These are especially important for groups such as homosexuals and the handicapped, whose families may share societal prejudices, and who may not know appropriate norms and behaviors. The family also transmits resources and reinforces behaviors that influence the kinds of experiences its members will have in other social institutions. In this sense, the family can be a significant bridge to other social institutions and processes, although alternative primary group structures are important when the family is unable to socialize for or is hostile toward a particular group. Here the potential clash between majority and minority group values and identities is seen again, and all social institutions tend to reinforce and perpetuate majority beliefs and structures.

The ways in which families utilize resources and values influence their members' group identities and ability to modify their group memberships. The degree to which diverse group values are emphasized and the degree to which they are related to majority group values influence family members' aspirations, identifications, and behaviors. Resources may be utilized to emphasize diverse group solidarity, or to provide linkages to opportunities outside of the group. Many European ethnic groups specifically sought to reduce ethnic identities when they first arrived in this country. It was believed that this would promote social acceptance and economic success. Family resources may also be used to influence choices about entering or remaining in groups, as when family resources are used to either facilitate or prevent a battered wife's movement out of the marital situation.

The educational institution also socializes people, and transmits the knowledge and skills needed to function effectively in various social structures. The acquisition of such knowledge, values, and skills affects the ability of people to function in other social institutions, especially the economic and political institutions. Members of diverse groups need to learn somewhat different knowledge and skills in order to relate their cultural and resource situations to majority-oriented social institutions. This may not occur when educational structures are themselves dominated by majority group values, knowledge, and skills that ignore the knowledge and learning patterns used in diverse groups. Lower-class children find it difficult to relate to books that portray middle-class lifestyles, while intelligent Spanish-speaking students are often labeled as ignorant by school personnel that cannot speak their language. Educational structures that ignore the needs and existing knowledge of members of diverse groups may also generate conflicts and anxieties that interfere with self-concept development and group socialization. Subjected to ridicule because of his or her looks and speech accent, for example, the Korean American child may withdraw socially and internalize a negative self-concept.

While majority-dominated educational systems can be obstacles to the functioning of diverse group members, they can also facilitate changes in majority-minority group relations. Learning knowledge, values, and skills useful in the social institutions and social organizations of the larger society allows diverse group members to function effectively within them. These institutions and organizations can then be used to achieve societal change and to obtain resources that are needed to gain more power or reduce social disadvantages related to minority group standing.

The economic, political, and religious social institutions can be analyzed in a similar way with respect to their perpetuation of majority group power and their potential for achieving social change. The economic institution perpetuates majority-minority inequality through resource and opportunity allocation, yet offers opportunities for change through social mobility mechanisms. The political institution serves to channel access to decisionmaking opportunities so that majority and other power groups continue to control significant social policy. On the other hand, coalitions and representative decisionmaking structure may be used to at least partially redistribute power and resources. The religious institution may be used to legitimate existing social arrangements and divert pressure for change through a focus on otherworldly goals. It may also serve as a goad to greater equality of resource distribution and opportunity by reinforcing basic human values of equality and justice.

Finally, the social welfare institution has particular relevance for the institutionalization of majority-minority relationships. The effects of disadvantage based on differentiation and stratification are moderated to some degree through social welfare efforts to provide curative services. Preventive and rehabilitative efforts aim to alter social relationships that systematically disadvantage members of diverse groups in terms of their ability to develop as individuals and as actors in a social system. Thus, the social welfare institution, like the other social institutions, functions to preserve inequality and disadvantage as well as to eliminate human diversity as a basis for disadvantage.

Differentiation and Stratification

When people are grouped according to biological or cultural characteristics, social arrangements can be affected in two ways. Simple social differentiation may be based on a division of labor, whereby those with special abilities perform relevant tasks but all groups are evaluated and treated equally (this model was exemplified in the early kibbutz). A second possibility is for differentiated groups to be socially stratified, so that some groups are valued more highly than others and therefore treated in an advantaged way. This pattern is the one most commonly seen in the technologically sophisticated societies of today, including the United States. When social stratification exists, the characteristics used to assign people to diverse groups become important factors in influencing people's life experiences and opportunities.

Stratification results in the creation of majority and minority groups based on access to social power. Majority group standing may also be based on numerical superiority, but size of group is not necessarily related to access to social power. In the United States, whites are a numerical as well as a power majority group. Women, on the other hand, are a numerical majority but a power minority. In terms of effects on life experiences, access to power is far more important than sheer numbers. Numerical strength can be mobilized in order to increase the power of minority groups, but this is generally dependent on the development of a strong group identity and effective coalitions among diverse minority groups.

A system of social stratification usually results in a *social class* structure. Once established, social class becomes closely correlated with life chances, lifestyles, and experiences in the social structure.

Therefore, members of social classes come to be seen and treated as members of different groups in much the same way that members of different ethnic groups are seen and treated differentially. Social class is primarily determined by occupational, educational, and residential roles, and the prestige and income that are derived from them. While the roles upon which social classes are defined are partially achieved, diversity often functions to restrict the potential achievement of roles. Ascribed characteristics, such as race, age, sex, and ethnicity, are often used to block educational and occupational attainment. As a result, these characteristics are correlated with social class level. We have also seen how social institutions function to mediate between role allocation, achievement, and social class by gradually shaping the resources, opportunities, and expectations of members of diverse groups.

Social class can be seen as a mechanism of social and economic exploitation to the degree that its component roles are ascribed. Once class membership is attained, it directly affects economic and social experiences. Members of lower social classes have the least choice about the conditions under which they live and work. The social and other rewards they receive for their work are minimal. The limited financial rewards combine with little social recognition to create feelings of alienation, powerlessness, and lack of self-worth. A circular process results: diverse group characteristics are used to channel people into positions that are then used to determine their social class. Since members of many groups are directed into positions that are poorly valued, they get few rewards and occupy lower-class ranks. Lower-class standing, therefore, comes to be associated with diverse groups, and stereotypes are reinforced.

The impact of social class on the life experiences of people is most readily seen in terms of life chances and lifestyle. Life chances refer to access to those resources necessarily for good health and personal security. All of the commonly used measures of life chances show that the lower the social class, the less one's chances for a healthy, secure life. For example, the lower the social class the higher the incidence of mortality, illness, and crime, and the lower the incidence of adequate medical treatment, adequate housing, and proper nutrition. Lifestyle refers to the satisfaction derived from social activities, the degree of control over one's own life, and distinctive ways of performing life tasks. There are identifiable differences between social class lifestyles in terms of such measures as child rearing, marriage patterns, leisure activities, political involvement, organizational memberships, occupational stability, friendship networks, and perceived life satisfaction. Generally speaking, the lower the social class, the less the involvement in affairs outside the family, the perceived life control and satisfaction, and the feelings of security. Clearly, then, to the degree that diverse group membership is related to social class, it is a significant factor in determining life patterns and the distribution of advantages and resources.

The characteristics that a society uses to differentiate and stratify people are frequently imbued with stereotypical behaviors which, as noted above, are perpetuated through social roles and social institutions. These stereotypes form the basis for prejudicial attitudes that are then readily translated into discriminatory behavior that ignores individual uniqueness and abilities. *Prejudice and discrimination* are often built on stereotypes that emphasize seemingly dysfunctional or undesirable aspects of a type of diversity. This is, of course, a type of ethnocentrism. However, it is then difficult to break out of these negative attitudes and behaviors to identify the strengths of diversity and the individual differences that exist within a diverse group.

Prejudice and discrimination are closely related to the economic factors that underlie stratification, and are often used to justify such stratification. Diverse group members are allocated roles that exclude and exploit them. This preserves the economic and social advantages of the majority group, but leads to lifestyles for minority groups that are predictably deprived and that are then used to justify the allocation of disadvantaging roles (the process of blaming the victim). Diverse group members are increasingly seen in a dehumanized way, reinforcing prejudicial attitudes and making it increasingly easy to discriminate against them. The aged, channeled into nursing homes that emphasize their needs rather than their strengths, are easily seen as faceless room occupants waiting to die rather than individuals eager to live.

Economic and political forces may be used to discourage attempts to preserve and transmit accurate and positive knowledge about diverse groups. History books that perpetuate myths about lawless American Indians, about historical events that seemingly included no blacks, or about arts that seem to have no women artists are all cases in point. These distortions make it difficult for diverse group members to appreciate their own heritage, and work against efforts to organize for the promotion of group awareness and for the resistance of further economic and social oppression. Without such awareness and organization, there is little likelihood that the existing system of majority power will be seriously challenged.

Mechanisms of Social Control

The denigration of diverse groups resulting from socialization and prevailing social stratification structures promotes fragmentation within and between these groups. Homosexuals, for example, are frequently too unsure of their own strengths and too frightened of retribution to organize on their own behalf. Lack of internal organization then makes it difficult to band together with other groups, such as feminists, who share similar problems (in this example, the effects of sexism). Individaul members of denigrated groups are controlled because they see themselves as inadequate and undesirable, so that they never even try for certain goals—college, child rearing, applying for a job, and so on. The fear of organizing together and the perception of self as inadequate promote the cooptation of diverse group members by majority groups, and this further fragments the diverse group. The token woman, black, Asian American, or senior citizen may be very reluctant to jeopardize his or her advantaged position by advocating for his or her group. The presence of such people is then used to demonstrate that the groups in question are not victims of discrimination.

Social control of diverse groups is further sought through societal models of group relationships that emphasize the melting pot rather than pluralism. Pluralism is said to generate conflict, while the melting pot is presented as resulting in harmony through the melding of groups into one equal whole. However, minority groups are less able to insure the inclusion in this whole of what they consider to be essential, so their sense of history and identity may be greatly reduced. Conflict has developed when diverse groups have resisted attempts to forcibly amalgamate and assimilate them and insisted instead on a pluralistic model of intergroup relations (enforced through a series of civil rights efforts, especially by women and blacks). This suggests that some basic economic and political changes in the existing social structures will be needed before pluralistic models are accepted and the integrity of diverse groups assured.

Even pluralism, however, will not solve the conflict generated by the rise of meritocracies and the single-minded devotion to bureaucracies. Diverse cultural groups have a variety of strategies by which people interact and a variety of priorities that direct behavior. This diversity is poorly accommodated in systems that use evaluative criteria that are unrelated to cultural values. Higher educational degrees, for example, are only one type of indicator of competence, in part because social institutions have functioned to exclude diverse group members from programs of higher education. Bureaucratic procedures that group members see being imposed on them for social control purposes may also violate group values and behavior. The poor have frequently expressed this view with respect to ways in which income maintenance and social service programs are delivered.

PROFESSIONAL RESPONSES TO DIVERSITY

It has often been noted that the social welfare institution functions in part as an agent of social control, and earlier in this chapter the ethical problems this creates for social workers were mentioned. There has traditionally been very limited input into decisionmaking about social welfare services and service delivery strategies from members of diverse groups, who would suggest service delivery structures related to the reality of their lives rather than to psycho-dynamic models or existing service networks. As a result, many needs of various diverse groups are being met ineffectively. Many services are perceived as irrelevant by those who need help; stereotypes about diverse groups are being perpetuated; service delivery systems are often perceived as demeaning and destructive of personal, group, and cultural integrity; and helping systems often conflict with and even destroy existing helping networks that are more suitable to the needs and wishes of members of diverse groups.

For the above reasons, social welfare structures can easily become dysfunctional for members of diverse groups. When this occurs, they function as yet further ways in which majority groups exploit and oppress minority groups. For example, the creation of programs without involving users may be seen as a way of using societal resources to provide jobs for groups that have access to them rather than to help those who are most disadvantaged. As long as societal definitions of need primarily reflect majority group values and perceived realities, and as long as services are developed to meet needs that are defined in this way, the social welfare institution will impede, at least in part, the goal attainment of members of diverse groups. The same is true when services are based on strategies for meeting needs that are not at least partially derived from input by those who will use or be most affected by them.

Social work as a profession is inevitably affected by its social welfare context, but can nevertheless develop interventive strategies that acknowledge and utilize human diversity. Professional ethics support efforts to involve client groups in service planning and delivery. Respect for individual, group, and cultural differences is also indicated, as is the understanding that "starting where the client is" includes the existing social and cultural environment. As practitioners assess life goals and resources available to attain them, the differences between diverse groups and among members of single group need to be part of service planning. The resources that exist within different groups need to be incorporated into interventive plans, with additional resources developed being consistent with and supportive of existing group resources.

Social change strategies must be built on knowledge about diverse groups, rather than on stereotypes that often distort perceptions of needs and resources. This knowledge strengthens an understanding of the ways in which social institutions and formal organizations can be sources of prejudice, discrimination, oppression, and exploitation. Understanding the operation of social institutions and formal organizations supports special efforts to change them in order to reduce the disadvantage that many diverse groups experience within and because of them. Finally, there must be unequivocal support for the value of human diversity. The strengths that persons bring with them as a result of their genetic, cultural, and social backgrounds are the basic resources that social workers use in practice. To ignore or undermine these strengths is to waste resources as well as to violate the integrity of each unique individual.

ISSUES OF CURRICULUM IMPLEMENTATION

Implementing a human behavior and the social environment approach like the one in this chapter requires that a wide range of social and biological science content be covered, and that it be integrated and placed within a distinctively social work frame of reference that explicates its practice utility. This section will suggest ways of assessing necessary content and strategies for sequencing, integrating, and focusing this content so that it relates to the needs of baccalaureate social work practitioners.

Assessing Necessary Content

Most curriculums have some content in several areas relevant to the development of a human diversity framework, and the extent and orientation of this content should be carefully assessed. These areas include the following:

1. *Content about human difference*—Content regarding the biological bases of difference as well as the cultural and lifestyle differences that groups develop as they seek to accomplish life goals is relevant, especially if presented in an objective framework of cultural, lifestyle, and biological relativity. Such content may be covered in social work, biology, psychology, sociology, history, and anthropology courses, among others.
2. *Content about the effects of human difference on behavior and life experiences*—Substantive content about the variations in behavior that characterize different groups is useful, especially if

analyzed to show how such behavior is a response to predictable life cycle needs as well as needs and objectives unique to a particular group. The degree to which various types of behavior are or are not genetically programmed or otherwise affected by biological factors is also useful content. Courses in social work, biology, history, sociology, anthropology, foreign language, and English literature frequently include aspects of this content.

3. *Content about the effects of social institutions on behavior and life experiences*—Understanding the differential impact of social institutions on various groups, and the ways in which power is used to preserve privilege through social institutions is very relevant. Courses that provide a sound foundation in understanding the structure of social institutions as well as their interrelationships are especially helpful. This content is frequently taught in social work, sociology, political science, and economics courses.

4. *Human development content*—The degree to which teaching in the area of human development, especially life cycle experiences and personality development, reflects diverse cultural, biological, and lifestyle experiences is important to assess. This content is often taught in social work, psychology, education, human development, and sociology courses.

5. *The learning environment*—The impact of the total learning environment on the recognition and valuing of human diversity needs to be examined. Diversity among faculty and students, exposure to diversity in the community, and the degree to which program and college or university procedures facilitate the activities of diverse groups are all areas to explore.

Focusing on Practice

As with any practice-related curriculum content, the human behavior and the social environment framework described in this chapter must permeate the entire curriculum. Even if there are one or more courses that specifically address human behavior and the social environment content, they cannot stand alone; they must be reinforced by content throughout the social work curriculum and learning environment.

For the purpose of examining strategies for building a sequential, cumulative, integrated curriculum, the curriculum can be divided into four parts.

Supporting Courses. These are courses required by the social work program that teach essential foundation content but that are outside of the social work program. If the assessment of existing content results in the identification of content in supporting courses that lays the foundation for and reinforces the conception of human behavior and the social environment within a human diversity framework proposed here, the major task is making that content explicit. Negotiations with the faculty of the appropriate courses should help them understand the relevance of the specified content to the human diversity framework being sought. Making them aware of the importance of their course content to the social work program ought to assure its consistent presentation each semester. It should also enable faculty to reinforce the linkages between the various parts of the content for students and, as far as possible, to relating it to social work (or allow students to do so through course papers or other projects).

Human Behavior and the Social Environment Courses. If assessment reveals that there is little explicit recognition of human diversity in foundation course content and the whole educational milieu, the social work program has to take action to insure such content. Hopefully, program faculty would meet with faculty who teach foundation courses to discuss the desirability of such content. This approach has the added benefit of strengthening linkages between social work and other programs/departments. If such discussions are not successful, as a last resort, the social work faculty may need to teach the content themselves, in which case the materials in this chapter should be helpful in developing a course or courses. If, on the other hand, assessment reveals a considerable amount of relevant content in supporting courses, the program has one primary task, and two options for accomplishing it. The task is to insure that the content is integrated into a coherent, practice-related human development and the social environment framework. This can be done either through the use of all the social work courses, or by having a social work course specifically for this purpose that is then reinforced by all the other social work courses.

Whichever alternative is selected, the curriculum must address the content in an explicit, carefully sequenced, and integrated way. The conceptual aspects of the framework must be learned before the analytical framework itself. Mastery of the framework must in turn precede attempts to use it to understand human development experiences and the operation of the social environment. Hopefully, this chapter will be helpful in identifying major concepts, the way they can be used to develop an analytical framework, and the way the framework can be used to understand social situations.

Social Work Courses. Each course in the social work program must strengthen the student's ability to understand human behavior and the social environment in a human diversity framework. Courses that address history need to include the experiences and contributions of diverse groups. Understanding social welfare as an institution must include its operation with respect to identifying and meeting the needs of different groups. Social policy and research should also relate to strategies for communicating with and involving many different kinds of groups in need assessment, decisionmaking, and evaluation. Finally, practice must be seen as skill that utilizes the rich resources of different groups of people, building on an ethical stance that values and respects diversity.

The Learning Environment. Generating a human development and the social environment framework built around human diversity does not occur only in the classroom. Students should be made aware of their own differences, and those of the faculty and fellow students. They must see them as an integral part of themselves and others, and recognize how they affect behavior. They should also see policies and procedures that provide the resources needed if all kinds of people in the program are to succeed. These include planning for the physically handicapped, alternate teaching and testing procedures for those from different cultural backgrounds if needed, an absence of implied or overt denigration of certain groups, and models of cooperative goal attainment between members of different groups. A program that ignores the diversity within its own environment in its daily functioning teaches students that classroom learning about diversity has no meaning and undermines the basic commitment to the relationships between knowledge, values, and skills that exists in baccalaureate professional social work practice and education.

CONCLUSION

Human development occurs through the interplay of biological, cultural, and social forces. The interaction of these forces is constantly changing as social expectations and resources change through the life cycle, and as group memberships change. Because human development is so heavily dependent on socialization, the diverse groups to which people belong are critical to their growth experiences. The processes by which people are allocated to or choose groups underlie group experiences. These experiences in turn are related to the possession of diverse biological and cultural characteristics that are used to create social arrangements that structure life chances and lifestyles. These experiences also impact on the ability of people to develop secure self-identities and group affiliations that then support functional behavior toward the attainment of life goals. An understanding of the interaction of people, their diverse group contexts, and the social institutions and formal organizations of society is fundamental to social work practice that respects and builds on existing human and social resources.

NOTES

1. This is a long-standing, ongoing issue in social science research, and has an extensive relevant literature. A current examination of it within a social work context may be found in Ramón Valle and Lydia Mendoza, *The Elderly Latino* (San Diego: Campanile Press, 1978).

2. Many research questions have become clouded by this problem, the effects of school desegregation being a recent example. Another even more current example is research on child care and family behavior, ably addressed in Alison Clarke-Stewart, *Child Care in the Family* (New York: Academic Press, 1978), especially in the preface and Chapters I and IV.

3. The terminology used to refer to the multiplicity of racial and ethnic groups in the United States is flexible, constantly changing, and subject to regional variations. Four major generic terms will be used in this chapter. "Blacks" refers to Black Americans of African descent. "Native Americans" refers to American Indians, Eskimos, and Hawaiians. "Asian Americans" refers to Americans of Asian descent, including Japanese Americans, Chinese Americans, Philippine Americans, Thai Americans, and Vietnamese Americans. "Hispanic" (an Eastern term) and "Latino" (a Western term) refer to Americans with Spanish cultural roots, including Puerto Ricans, Mexican Americans (Chicanos), and Cuban Americans. Other racial and ethnic groups will be individually referred to, such as Italian Americans.

4. In referring to groups differentiated on the basis of sexual or affectional preference, the generic terms used in this chapter are heterosexual and homosexual. More specifically, homosexual men are called gays and homosexual women are called lesbians.

5. Norton, Delores, ed., *The Dual Perspective: Inclusion of Ethnic Minority Content in the Social Work Curriculum* (New York: Council on Social Work Education, 1978).

ANNOTATED BIBLIOGRAPHY

These references are intended primarily for the use of faculty members developing course content in areas discussed in this chapter, although many works listed here may also be useful to students. References are provided that are unusually helpful in developing an appropriate analytical framework, or that provide substantive and affective knowledge about various types of diversity.

This is a very selective bibliography that attempts to identify some seminal works that can then be used to obtain other references.

Foundation References

The one work that comes closest to capturing the approach discussed in this chapter is Myrtle Reul, *Territorial Boundaries of Rural Poverty* (E. Lansing, Mich.: Michigan State University, 1974). It attempts to combine an analytical framework for understanding human behavior and the social environment within a human diversity perspective with first-person accounts of the life experiences of members of various diverse groups. It specifically covers the practice implications of the theory and first-person accounts discussed in the book. Since this book is not commonly known or used, those persons having difficulty locating it may want to order directly from the publisher: Bulletin Office, Box 231, Michigan State University, East Lansing, Michigan 48824. The cost is $6.50 per copy, including postage.

Two useful books that deal with the relationship between biological and social behavior, a topic of fundamental importance for understanding human development and human diversity, are Allen Mazur and Leon Robertson, *Biology and Social Behavior* (New York: Free Press, 1972); and Vernon Reynolds, *The Biology of Human Behavior* (San Francisco: W.H. Freeman, 1976).

The best example of a text specifically written for students on human behavior and the social environment courses is Anderson and Carter, *Human Behavior in the Social Environment*, rev. ed. (Chicago: Aldine, 1978).

REFERENCES

Banks, James A. *Teaching Strategies for Ethnic Studies*. Boston: Allyn and Bacon, 1975.

Berkowitz, Monroe. *Public Policy Toward Disability*. New York: Praeger, 1976.

Bell, Allan P., and Martin S. Weinbert. *Homosexualities: A Study of Diversity Among Men and Women*. New York: Simon and Schuster, 1978.

Billingsley, Andrew. *Black Families in White America*. Englewood Cliffs, N.J.: Prentice-Hall, 1968.

Brown, Howard. *Familiar Faces, Hidden Lives*. New York: Harcourt, Brace, Jovanovich, 1976.

Brown, Rita Mae. *Rubyfruit Jungle*. New York: Bantam Books, 1977.

Cafferty, Pastora San Juan, and Leon Chestang, eds. *The Diverse Society: Implications for Social Policy*. Washington, D.C.: National Association of Social Workers, 1976.

Chesler, Phyllis. *About Men*. New York: Simon and Schuster, 1978.

Clarke-Stewart, Alison. *Child Care in The Family*. New York: Academic Press, 1978.

Cohen, Shirley. *Special People*. Englewood Cliffs, N.J.: Prentice-Hall, 1977.

Coser, Lewis. *The Functions of Social Conflict*. Glencoe, Ill.: Free Press, 1956.

David, Deborah, and Robert Brannon, eds. *The Forty-Nine Percent Majority: The Male Sex Role.* Reading, Mass.: Addison-Wesley, 1976.

Duberman, Lucile. *Social Inequality: Class and Caste in America.* Philadelphia: J. Lippincott, 1976.

Fanon, Franz. *Wretched of the Earth.* New York: Grove Press, 1966.

Goffman, Erving. *Stigma.* Englewood Cliffs, N.J.: Prentice-Hall, 1963.

Goodman, Bernice. *The Lesbian: A Celebration of Difference.* New York: Out and Out Books, 1977.

Howard, Jane. *A Different Woman.* New York: E.P. Dutton, 1973.

Kalish, Richard. *Late Adulthood.* Belmont, Calif.: Wadsworth, 1975.

Knowles, Louis, and Kenneth Prewitt, eds. *Institutional Racism in America.* Englewood Cliffs, N.J.: Prentice-Hall, 1970.

Lerner, Gerda, ed. *Black Women in White America.* New York: Vintage, 1972.

Lidz, Theodore. *The Person.* New York: Basic Books, 1968.

Marinelli, Robert, and Arthur E. Dell Orto, eds. *The Psychological and Social Impact of Physical Disability.* New York: Springer Publishing, 1977.

Norton, Dolores G., ed. *The Dual Perspective.* New York: Council on Social Work Education, 1978.

Rothman, Jack. *Issues in Race and Ethnic Relations.* Itasca, Ill.: F.E. Peacock, 1977.

Sheehan, Susan. *Welfare Mother.* New York: Saturday Review Press, 1975.

Silverstein, Charles. *A Family Matter.* New York: McGraw-Hill, 1977.

Somerville, Rose. *Intimate Relationships.* Englewood Cliffs, N.J.: Prentice-Hall, 1975.

Troll, Lillian. *Early and Middle Adulthood.*, Belmont, Calif.: Wadsworth, 1975.

U.S. Department of Commerce. *Social Indicators 1976.* Washington, D.C.: U.S. Government Printing Office, 1977, stock no. 041-001-00156-5.

Valle, Ramón, and Lydia Mendoza. *The Elderly Latino.* San Diego: Campanile Press, 1978. This is one of a series looking at aging in various racial and ethnic contexts, with particular relevance to social work. The other works in the series are: Frank Dukepoo, *The Elderly American Indian*; E. Percil Stanford, *The Elder Black*; Eva Cheng, *The Elder Chinese*; Wesley H. Ishikawa, *The Elder Guamian*; Karen C. Ishizuka, *The Elder Japanese*; Roberta Peterson, *The Elder Philippino*; Wesley H. Ishikawa, *The Elder Samoan.*

van den Berghe, Pierre. *Age and Sex in Human Societies: A Bio-Social Perspective.* Belmont, Calif.: Wadsworth, 1973.

Whitehurst, Carol. *Women in America: The Oppressed Majority.* Santa Monica, Calif.: Goodyear, 1977.

Williams, Juanita H. *Psychology of Women: Behavior in a Bio-Social Context.* New York: W.W. Norton, 1977.

Chapter Eleven

Social Policy and Social Services
Winifred Bell

INTRODUCTION

Social policy and social services deal with that part of the curriculum that examines, analyzes, and evaluates social problems, social policies, and the social welfare system in their societal, historical, and organizational context. This area helps to lay the knowledge base for professional practice and contributes to the development of professonal identity and a commitment to ethical practice and social reform. It carries a particular responsibility for acquainting students with the history, values, interrelationships, and impacts of social welfare institutions, and their wide-ranging roles for social workers, especially in behalf of the vulnerable, handicapped, and powerless members of society. Teaching in this area should aim to inspire an enduring service commitment and the wish to become part of the continuing effort to bring about the reforms necessary to realize social justice. This chapter will explore curriculum design and content in the area of social policy and social services that help achieve this teaching goal.

Understanding individuals within their situation requires knowledge of the economic, political, and normative forces that shape the social structure, and an awareness of their differential impact on and perception by different socioeconomic classes and ethnic, racial, religious, age, and sex groups in the population. It is particularly important for students to understand the nature, dynamics, and contradictions of the American system, the ways it falls short of ideal societal values, and what it owes to diversity. This understanding is essential if they are to respond sensitively and realistically to the hurts, perceptions, and potentials of the many different individuals and groups they will encounter in practice.

Knowledge of where the society has been and where it appears to be going is equally relevant to competent social work practice, for both what has happened and what people yearn for or fear influence their present behavior. Similarly, knowing the history and hopes of member groups in the population and how they differ and coincide, sheds light on their current situation, needs, and problem-solving potentials and preferences.

Competent problem assessment and planning requires the skill to distinguish between the types of situations. The first type is one that service users and social workers can directly affect through their own collaborative efforts or with the help of other community services. The second type of situation is one that will require procedural, regulatory, or legal changes, or the creation of new community resources. Thus, skill in recognizing gaps in services or in documenting adverse organizational and policy impacts on people is as fundamental to good practice as collecting and analyzing facts regarding intrafamilial patterns and tensions.

ISSUES OF CURRICULUM DESIGN

Because of the breadth of knowledge encompassed by the social policy and social services segment of the curriculum, there is a temptation to organize broad survey courses or to deal with principles at a very high level of generalization. While the material may be "covered" in this manner, it provides little opportunity for inexperienced students to make meaningful connections between principle and practice or between the past and the present. Even with the more bridging analytic approach, there is sometimes greater emphasis on the *models* of analysis than on the *goals* of analysis, as though the educational mission were simply to develop mental agility. To guard against these pitfalls, it helps to keep in mind that the knowledge base and systematic ways of organizing knowledge form only one part of the whole. Unless students are actively involved in making connections between the constraints that societal, institutional, program, and practice shortcomings impose on people in their daily lives, the knowledge base, however rich, will be of little use in practice.

Thus, it is not sufficient to know the problems of society. Students also need the desire to bring about reform and the practice skill and knowledge necessary to aid this process. To this end, the connections between principle and practice should be explicit. Students should learn, for instance, that they are indeed participating in the policy-making process in their society when they carry out intake functions, treat people with respect or indifference, use community social services appropriately and energetically in behalf of service consumers or fail to do so, and carry out agency reporting functions carefully or carelessly.

In other words, students should learn to reason both inductively and deductively. Not only are the same responses to situations apparent in many individuals and groups, but also the plight of a given individual or group is generally mirrored in others. For every service user who is adversely affected by some policy or regulation or who encounters obstacles in securing services because of their fragmentation, complexity, location, or delivery style, there are usually many others with similar experiences. When students are taught to examine the whole problem in its various manifestations, to differentiate between the exogenous and endogenous forces that generate and sustain it, and to develop skills in dealing with both aspects, they may more often avoid two problems that plague professionals in practice. The first is often called "bureaucratic burnout," which is the temptation, when institutional gaps or inadequacies cause too much frustration, to lose service commitment and begin blaming the victim. The other problem is an inclination on the part of the professional to deal with one person, group, or situation at a time without seeing the broader policy and organizational implications that sometimes only insiders are in the position to correct or to bring to the attention of those who can do so.

Social policy and social service courses that keep the interface of persons and institutions, persons and the social structure, and persons and their situation in constant focus help to build bridges that can only influence practice and morale for the better. Even when reform cannot be effected in time to relieve the individual condition, professionals and service users can take the first and essential step toward reform by accurately documenting their adverse experiences and channelling reports to decisionmakers. Professionals are more apt to take this step when the educational model to which they were exposed incorporated it as a normal and intrinsic part of good practice.

In their courses, students should learn about the accomplishments and favorable impacts of social welfare programs and policies as well as their faults. It is by keeping the virtues and shortcomings in perspective and developing insight into the genesis of each that beginning professionals become realistically involved in change efforts.

The ability to evaluate their own practice will be heightened as students are exposed to the literature showing how the mastery of agency policies and procedures directly affects the quality of service. This is especially apparent in large public agencies where beginning professionals are most likely to be employed. Often, one of their first experiences will be an encounter with complex regulations that they must learn reasonably well to be at all helpful to either the agency or service users. While university education should not substitute for in-service training or take over that mission, university courses can instill a respect for "hard facts" and familiarize students with basic policy information. This includes the broad characteristics and missions of state plans and agency manuals, and sources of information on public and voluntary services at the local, state, and federal levels. Students must be able to anticipate the reality pressures of agency life and methods of coping with them effectively. In this connection, it is helpful to collect accounts of specific workers who have made a difference for service users by careful study of agency manuals and even heroic insistence on protecting the constitutional rights of families.

Oral and written assignments in social policy and social services courses are designed to improve a range of communication skills. They provide opportunities for oral group presentations that prepare students for the collaborative efforts that pervade social work practice and on which much of its strength depends. These courses also improve the ability to carry out future responsibilities for communicating clearly, accurately, and coherently with service users, supervisors, professional colleagues, public officials, and community groups. Individual written reports provide experience in preparing concise, logical analyses and interpretations. Students who have searched for illuminating studies of the impact of institutions on the people they serve will have a greater appreciation for accurate and methodical record keeping. If they have examined and evaluated annual reports from the service sector, they will be alert to the importance of asking significant questions and monitoring program effectiveness year in and year out. When they have been exposed to the delays in reform resulting from ambiguous or insufficient communication from social welfare professionals, they will be more apt to approach their letter writing, case summaries, plans for action, research assignments, and even their initial data collection tasks with a greater sense of purpose and urgency.

The relevance of social policy and social services courses for practice is especially clear in the advocacy and social action roles. Both consist of far more than impassioned pleas in behalf of service users or frenetic social protests. They require the ability and knowledge base necessary to gain a thorough mastery of the issue at hand, to approach the social agency network (or law-making body) with an expert grasp of the structure, function, and distribution of power, and to negotiate from facts with skill and reason, making appropriate use of professional organizations and other influence groups in the process. Even beginning courses can provide the opportunity to gain experience in panel discussions of public issues after well-organized study by groups of students. In addition, many colleges and universities are located in an area where attendance at legislative hearings, preparation of background papers on specific issues of legislative concern, or analysis of the decisionmaking process are feasible.

FOUNDATION CONTENT

Social work students need background knowledge of the societal forces that interact and reinforce each other to generate social problems, stratify societies, produce conflict, and order and constrain the solutions that will be acceptable and feasible at any given time or place.

Theoretical and Comparative Courses

Theoretical and comparative courses in the social sciences are particularly germane since the systematic comparison of theories and conceptual schemes lifts students from a "lay view" to a scientific and scholarly perspective. In the process, horizons are broadened, hidden assumptions and biases are exposed and corrected, and students are introduced to some of the finest minds of our times and their patterns of reasoning. Theoretical courses illuminate how the central issues, areas of concern, and research questions shift from one social science to another and yet reflect similar societal values. They present the university as a forum for the lively and enlightened clash of ideas, and develop the ability of students to participate in this discourse. They also provide organizing principles for ordering the myriad of facts and perspectives that students are expected to accumulate, comprehend, and integrate.

A comparative approach can be provided either by studying with scholars of different ideologies and central concerns or by being exposed to theoretical courses in a variety of social sciences. There is particular merit in courses that are designed to compare and assess belief systems and patterned social responses in different societies or in various ethnic and racial groups. These systems and responses may concern kinship patterns, socialization patterns, achievement values, political ideologies and participation, religious beliefs, women's roles, treatment of minorities, and economic organization. Such courses help students gain a perspective on their own life experiences and usually illuminate more clearly than others the remaining areas of ignorance and ambiguity. By bringing the role of values into sharper focus, they help students to differentiate more easily and surely between fact and assumption. Liberal education and foundation courses, in other words, are expected to help students better understand their complex world, to stimulate their critical faculties, and to enhance their tolerance for ambiguity.

Setting Priorities

Some social science theories, modes of analysis, and subject areas may be more relevant than others for social workers. However, before considering priorities, it should be kept in mind that at most colleges and universities students are drawn to the "great teachers" who irrespective of their discipline have the ability to open windows on the world and to catch students up in the excitement of learning. In the best sense of the term, such teachers become significant role models whose contribution to learning far surpasses the importance of their discipline as a foundation for social work. It should also be recognized that the strength of the various social science faculties differs from one campus to another, and this too should influence faculty advising and the setting of priorities.

All other factors being equal, most social service and social policy faculty probably agree that sociology, economics, and political science are all of great importance to social workers. Within these broad rubrics, however, there are still many alternatives. In guiding students through the maze, faculty would do well to identify those social science theories that most usefully underpin and reinforce the specific goals and objectives of their social work curriculum. For example, when the curriculum is specifically designed to help students understand and explore the ambiguities, conflicts, contradictions, and discrimination in their society, few sociological theories are so helpful as functional analysis. More specifically, Merton's paradigm for manifest and latent functional analysis has served as the model for some unusually insightful and influential social welfare studies. By alerting scholars to the importance of identifying and measuring the *full* range of consequences of any particular social welfare law, program, policy, or procedure on all persons, groups, and institutions it touches, Merton's work has generated remarkably realistic and useful investigations of the contradictory impacts of our major social welfare programs and their societal roles.

In a similar way, functional analysis has focused attention on the importance of examining the full span of decisionmaking—from policy formulation, interpretation, and regulation to discrete implementing procedures at the grass-roots level—before arriving at conclusions about the "net balance" of consequences. As scholars using this approach have learned, what appears to be a most promising reform can turn out—for predictable groups—to be just another reinforcement of a discriminatory social structure that social workers have supported, even if unknowingly.

Studying the theory and using the paradigm, in other words, provides insight into the nature of the society and its social structure and value system. It also pinpoints the precise mechanisms used in given instances to support the status quo and to defeat reform efforts. This information in turn guides the way toward more realistic and effective reform efforts. When students see the entire sweep from theory-based research through reform, the very demanding and disciplined work required for professionals at each stage, and the many different professional roles involved in the process, only a felicitous influence on their development as professionals can result.

In identifying foundation courses that will be most useful, the important goal to keep in mind, as illustrated above, is to help students to secure a logical underpinning of social science knowledge for their particular social work curriculum. The interrelationship of theory and practice must be understood and integrated to help students succeed in their future professional roles. With crowded schedules, students cannot possibly study all that would be useful, but at the very least, faculty advisors should be guided by the idea that a broad theoretical and comparative base in the social sciences is important to social workers.

Economics Courses

As far as economics is concerned, some faculties will feel that it is the most crucial social science base if students are to understand the relationship between social values, social policy, and the distribution of economic resources and opportunities. To make effective linkages with practice and to be prepared to provide realistic help to families, students should know how the economic system functions and how it impacts on different groups in the population at various stages in business cycles. To this end students should learn about the distribution of wealth and income and employment and unemployment, and how each is measured. They should know about the various schools of economic thought on the relationship between unemployment and inflation, the implications and problems of the tax system, and the significance of the increased concentration and mobility of industry.

At a different level, but a very useful one, students are increasingly advised to study consumer economics. They will then be better prepared to help with the financial, budgetary, and credit problems encountered in practice. They will also be better informed about community resources that may be useful in solving problems in this area.

Political Science Courses

Students often arrive at college without any clear notion of the structure, respective functions, interrelationships, or decisionmaking processes of local, state, or federal governments. Both the knowledge and participatory attitudes that come from studying political science are basic to good citizenship, intelligent and informed participation in the legislative affairs of professional organizations, and social work policy and action roles. Therefore, at least an introductory course in political science would seem to be almost essential for students who arrive without a sufficient background in this area.

Needless to say, social work faculty will need a rich background in the social sciences so that they can identify and fill gaps in knowledge as needed, and make insightful applications of theory. The needs of students and faculty add up to a very large mandate to be discharged within tight schedules and severe time constraints. One feasible solution used by social work faculty is to choose texts for introductory courses in social welfare that are solidly based in social science theory. By exposing students to the economic, political, and sociological forces in their society and to the way they have shaped social welfare institutions, such texts help to fill gaps in knowledge that would otherwise only be filled by discrete courses in each of the social sciences. In the process they also serve as excellent citizen education for students from other disciplines.

SUBSTANTIVE CONTENT ON CONTEMPORARY SOCIAL WELFARE

Social Welfare in the United States

At the outset students need an introductory overview of modern social welfare in the United States. It should include:

1. how social welfare is defined, the types of activities it embraces, and how they differ depending on whether they represent responses to common human needs or individual and social problems;

2. societal forces (including values) that play a dominant role in shaping the social welfare system and allocating resources;

3. societal functions of social welfare;
4. parameters of the system, for example, organizational auspices, target groups, universal or selective eligibility conditions, provision of cash benefits and/or services, and delivery patterns;
5. social welfare expenditures, and allocations among program components, levels of government, public and private sectors;
6. patterns of financing and their implications for adequacy and equity;
7. distribution of benefits and services by income, racial, ethnic, age, marital, and work status, and residence.

Students will emerge with a better understanding if this subject is handled comparatively, so that similarities and differences in social welfare planning, programs, delivery patterns, and investment between other nations and the United States are highlighted, as well as the similarities and differences among our specific programs. This approach not only immediately shifts locally oriented students to a broader perspective, but also exposes them to values and program options that many never have encountered previously. The comparative approach also affords opportunities to introduce the many collaborative international studies, problem-solving efforts, and organizations in social welfare. This begins the process of relating students to the wide range of professional reference groups and their role in international social work and social reform.

Social Problems, Needs, and Resources
The distinction between social problems and social needs is particularly important at the undergraduate level, since many beginning professionals will work in agencies that serve "normal" people who have commonly encountered needs that they cannot satisfy through their own efforts. The future of social work, too, would appear to hold increased opportunities of this type, as community services expand to meet the long-recognized developmental and social needs of all age levels and the seriously neglected inner cities.

One educational objective should be to move students from the lay view of social problems as cancers on an otherwise healthy organism to a more scientific, theoretically sound, and realistic orientation. Many social policy and social services teachers find that the problem of poverty continues to provide the most fruitful opportunities for this type of exploration. It helps students to examine their attitudes toward the poor and to identify their hidden assumptions about the causes of poverty. It provides insights into the close bond between values, social structure, and social problems. The problem of poverty is a natural bridge to knowledge about the labor market, political and economic organization and power, and the different impacts of economic and social structure on various ethnic, racial,•age, and sex groups. In addition, it is a subject on which most college libraries have reasonably good collections, including the basic government documents and journals that social workers must rely on so heavily. These include the *Current Population Reports* from the Bureau of the Census, the *Social Security Bulletin*, and the *U.S. Statistical Abstract*. Finally, the problem of poverty provides an excellent integrating experience in weighing the role that our failure to meet the common social needs of all citizens plays in creating social problems.

Community Social Services

An important educational objective, best discharged if the subject is handled early in the curriculum, is to help students make career choices, including whether or not to enter the profession. Another objective is to lay a groundwork of knowledge for field practice. Students will gain more from their field experience if they begin with some background knowledge about 1) different fields of activity; 2) the diverse populations, situations, and problems served and to what end; 3) delivery patterns; 4) social work roles in total institutions and community-based agencies; 5) the implications of working in settings hosted by other professions; and 6) the "linkage" agencies in the social welfare network. A third major objective is to acquaint students with the history of social welfare programs and the emergence, status, and ethics of the social work profession. This promotes an identification with age-old efforts to resolve social and personal problems through social welfare interventions and begins the development of the "professional self."

While survey courses have often been developed to discharge these missions, many undergraduate faculty are finding that they are best accomplished in settings courses (e.g., child welfare, mental health, mental retardation, family counseling, aging, and corrections). These courses provide the opportunity to delve deeply into one set of problems, the needs of one age group, or one service network, and thus help to counterbalance the many survey courses confronting undergraduates everywhere. Settings courses also serve as excellent integrating tools since they provide the opportunity to examine in depth unmet needs, social problems, social policies through time, social welfare organizations, methods of intervention, and social reform. Courses of this type may be viewed as part of the social policy and social services offerings or as part of the offerings in methods of intervention. However the curriculum is organized, though, and whatever the primary mission of these courses is, their integrating mission should be kept in mind.

The Law and Social Work

Relationships between the law and social work will sometimes be handled at the undergraduate level within the course offerings of the social work program itself. Other programs will draw upon resources available in law faculties or elsewhere in the college or university. Of particular importance is knowledge of the relationship between individual and family rights and the social services, laws of evidence as they especially pertain to child neglect, abuse, or delinquency, and the litigation process as it occasionally involves social workers. In addition to the cognitive mission, it is important for students to learn what lawyers and judges expect and need from social workers and learn how to collaborate successfully with them in behalf of service users.

Complex Organizations and
Bureaucratic Skills

Finally, students need to learn about complex organizations and to develop the bureaucratic skills that help professionals capitalize on the possibilities of organizational life and neutralize its stresses and dangers, to paraphrase Robert Pruger. He further suggests that teaching in this area should aim to help young professionals establish and maintain the most creative relationship possible with their working environment. To this end he proposes that teachers focus on the following themes:[1]

1. Large organizations have both strengths and weaknesses. Despite shortcomings they do some things very well that other forms of organization cannot accomplish at all.
2. Despite claims to the contrary, change is constantly occurring in large organizations, although often very quietly and too slowly. Nonetheless, opportunities exist for people within the system to influence it for better or worse, and students should be taught to expect change as well as stability and to be sensitive to the harbingers of change.
3. "Winning or losing is fundamentally a matter of the right behavior at the right time."[2] When change is in the wind, creativity, goal-oriented behavior, and independent, sound professional judgment come into the forefront.
4. Responsible professional behavior earns respect, conserves energy,

and brings more satisfaction in large organizations than its opposite. Conversely, large organizations have highly developed skills in neutralizing emotional outbursts and walling off discontents. The likelihood of being selected for interesting special assignments as well as the chance for promotion become dimmer with each emotional outburst.

5. One of the most ubiquitous needs of professionals in large organizations is evidence that they can influence the system, instead of simply being directed by it. What is less obvious is how often the outcome is determined by the individual worker, not the organization. From their first day of work, the way professionals present themselves determines in part whether they become active participants or passive instruments. Social work education should anticipate the range of worker patterns and their predictable outcomes so that students will be better prepared for bureaucratic life.

Students must also learn to recognize the organizations that are least likely to change in significant ways, so that they can make wise decisions about where they want to work and when they want to leave one job for another. Fortunately, more attention is now being directed to systematic ways that low- and middle-level employees can help to bring about organizational change, so that it will not remain solely the prerogative of management. Finally, students should learn that, like their education, the disciplined, goal-directed mastery and use of knowledge is a powerful weapon virtually everywhere in the world of professional work. Professionals who look beyond their daily assignments, try responsibly to fit their jobs into the whole, and strive toward excellence experience greater satisfactions and have better than average chances of realizing career goals. As in other areas of life, achievement is generally directly related to effort invested.

ANALYTIC CONTENT: SELECTION OF FRAMEWORK FOR ANALYSIS

An analytic approach seeks to organize material logically and conceptually, rather than chronologically. The hope is that by highlighting major issues, interrelationships, and differences and commonalities, content will become more meaningful and students will become more actively engaged in the learning process. This approach also seeks to provide the necessary knowledge base in ways that bring about changes in attitude and develop the disciplined analytic and evaluative skills that professionals need in practice.

In planning courses in this mode, faculty face two tasks: 1) to select and organize course content so that the landmarks of social welfare are covered and the big issues addressed, and 2) to do so in ways that the framework for analysis becomes part of the lesson. As many educators have found, it is not always easy to keep these two objectives in balance, and when skeletel framework takes precedence, the sheer variety of fascinating models and the fun of playing with them can seriously limit the cognitive gains for students. This is especially true when many subject areas and levels of emergence are involved.

Experience suggests that the search for and selection of suitable frameworks for analysis is easier and more successful when a few principles are kept in mind:

1. While there is an abundant supply of analytic models reflecting different theories and serving different objectives, many undergraduate students appear to make better progress if they have repeated experience with a few of the best models that educators can locate or design, rather than being exposed to a large number.
2. A simple uncluttered framework has more merit at the undergraduate level than complex models. What this means in practical terms is that the analysis should highlight the chief parameters of programs, policies, or organizations and the big issues or processes, rather than clutter the discussions with endless details.
3. When one excellent group of theorists has developed analytic models that fit a number of subject areas covered in social policy and social services, as is true, for example, of the functional analysts, relying primarily on their models may well reinforce learning and facilitate integration. This is not to suggest that undergraduate educators should ever succumb to the temptation to grant a monopoly (as was virtually the case with Freudian models at an earlier stage in social work education), but simply to alert faculty to one approach that facilitates integration.[a]
4. To be relevant and useful, a framework for analysis should include the variables of greatest moment to social workers. This means that the wide range of efficiency, Program, Planning, and Budgeting Systems (PPBS), and input-output models, as they have been

[a]For instance, the same body of theory generated Merton's paradigm for the analysis of manifest and latent functions, Goode's model for analyzing illegitimacy, family structure, and role theory, Rothman's model for studying the closed institutions of the nineteenth century, and Piven and Cloward's model for analyzing the functions of public welfare. Similarly, Bell used Merton's paradigm in her study of Aid to Dependent Children, and Cumming used functional analysis as her model for studying the impacts of community social service networks.

developed to date, may be less insightful for many purposes than models that include such key variables as humanistic values, ethics, and reform objectives.

5. To be useful in social work education, the framework for analysis should also include consideration of what happens at the interface of social welfare institutions and the broader society and at the interface of organizations and potential as well as actual service consumers. In other words, the social welfare system is not a closed system, nor is ever likely to become one. What is required in models is a specific linkage that accounts for the interactions under study.

Finally, it should be kept in mind that designing models for analysis helps educators to fit the analysis to their style and purpose or to the special needs of students. There is no reason to rely on existing models unless they perfectly fit the need and occasion. Every model was created by someone, and if none quite fits the task at hand, this is more than sufficient reason for faculty and students to design new and more appropriate, insightful ones.

NOTES

1. Pruger, Robert, "Bureaucratic Functioning as a Social Work Skill," in Baer, Betty L., and Ronald Federico, *Educating the Baccalaureate Social Worker*; Report of the Undergraduate Social Work Curriculum Development Project (Cambridge: Ballinger, 1978), pp. 143-68.

2. Ibid., pp. 149-68.

REFERENCES AND BIBLIOGRAPHY

Abbot, Grace. *Child and the State*, 2 vols. Chicago: University of Chicago Press, 1938.

Bell, Winifred. *Aid to Dependent Children*. New York: Columbia University Press, 1965.

Bennis, W. "When to Resign." *Esquire* 77, 6 (June 1972):143-45, 188-90.

Blau, Peter M., and Marshall W. Meyer. *Bureaucracy in Modern Society*, 2nd ed. New York: Random House, 1971.

Billingsley, Andrew, and Jeanne Giovannoni. *Children of the Storm*. New York: Harcourt, Brace, Jovanovich, 1972.

Boskin, Joseph, ed. *Issues in American Society* (Encino, Calif.: Glencoe, 1978.

Brager, George, and Stephen Holloway. *Changing Human Service Organizations: Politics and Practice*. New York: Free Press, 1978.

Chessler, Phyllis. *Woman and Madness* Garden City, N.Y.: Doubleday, 1972.

Chu, F., and S. Trotter, eds. *The Madness Establishment.* New York: Grossman, 1974.

Culbert, S. *The Organization Trap and How to Get Out of It.* New York: Basic Books, 1974.

Cumming, Elaine. *Systems of Social Regulation.* New York: Atherton, 1968.

Etzioni, Amitai. *Modern Organizations.* Englewood Cliffs, N.J.: Prentice-Hall, 1964.

Etzioni, Amitai, ed. *A Sociological Reader on Complex Organizations.* New York: Holt, Rinehart, Winston, 1969.

Finch, W. "Social Workers versus Bureaucracy." *Social Work* 21, 6 (September 1976):370-76.

Gil, David. "A Systematic Approach to the Analysis of Social Policy." *Social Service Review* 44, 4:411-26.

Gil, David. *Unravelling Social Policy.* Cambridge, Mass.: Schenkman, 1973.

Gil, David. *Violence Against Children.* Cambridge, Mass.: Harvard University Press, 1970.

Gilbert, Neil, and Harry Specht. *Dimensions of Social Welfare Policy.* Englewood Cliffs, N.J.: Prentice-Hall, 1974.

Gilbert, Neil, and Harry Specht, eds. *The Emergence of Social Welfare and Social Work.* Itasca, Ill.: F.E. Peacock, 1976.

Ginsburg, Helen. *Poverty, Economics, and Society* (Boston: Little, Brown, 1972.

Goode, William J. *World Revolution and Family Patterns.* New York: Free Press, 1963.

Gordon, David, ed. *Problems in Political Economy.* Lexington, Mass.: D.C. Heath, 1971.

Green, A.D. "The Professional Social Worker in Bureaucracy." *Social Service Review* XL, 1 (March 1966):71-83.

Hanlan, A. "Counteracting the Problem of Bureaucracy in Public Welfare." *Social Work* 12, 3 (July 1967):88-95.

Hasenfeld, Yeheskel, and Richard A. English, eds. *Human Service Organizations.* Ann Arbor: University of Michigan Press, 1977.

Huber, Joan, ed. *Changing Women in a Changing Society.* Chicago: University of Chicago Press, 1973.

Huber, Joan, and H. Paul Chalfant, eds. *The Sociology of American Poverty.* Cambridge, Mass.: Schenkman, 1974.

Kadushin, Charles. *Child Welfare,* 2nd ed. New York: Macmillan, 1974.

Kahn, Alfred J., and Sheila Kamerman. *Social Services in International Perspective.* Washington, D.C.: U.S. Government Printing Office, 1977.

Kamerman, Sheila, and Alfred J. Kahn. *Social Services in the United States.* Philadelphia: Temple University Press, 1976.

Kaplan, Gerald. *Support Systems and Community Mental Health.* New York: Behavioral Publications, 1974.

Katz, Daniel, et al. *Bureaucratic Encounters: A Pilot Study in the Evaluation of Government Services.* Ann Arbor: University of Michigan, Institute for Social Research, 1975.

Mailick, S., and E.H. Van Ness. *Concepts and Issues in Administrative Behavior.* Englewood Cliffs, N.J.: Prentice-Hall, 1962.

Mazer, M. *People and Predicaments.* Cambridge: Harvard University Press, 1976.

Meltsner, A. "Bureaucratic Policy Analysts." *Policy Analysis* 1, 1 (Winter 1975):115-31.

Merton, Robert K. *Social Theory and Social Structure*, rev. ed. New York: Free Press, 1957.

Merton, Robert K., and Robert A. Nisbet. *Contemporary Social Problems*, 2nd ed. New York: Harcourt, Brace and World, 1966.

Morales, Armando, and Bradford M. Sheafor. *Social Work: A Profession of Many Faces.* Boston: Allyn and Bacon, 1977.

Morris, Robert. *Toward a Caring Society.* New York: Columbia University School of Social Work, 1974.

Offenbacher, Deborah I., and Constance H. Poster, eds. *Social Problems and Social Policy.* New York: Appleton-Century-Crofts, 1970.

Pappenfort, Donnell M., Dee Morgan Kilpatrick, and Robert W. Roberts, eds. *Child Caring: Social Policy and the Institution.* Chicago: Aldine, 1973.

Piven, Frances Fox, and Richard Cloward. *Regulating the Poor.* New York: Random House, 1971.

Platt, Anthony. *The Child Savers: The Invention of Delinquency.* Chicago: University of Chicago Press, 1969.

Pumphrey, Ralph E., and Muriel K. Pumphrey, eds. *The Heritage of Social Work.* New York: Columbia University Press, 1961.

Rivlin, Alice M. *Systematic Thinking for Social Action.* Washington, D.C.: The Brookings Institution, 1971.

Romanyshyn, John M. *Social Science and Social Welfare.* New York: Council on Social Work Education, 1974.

Rothman, David. *The Discovery of Asylum.* Boston: Little, Brown, 1971.

Ryan, William. *Blaming the Victim*, rev. ed. New York: Vintage Books, 1976.

Sidney Hillman Foundation Reprint Series. Up to 100 copies of issues are available on request without charge. This reprint series consists of an outstanding collection of public affairs articles, particularly in social and economic areas. Write for a list of reprints to the Sidney Hillman Foundation, 15 Union Square, New York, N.Y. 10003.

E.g., Ginsburg, Helen. *Needed: A National Commitment to Full Employment*, No. 40. Levison, Andrew. *The Working Class Majority*, No. 39. McKeever, Porter. *The Role of the U.S. in the World Community*, No. 38.

Special Task Force to the Secretary of Health, Education and Welfare. *Work in America.* Cambridge: MIT Press, [1974].

Sullerot, Evelyne. *Woman, Society, and Change.* New York: McGraw-Hill, 1967.

Titmuss, Richard M. *Commitment to Welfare.* London: George Allen & Unwin, 1968.

Townsend, Peter, et al. *The Fifth Social Service: Nine Fabian Essays.* London: The Fabian Society, 1970.

Townsend, Peter, et al. *Social Services for All? Eleven Fabian Essays.* London: The Fabian Society, 1968.

Weinberger, Paul E., ed. *Perspectives on Social Welfare*, 2nd ed. New York: Macmillan, 1974.

Wilensky, Harold L. *The Welfare State and Equality*. Berkeley: University of California Press, 1975.

Willie, C., and B. Brown. *Racism and Mental Health*. Pittsburgh: University of Pittsburgh Press, 1973.

Appendix
List of Participants in
the Curriculum
Development
Workshops

ALASKA

Mary Lee Nicholas
University of Alaska-Anchorage

ARIZONA

Donald F. Fausel
Arizona State University

ALABAMA

Sara Bell Allen
University of Alabama

Norman Eggleston
University of Alabama in
  Birmingham

Quinton Gresham
Talladega College

Ruffer Johnson
Tuskegee Institute

Virginia R. Jones
University of Montevallo

Jack Sellers
University of North Alabama

CALIFORNIA

Maurice B. Hamovitch
University of Southern California

A. Dean Pierce
California State University at
   Long Beach

David Shipp
San Francisco State University

Bernard Thorsell
California State U.-Northridge

COLORADO

Bruce Hall
Colorado State University

CONNECTICUT

George A. Appleby
Southern Connecticut State
   College

Donald W. Berghuis
Hartford Connecticut Board of Education
Hartford, Connecticut

Ken Byklos
Sacred Heart University

Sister Maria Joan O'Neil
St. Joseph College

Debbie Polidy
St. Joseph College

DELAWARE

Funmi Odekunle
Delaware State College

DISTRICT OF COLUMBIA

Sandra Sutherland Fox
The Catholic University of America

Jacqueline Marie Smith
Federal City College (University
of the District of Columbia)

FLORIDA

L. Yvonne Bacarisse
Florida Internation University

Mary N. Hall
University of West Florida

Joyce S. Wando
Florida Technological University

Victoria Warner
Florida A&M University

GEORGIA

Jo Callaway
Tift College

Edward Jacobs
Southern Region Educational
Board
Atlanta, Georgia

Ray Mills
The University of Georgia

Christine Wren
Northeast Georgia Community
Mental Health Center
Athens, Georgia

HAWAII

Winifred Ishimoto
University of Hawaii

Riki G. Lambert
Brigham Young University
Hawaii Campus

IDAHO

Doug Yunker
Boise State University

ILLINOIS

Martha E. Brelije
Southern Illinois University
   at Carbondale

Judith Cingolani
Southern Illinois University
   at Edwardsville

Robert Constable
University of Illinois-Chicago
   Circle

Margaret Dwyer
Loyola University at Chicago

Marjorie Mayo
Roosevelt University

James P. McCabe
College of St. Francis

Betty I. Moore
Augustana College

Gary L. Shaffer
University of Illinois-Urbana

INDIANA

Cyrus S. Behroozi
Indiana University

Chester J. Carpenter
Indiana State University

John P. Crowley
Saint Francis College

Phyllis J. Day
Purdue University

Judith P. Dieter
Marion College

Alice W. Dorn
Anderson College

Charles D. Halbrook
University of Evansville

David Harley
Goshen College

Harry Macy
Ball State University

Marilyn McQueen
Taylor University

Clarence Rivers, Jr.
Valparaiso University

IOWA

Stephen M. Aigner
Iowa State University

Brunhilde Eska
University of Northern Iowa

Marvin Fagerlind
Loras College

M.W. Funk
Wartburg College

Grafton H. Hull, Jr.
Morningside College

Pat Johnson
Luther College

Wayne Johnson
University of Iowa

Sylvia Kuennen
Briar Cliff College

Helen Ormsby
University of Northern Iowa

John (Jack) Pauley
Psychiatric Hospital
University of Iowa

Jackie Pray
Graceland College

John Rogers
Mount Mercy College

KANSAS

Elwin M. Barrett
Wichita State University

John Bower
Tabor College

Bill Lockett
Mid-America Nursing Center, Inc.
Wichita

David Norlin
St. Mary of the Plains College

Paul C. Pelletier
Kansas State University-Manhattan

Chris Petr
Baker University

Ruth Porisch
Bethany College

Rick Spano
University of Kansas

KENTUCKY

Wallace Baggett
Murray State University

Robert L. Berger
Thomas More College

Will R. Berry
Western Kentucky University

Robert Brewster
New Port, Kentucky

Doug Burnham
Eastern Kentucky University

Ed Francel
University of Louisville

Geraldine Hall
Christian Service Ministry
Morehead, Kentucky

Thomas O. Johnson
Ashbury College

John W. Landon
University of Kentucky

Ted A. Marshall
Morehead State University

Rosetta Mauldin
Northern Kentucky University

Ethel L. McLendon
Kentucky State University

Frances Parrish
Spalding College

Janet Rankin
Department of Human Resources
Frankfort, Kentucky

Joseph Sheehan
Northern Kentucky State University

M. Trueheart Titzl
Spalding College

LOUISIANA

Millie Charles
Southern University of New
    Orleans

MAINE

Joseph Kreisler
University of Maine at Portland-
    Gorham

Julia Watkins
University of Maine at Orono

MARYLAND

Lavetta C. Alston
Bowie State College

Mary Ellen Elwell
Western Maryland College

Lynnda Kratovil
Methodist Board of Child Care
Baltimore, Maryland

Robert P. Long
Salisbury State College

Malinda Orlin
University of Maryland

MASSACHUSETTS

Sister Neonilla Barrett
Regis College

Ruth C. Bullock
Eastern Nazarene College

Brenda Davies
Children's Protective Services
Boston, Massachusetts

Paul D. Hand
Anna Maria College

David P. Kemple
Metropolitan College-Boston
  University

MICHIGAN

Faye Y. Abram
Marygrove College

Thomas J. Blakely
Narareth College of Kalamazoo

Jack L. Chapis
Central Michigan University

Fred M. Cox
Michigan State University

Cornell DeJong
Northern Michigan University

Clyde Gehrig
Alma College

Rodney Mulder
Grand Valley State Colleges

James C. Piers
Hope College

Reger C. Smith
Andrews University

MINNESOTA

Betty Bothereau
Mankato State University
Mankato, Minnesota

Don W. Crompton
Bemidji State University

Florence Finnicum
University of Minnesota

Burt Galaway
University of Minnesota, Duluth

Dwight Jessup
Bethel College

Douglas M. Lemons
College of St. Scholastica

Judith A. Miller
Colleges of St. Catherine
   & St. Thomas

Wayne R. Sandee
Mankato State University

Helen Yesner
University of Minnesota-
   Minneapolis

MISSISSIPPI

Elaine H. Cooper
Mississippi State University

Robert I. Gilbert
Mississippi University for Women

Lula King
Jackson State University

Gary R. Mooers
University of Mississippi

Abdul Rahmaan Abd Raheem Muhammad
Mississippi Valley State University

June Allen Pegues
Delta State University

Ann Stanford
Social Work Services, VA Hospital
Jackson, Mississippi

MISSOURI

Margaret Jane Allen
Missouri Western State College

Vincent Faherty
University of Missouri

Marsha Hoffman Rising
Southwest Missouri State
   University

Robert E. Roselius
Missouri Valley College

Charles R. Shapiro
Avila College

Joan Smith
Saint Louis University

J. Paul Walsma
Saint Louis University

MONTANA

Steven R. Cole
Montana State University

John Spores
University of Montana

Joan Porter
Montana State University

NEBRASKA

Louis Heider
Concordia College

Milt Hofstad
Kearney State College

Lucille F. Zelinsky
University of Nebraska at Omaha

NEVADA

Joan Buchanan
Nevada State Welfare Division
Carson City, Nevada

Marlene Chrissinger
University of Nevada-Las Vegas

Barbara W. Larsen
University of Nevada-Reno

NEW JERSEY

Miriam Dinerman
Rutgers University

George D. Metrey
Kean College of New Jersey

Emma Quartaro
Seton Hall University

Greta L. Singer
Monmouth College

Gene E. Webb
Fairleigh Dickinson University

NEW MEXICO

Alvin L. Sallee
New Mexico State University

Facundo B. Valdez
New Mexico Highlands University

NEW YORK

Rosyln F. Gerald
Niagara University

Leonard Gravitz
Rochester Institute of
Technology

Gerald M. Gross
Syracuse University

Ivory Holmes
Adelphi University

Jeanne Hunzeker
Adelphi University

Bonita H. Mayer
State University College at
Brockport

Robert Rivas
SUNY at Albany

Linda Sallett
Utica College of Syracuse
University

Carl A. Scott
CSWE

Tom Stirton
Long Island University
The Brooklyn Center

John Toscano
Vanderhayden Hall
Troy, New York

Philip Wilson
Long Island University

NORTH CAROLINA

John R. Ball
East Carolina University

Patricia Ramsey
Meredith College

Idonna Russell
North Carolina State University

Virginia J. Stephens
University of North Carolina
 at Greensboro

Carolyn R. Thompson
Mars Hill College

Sterling Whitner
Livingstone College

NORTH DAKOTA

Myrna P. Haga
University of North Dakota

OHIO

Evan Bertsche
Bowling Green State University

Marlene Carne
Montgomery County Bd. of Mental
 Retardation
Dayton, Ohio

Philip R. Engle
Wright State University

Frank Longo
Ohio State University

Marilyn Rifkin
University of Cincinnati

Margaret Sebastian
Ohio University

Mildred Seltzer
Miami University

Eliot R. Shimer
Capitol University

OKLAHOMA

Julia Norlin
University of Oklahoma

Jana Sue Springer
Tulsa University

OREGON

Myra S. Miller
University of Oregon

Ralph A. Schmoldt
Concordia College

PENNSYLVANIA

Bill Bolosky
California State College

William C. Boor
Shippensburg State College

Elaine Clyburn
Villa Maria College

Charles Y. Furness
Philadelphia College of Bible

Sheldon R. Gelman
Pennsylvania State University

Ruth Glosser
St. Francis College

Deborah S. Hammond
Slippery Rock State College

Edward T. Kelleher
Lock Haven State College

Edward G. Kuhlmann
Eastern College

Lecie Machell
Cedar Crest College

Charles M. Murphy
Gannon College

Eugene Myers
Conemaugh Valley Memorial
    Hospital
Johnstown, Pennsylvania

Kathleen E. Nuccio
College Misericordia

W. Sherman Perry
Temple University

William Pollard
University of Pittsburgh

Sharon H. Raffield
Elizabethtown College

Sister Rita K. Sperka
Holy Family College

Patrick Wardell
Pennsylvania State University

PUERTO RICO

Luz E. Lopez de Colon
Inter American University

Sister Mary Totti
Catholic University of Puerto
    Rico

Zulma Zelez de Urrutia
University of Puerto Rico

RHODE ISLAND

Myra R. Jones
Rhode Island College

Peter D. Salvatore
Providence College

Bruce Thompson
Roger Williams College

SOUTH CAROLINA

Eva M. Njoku
Benedict College

Ruby Clowers Sulton
South Carolina State College

SOUTH DAKOTA

Louise C. Johnson
University of South Dakota

Bob Maffs
Sioux Falls College

G. Raybell
Mount Marty College

Harriet Scott
Augustana College

Ginger Wintemute
Dakota Wesleyan University

TENNESSEE

Tommie F. Brown
University of Tennessee at
    Chattanooga

Virginia Lea Fitch
East Tennessee State U.

Morris D. Klass
Memphis State University

Annie B. Martin
Tennessee State University

Captolia D. Newbern
Lincoln Memorial University

Betty H. Rasberry
University of Tennessee at
    Martin

C. Benny Reed
East Tennessee State University

Sue Sanders
Lincoln Memorial University

Paul Schwartz
Memphis State University

A.T. Tanner
Lambuth College

Eugenia P. Turner
Department of Human Services
Nashville, Tennessee

TEXAS

Hermila Anzaldua
Pan American University

Albert Barstis
Texas Woman's University

Julia Burkart
West Texas State University

Deanna Burrell
Texas Southern University

Linda Carmicle
The Galaxy Center
Garland, Texas

C.J. Collins
Our Lady of the Lake University

William L. Culp
Abilene Christian University

Mary Cunningham
University of Texas at Austin

Preston M. Dyer
Baylor University

Fannie Belle Gaupp
North Texas State

Elmer L. Good
Southwest Texas State University

George K. Herbert
University of Texas at Austin

Mary Hisanaga
New Lives Program
Ft. Worth Independent School
    District
Ft. Worth, Texas

Margaret McCowen
University of Texas at Arlington

Felife Peralta
University of Texas, El Paso

Mary Ann Ramsey
Department of Human Resources
Austin, Texas

Nettie Scott
VA Hospital
Waco, Texas

Gerda H. Smith
Houston Baptist University

Ann Strong
St. Edward's University

Robert Ward
Department of Human Resources
Waco, Texas

Colleen Williams
Our Lady of the Lake University

UTAH

Nile D. Meservy
Utah State University

E. Gene Shumway
Brigham Young University

Jack L. Stokes
Southern Utah State College

VIRGINIA

David Beverly
Virginia Commonwealth University

Judith Jhirad-Reich
George Mason University

Ervin Mast
Eastern Mennonite College

Mary H. Pegram
Averett College

Lea B. Pellett
Christopher Newport College

Dorothy Ragsdale
Central State Hospital
Peterburg, Virginia

Martin Schwartz
Virginia Commonwealth University

Wanda Scott
Western State Hospital
Staunton, Virginia

George C. Stonikinis, Jr.
Longwood College

David B. White
Virginia Intermont College

WASHINGTON

William Berleman
University of Washington

Rose Blanchard
Eastern Washington State College

William H. Gilbertson
Pacific Lutheran University

John Schiller
Pacific Lutheran University

WEST VIRGINIA

Sung Lai Boo
West Virginia University

Mary L. Heiser
West Virginia State College

Deborah S. Prather
Shepherd College

William Roberts
Glenville State College

Rosa Thompson
Department of Welfare
Bluefield, West Virginia

Ted Tuel
Department of Welfare
New Martinsville, West Virginia

Buford Young
Concord College

WISCONSIN

William Egan
Village Church Adult Day Care
Milwaukee, Wisconsin

Carolyn Konle
Marquette University

Ann L. McLean
University of Wisconsin-Oshkosh

Lois Miranda
University of Wisconsin-Oshkosh

Katharine H. Ostrander
Newport College, Salve Regina

John P. Rader
Carroll College

Joan Robertson
University of Wisconsin-Madison

Robert P. Scheurell
University of Wisconsin-
  Milwaukee

Carol Schulke
University of Wisconsin-Oshkosh

Mary Ann Suppes
Mount Mary College

James Wallus
Tomah Veteran Administration
  Hospital
Tomah, Wisconsin

Jane Ward
Viterbo College

Charles M. Young
University of Wisconsin-
  La Crosse

WYOMING

James R. Wiebler
University of Wyoming

Index

About the Editors

Betty L. Baer, who was the director of the Undergraduate Social Work Curriculum Development Project, is on the faculty at West Virginia University. In addition to developing that university's undergraduate social work program within the School of Social Work, she has also served as acting dean of the school. She is active in several bodies of the Council on Social Work Education, and is in demand as a consultant by many baccalaureate social work programs. She was also instrumental in creating the Association of Baccalaureate Program Directors. Her practice experience includes extensive community-based work.

Ronald C. Federico is director of the Baccalaureate Social Work Program at the University of Cincinnati, and was project associate of the Undergraduate Social Work Curriculum Development Project. He is active as a site visitor and consultant to baccalaureate social work programs, and is the editor of the Association of Baccalaureate Program Directors newsletter. He has published in the areas of social work and sociology. He was previously on the faculty at the University of North Carolina at Greensboro.

About the Contributors

Dr. Winifred Bell, professor at Cleveland State University, has had a long and distinguished career in social work practice and social welfare research, writing, and teaching. She has held significant positions in the government, on national and international committees, and at major universities, and she has been active as a consultant for a variety of social welfare agencies. Her many publications have provided important insights into several areas of social welfare policy.

Dr. Katherine Hooper Briar is an assistant professor at Pacific Lutheran University. In addition to her teaching responsibilities, she is director of the Child and Family Welfare Project, and a Jail Employment and Social Services Project. She has worked as a consultant to a variety of organizations and served as a delegate to the 1978 White House Conference on Balanced National Growth and Economic Development. Her publications include a forthcoming book on the effects of unemployment on workers and their families.

Jacqueline D. Fassett is director of social services at the Sinai Hospital in Baltimore, Maryland. She is also First Vice President of the National Association of Social Workers and has been an active participant in the Undergraduate Social Work Curriculum Development Project from its inception.

Dr. Herbert H. Jarrett is the director of the undergraduate social work program at the University of Georgia. He has conducted research in the areas of competency-based education and has published several articles on social work education. He has been active with the Council on Social Work Education in doing site visits and has been a consultant for several baccalaureate social work programs. His social work practice background includes work in the fields of mental retardation and mental health.

Laura B. Morris is the director of community relations for the Digital Equipment Corporation in Boston, Massachusetts. She was formerly director of family advocacy for the Family Service Association of Boston, and has had extensive experience with the Massachusetts Department of Public Welfare in a planning capacity. She was involved in the work of the Undergraduate Social Work Curriculum Development Project from its inception.

Dr. Edna T. Roth, professor of social work at Virginia Commonwealth University, was previously on the faculties of the University of Kentucky and Case Western Reserve University. She is widely recognized for her teaching skills and has held a number of institutes and workshops on social work practice methods and theory. She has also had extensive practice experience in the family service field.

Dr. Bradford W. Sheafor is professor and director of the social work program at Colorado State University. Formerly, he was associate dean of the School of Social Welfare at the University of Kansas. He is secretary of the Council on Social Work Education and has served that organization as well as the National Association of Social Workers in a number of capacities. His publications include a recent, widely used introductory social work text. He was active in the work of the Undergraduate Social Work Curriculum Development Project during the entire grant period.

Ramón Valle is an associate professor at San Diego State University, where he also has major responsibilities in the Center on Aging. In addition to his activities with various commissions of the Council on Social Work Education, he has been active in providing service delivery to elder members of minority groups, especially Latino elderly. His publications have covered this area as well as program evaluation and teaching effectiveness.

Fay Coker Walker is an assistant professor at Mars Hill College in North Carolina, from where she is currently on leave to pursue advanced study. Her practice experience has been in health-related areas, and her major research interests include rural social work and undergraduate social work teaching effectiveness.